Legacies of the Collapse of Marxism

John H. Moore
Editor

GEORGE MASON UNIVERSITY PRESS
Fairfax, Virginia

Copyright © 1994 by
George Mason University Press
4400 University Drive
Fairfax, VA 22030

Distributed by arrangement with
University Publishing Associates, Inc.

4720 Boston Way
Lanham, MD 20706

3 Henrietta Street
London WC2E 8LU England

Library of Congress Cataloging-in-Publication Data

Legacies of the collapse of Marxism / John H. Moore, editor.
p.   cm.
Includes bibliographical references.
1. Post-communism—Former Soviet republics.   2. Post-
communism—Europe, Eastern.   3. Nationalism—Former Soviet
republics.   4. Nationalism—Europe, Eastern.   5. Former Soviet
republics—Politics and government.   6. Europe, Eastern—Politics
and government—1989–   7. Former Soviet republics—Economic
conditions.   8. Europe, Eastern—Economic conditions—1989–
I. Moore, John Hampton, 1935–   .
JN6511.L37   1994
320.947'09'049—dc20   94–23348   CIP

ISBN 0–913969–71–0 (cloth : alk. paper)
ISBN 0–913969–72–9 (pbk. : alk. paper)

 The paper used in this publication meets the minimum requirements of
American National Standard for Information Sciences—Permanence
of Paper for Printed Library Materials, ANSI Z39.48–1984.

Contents

Preface

John H. Moore
George Mason University

The revolutions of 1989 ended the domination of the Communist Party in the former Soviet Union and throughout Central and Eastern Europe and were the beginning of the end of the Soviet Communist Party. The collapse of communist rule had another, deeper meaning: it signified the collapse of Marxism as the ideological foundation for a form of government now repudiated nearly everywhere east of the Oder-Neisse line.

This twin collapse and the end of Soviet hegemony and global influence that accompanied it have brought profound change throughout the world. The most immediate focal point was, of course, the former Soviet Union and the members of the Warsaw Treaty Organization. Revolutionary political change occurred, virtually overnight. Governments were tumbled, leaders thrown out or executed, and new governments formed. Where once there was one-party rule, now, in a kind of paroxysm of pent-up demand for self-determination, dozens of new political parties have been formed. Some of these consisted of old communists who reorganized under new banners, but many genuinely new alliances and ideological viewpoints emerged. From all of this turmoil, coalitions and strong single parties capable of governing are developing, but, like much of what is transpiring in Eastern Europe, the outcome is yet to be seen.

Economically, the changes in Eastern Europe have been slower but in some cases no less profound. Massive reforms intended to create market economies have been launched in several of the former bloc countries. In the process, the old economic systems were abandoned, again virtually overnight. The infrastructure required for market economic systems could not be developed as quickly; the result was severe economic distress, from which only a few signs of relief have appeared. COMECON disintegrated, producing an urgent need to re-align foreign trade patterns, a matter that contributed to the economic woes of the region. Inflation plagues the new economies, less severe in some than in others, but a very serious problem in several countries. Rapid growth of a new private sector based on the establishment of thousands of small businesses and some cases of successful privatization of former state enterprises are responsible for the recovery that has occurred. But, as with political change, the process of economic change is far from being concluded and the form of a stable outcome far from clear.

With such profound political and economic upheaval, social change has also been great. Old relationships have been severed and new ones just beginning to develop. The social support systems that existed under the former regimes, such as they were, have vanished, and inflation, economic restructuring, and recession have left many people in dire straits. Pervading the situation nearly everywhere is a sense of deep uncertainty about the future. Everything is in a state of flux, from political constitutions to courts of justice to law enforcement to interpersonal relations. Habits of thought developed through two or more generations are suddenly obsolete; new ideas and new outlooks on life are being thrust upon people who are ill-prepared by education, experience, or, in many cases, inclination to adopt them. Perhaps more than any other factor, it is the need to inculcate new ways of thinking and the difficulty in doing so that stands in the way of fundamental political and economic change in the former Soviet Union and the members of the old bloc.

But the changes wrought by the collapse of the Communist empire reach far beyond the confines of Eastern Europe and the former Soviet Union. The bipolarity that defined international relations for over forty years has vanished. The repercussions of this disappearance, scarcely conceivable four years ago, are still reverberating throughout the world. The roles of transnational organizations—NATO, OECD, CSCE, and the UN—are being redefined. The very concept of national security is under scrutiny. Some commentators believe that economic power should be the defining characteristic and would institute national policies seeking to insure it. Others see the need to refocus attention on renegade states and the threat they pose for peace and stability. Most agree that the end of the Cold War requires a revamping of policy and permits a substantial reduction in military preparedness. The resulting military downsizing in the United States is creating serious economic problems in many regions of the country and will undoubtedly contribute to similar difficulties in Western Europe and other parts of the world.

Old alliances are being reconsidered and new ones are emerging. The historic relationship between the United States and Japan is among the most prominent of the alliances that grew from the bipolar division of power. In the tacit agreement, the U.S. shielded Japan from the Soviet Union under its nuclear umbrella, while Japan refrained from building its own military might. With the need for the nuclear shield apparently dissipated, Japan appears to be taking a more independent line in both domestic and foreign policy.

Elsewhere, the world of Islam may be developing new alignments. The breakup of the Soviet Union has left potentially fertile ground for Muslim expansion in the former Soviet republics of Central Asia. The war in the Balkans, itself not unrelated to the disintegration of the former Soviet Union, may lead to new alliances based not on Islam but on Orthodoxy and traditional Slavic relationships. In many parts of the world, nationalistic feelings are surfacing, contributing to the need for a new understanding of national security.

* * *

Many more examples of changes resulting from the ending of Communist rule in the former Soviet Union could be adduced, and more will emerge in the future. They are all legacies of the collapse in the East, the subject of a conference held in Washington, D.C., in March 1992. The conference was organized by the International Institute of George Mason University in cooperation with the Institute for European, Russian, and Eurasian Studies of George Washington University. Approximately 65 scholars from the United States and Europe participated in the three-day meeting. The papers in this volume are the product of that conference.

Certainly no one had or could have had the prescience to foresee all of the ramifications of the 1989 revolutions, nor is the outcome evident today. The papers prepared for the conference are the products of authors writing in 1991, two years after the revolutions, well before the outlines of things to come began to emerge from the euphoria of the downfall of communism. No effort has been made to update them; indeed, the daily news is full of events that are forming the history of the transition from communism to the new states. These papers, then, represent the judgments of informed scholars assessing the implications of the most dramatic and far-reaching events since World War II.

In a historical *tour de force*, Leonard Liggio first links Russia with the settlement of North America through the interruption of the Russian fur trade through the Baltic cities that resulted from the wars of Ivan the Terrible and his successors. He reminds us of longstanding Russo-American relations dating from the time of the Russian settlements on the Pacific coast down to Theodore Roosevelt's involvement in the Treaty of Portsmouth that ended the Russo-Japanese War in 1906. He cites Brinton's application of his model of revolutions, proceeding from extreme radicalism to a search for stability, to Soviet history, arguing that Stalin produced a kind of bureaucratic stability after the radicalism of the Bolshevik revolution. Liggio draws parallels between the downfall of the Soviet state and the last days of the Roman Empire, and shows how the French Revolution provides lessons both for liberals, who see it as the model of anti-liberal government, and for Marxian socialists, who see it as a model for the successful seizure of state power. Since Ludwig von Mises had demonstrated the theoretical impossibility of socialism in the 1920's, and since the Bolsheviks must have been aware of this, Liggio argues that socialism was introduced in Russia not to improve the lot of the ordinary citizen but as a means of control. Finally, he shows how financial crises in the United States and other Western countries, brought about by profligate government spending, ironically played a role in the ultimate collapse of the Soviet system.

While Liggio focuses on the former Soviet Union, Rudolf Andorka analyzes the cause of the revolution and prospects for the future in his native land of Hungary. Andorka identifies a number of conditions and symptoms of social malaise that indicate deep underlying social decay, the sour foundation for revolution. Material living conditions were part of the problem in Hungary, although not as bad as in other East European countries. There was evidence of a basic lack of trust outside close circles of family and friends. Alcoholism and suicide rates were high and rising. There was great resentment of social inequities, of the degradation of moral standards, and of the lack of personal freedom. Andorka identifies several threats to the transition to a market economy and a democratic political order: a long and deep economic recession, the possible emergence of extremist political parties, and the lack of the institutions and traditions of a civil society. At the same time, he thinks that Hungary has assets that argue for optimism: experience with the market system through participation in the second economy that began in 1968, the relatively high level of education, the absence of ethnic minorities that might be a breeding ground for nationalistic fervor, and, not least, the experience of the failed 1956 rebellion, which stands as a model of the fight for democracy.

Nationalism is treated in several papers. Francis Fukuyama focuses on the history and prospects of Russian nationalism. He points out that Russian nationalism, both historically and currently, is far from uniform or monolithic, and devotes much of his paper to delineating differences among the views held by different nationalist factions. He traces the uneasy relationship between nationalist proponents and the Soviet authorities, noting that Bolshevism had a nationalist tinge despite its claims to universality and showing how nationalism was manifested in Soviet policy, particularly during the Brezhnev years. Fukuyama discusses the status of nationalist movements in Russia today, in which the ideas and writings of Alexander Solzhenitsyn play a prominent role, although not by any means expressing universally held views. He shows that there are now, as before, a variety of views among those who consider themselves Russian nationalists, ranging from more or less liberal thinkers who favor a market economy and Western-style parliamentary institutions to conservatives who have a distaste for markets and who would prefer an authoritarian form of government. As for the future of Russian nationalism, Fukuyama argues that the West owes a debt to Yeltsin for having pre-empted the nationalist position as a liberal nationalist. However, the failed coup of August 1991, in which conservative nationalists allied themselves with old-line communists in the army and the police, may have laid the groundwork for a more powerful nationalist movement by severing the link between it and the discredited communist party.

Craig Calhoun takes a different approach to the problem of nationalism, situating it in the context of theoretical discourses of democracy and the civil society. For him, a shift to a capitalistic economic system would represent only one part of the reform of the former communist societies. Capitalism may provide a framework within which societal integration can develop, but it is impersonal and limited to purely economic transactions. Lacking are the webs of interpersonal relationships and intermediary associations through which individuals can become part of society. Recognizing that conditions of modernity are fertile ground for the development of nationalism, Calhoun nevertheless strikes an optimistic note in arguing that nationalism is constructed, rather than primordial, and therefore no more real than other identities that people can claim. Where Fukuyama points to an uneasy relationship between communist regimes and nationalists, Calhoun goes a step further and argues that the regimes deliberately used nationalistic sentiments for their own purposes. He concludes that nationalism, potentially dangerous, must be mediated by the development of the institutions of civil society.

Nationalism is not congruent with ethnicity, of course, although ethnicity may play a role in the development of nationalist movements. Randall Collins and David Waller provide a theoretical analysis of ethnicity. Agreeing with Calhoun's view, they point out that nationalism is not primordial; nor, in their view, is ethnicity. In fact, their central thesis is that ethnicity—in terms of its strength and boundaries—is determined by geopolitics. They argue that geopolitical strength brings prestige to the dominant ethnic group in a state and thereby tends to extend its boundaries and influence within the state. Thus factors that determine geopolitical advantage will also influence ethnic strength within a nation. They proceed to set out such factors—size, resource advantage, marchland advantage, the avoidance of overextension—and to apply the theory to the emergent states of the former Soviet Union. In discussing Russia, for example, they conclude that it is likely to enjoy geopolitical success because of the favorable set of factors it possesses; accordingly, they predict that the prestige and influence of Russian ethnicity will grow. For that reason, they say, there should not be much in the way of additional ethnic secessionist movements. On the other hand, they predict continued ethnic clashes in the Caucasus because no state there will be strong enough to provide an ethnic group with enough prestige to attract others and thereby become dominant.

If ethnic movements or nationalisms based on ethnicity grow in the wake of the collapse of the communist empire, it is likely that minority groups will be subjected to discrimination or persecution. Thus the protection of minority rights takes on a new urgency, as Ambassador Petrus Buwalda emphasizes in his contribution to the volume. He traces the history of efforts to protect minority rights, including provisions resulting from the Congress of Berlin and the system created under the League of Nations. Minority rights are treated in the U.N. Charter's provision for human rights, but only as one of several aspects of human rights. Furthermore, the provision dealing with minority rights pertains to them on an individual, rather than group, basis. For Buwalda, although protection of individual rights is important, the problem of minority rights can be addressed effectively only if they are treated as groups. He acknowledges the problems involved with the group approach, noting in particular the problem of deciding who belongs to a given minority group, which he concedes has never been resolved. But he believes this problem can be solved and that any future approach should be based on the rights of minorities as groups. He suggests that the CSCE could serve as the organization for monitoring and protecting minority rights and notes the Dutch suggestion that a High Commissioner for Minorities be created in the CSCE for the purpose.

Three papers in the collection are devoted to economic aspects of the revolutions and subsequent transitions. James M. Buchanan develops a new analysis, based on economic theory, of the reasons for the differences in mental habits between people in developed market economies and those in the former Soviet Union so often implicated as factors retarding fundamental change in the East. Buchanan argues that the use of money, with its near-perfect fungibility, introduces an asymmetry into buyer-seller relations. Buyers, who come to market transactions with money, have a transactions advantage over sellers, who bring specific goods to the market. In situations where excess demand is absent (i.e., most market situations), this means that sellers must work hard to satisfy the demands of potential buyers. This is the typical situation in market systems and explains the prevalence of advertising and other marketing devices. In command economies of the Soviet type, however, money does not have this function because of chronic excess demand, itself inherent in such systems. Therefore sellers do not have the same incentives as in the typical market situation; this explains the poor service, lack of advertising, and other characteristic features of the old Soviet economy. Moreover, the chronic excess demand channels entrepreneurial activity into "non-money" channels: the means of influencing choices by other than market purchases. The diversion of entrepreneurial energy away from supply side activities may imply a longer transition period if Russian entrepreneurs are slow to shift from the one form of entrepreneurial activity to the other.

Peter Murrell attacks questions of the path of economic reform on the basis of the conservative political philosophies of Burke, Popper, and Oakeshott. In his interpretation of these works, he finds arguments against the development of blueprints for rapid, significant change from an existing social order to a new one. These arguments are based on the problems of knowing or understanding the actual workings of a social organization because of its great complexity and its long evolution through time, in which no single hand can be seen guiding the development of the system. In addition, the workings of any society depend on two kinds of knowledge: that in textbooks, labelled "technical" knowledge, which is general and without specific bounds, and that embodied in the experience and knowledge of individuals, labelled "practical" knowledge, which is not necessarily communicable in general. Practical knowledge is essential to society; change necessarily renders some practical knowledge obsolete, and the more radical the change, the more practical knowledge is destroyed. Thus there are strong arguments favoring what Popper calls piecemeal rather than Utopian social engineering. Murrell uses these points to argue that privatization should be carried out gradually rather than rapidly, and that worker management, in countries with experience with it (e.g., former Yugoslavia and Poland), should not be abandoned in the course of the transition but allowed to survive as an interim position on the way to a fully market outcome in the interest of preserving practical knowledge.

The issue of the speed of privatization is tackled by Anders Åslund. Indeed, this issue drew a great deal of attention during the conference discussions. Åslund discusses at length the capacity of the state to execute the policies and actions of economic reform. He concludes that the governments of the nations in transition are not well-equipped for this purpose. The resources that they can control are more limited than would be expected because of difficulties in raising revenue in the transition period. The bureaucratic systems are inefficient and ill-suited to the tasks at hand. Not only that, the quality of the state apparatus is poor: the personnel have inappropriate training and experience and are demoralized, and the structure of the system is wrong. The information available to the new governments is poor because the old systems were designed for entirely different purposes; furthermore, the information is likely to deteriorate as the private sector expands. All of this argues that the kind of fine-tuning suggested by Murrell is not a feasible policy, and part of the argument about the speed of privatization dwelt on this point. Åslund makes a set of recommendations about the role of the state in these circumstances, generally emphasizing the need to create a liberal (in the European sense) economic order, with the legal framework and institutions required for that purpose. He also recommends that the governments create stable and preferably convertible currencies and privatize as rapidly as possible.

Looking to the future, Daniel Chirot raises the fundamental issue of the future of liberalism in Central Europe. After discussing the causes of the fall of communism, he asks whether liberalism is destined to suffer the same fate as it did in the interwar period. To answer this, he advances several reasons for the collapse of liberalism then. He notes the absence of consensus regarding ideological models, the redrawing of national borders with all of its consequences for trade and economic well-being, and the existence of peasant problems in several countries. More fundamental, he says, was a strongly anti-liberal atmosphere that arose from the rejection of modernity and thus of liberal democracy and capitalism. He notes the presence of strong nationalist fervor, fueled by resentments of the West, throughout Central and Eastern Europe in the interwar period. Finally, he argues that leaders were driven to the right because they feared growing Soviet power on the left. Once having made these points, he can easily argue that circumstances today are quite different, and a more optimistic view can be taken. However, the Balkans may be an exception. Untouched by the Reformation and the Enlightenment, they do not have the intellectual traditions of liberalism. Now there are disturbing nationalist forces at large in the region, in some cases set loose and encouraged by former communist leaders. But the signs in the rest of Central Europe are positive enough, and the prevailing ideological current in Europe sufficiently liberal, that Chirot can conclude that these problems are likely to be contained. Of course, all of this remains to be seen.

The collapse of the Soviet Union vindicated the views of the small minority of intellectuals who had held it to be an inefficient, inhumane system destined or at least warranted to fail. But it was entirely at odds with those who had been so confident of its ultimate success and had defended it so ardently over the years, even up to the time of the collapse. Robert Conquest examines the reasons for what he calls the academic unwillingness to face reality. He argues that the basic habits of mind were set by the Webbs, whose views were molded in the first instance by a belief that socialism was the society of the future and that it existed in the USSR. This led them to excuse some of the reality and deny the rest. It also led them to accept as true the figures that were published by the Soviet regime. Both of these attributes have come down through the generations to the present day. Indeed, the willingness to accept the official data as true penetrated most work done on the Soviet system, including that of the Central Intelligence Agency. Conquest argues that most Sovietologists were social scientists—sociologists and economists—rather than historians, and so sought structural rather than essential explanations for what was observed. They were trained not to inject opinion into their work and were reluctant to utilize eye-witness accounts over the (false) official data. All of this led to a deep disparity between the Soviet Union described by social scientists based on these data and "scientific" models and the Soviet Union known to its citizens, to travelers, and to those who listened to emigres. In the end, Conquest says, the failure of Western researchers lay in a profound weakness of imagination. They simply could not imagine a regime in which millions of people could be tortured and killed or data could be literally invented. For someone who might harbor sympathies to the professed objectives of the communist state, this lack of imagination would be intellectually fatal.

The failure of Sovietologists to foresee the fall of communism is also discussed in Seymour Martin Lipset's contribution. In parallel with Conquest, he notes that Sovietologists in general were not useful in anticipating the developments of the last few years. He also attributes this to the fact that most belonged to the left-liberal side of the political spectrum, people who believed that the Soviet system would work because it should work. He points to others who did address the weaknesses of the system—a few Sovietologists and some prominent political figures, including Ronald Reagan and Daniel Patrick Moynihan. But these observations are secondary to the main thrust of Lipset's essay, most of which is devoted to the contrast between Marx's theory of history, which of course holds that socialism would emerge only after capitalism had produced an end to scarcity, and the Bolshevik interpretation of Marx. Lipset reviews the writings of many prominent old Marxists, revealing their deep skepticism about the feasibility of creating a socialist state in backward Russia and showing how they predicted its failure.

Of course, none of the Marxists or their modern counterparts set out a timetable for the collapse of the system. Lipset recalls that Lenin allegedly "danced in the snow" on the 71st day after the Bolshevik takeover because the regime had lasted longer than the Paris Commune. Of course, it lasted more than 70 years, becoming the stultifying bureaucratic monster that Rosa Luxemburg had foreseen, what Lipset terms a "sociological abortion." The collapse of Soviet communism put paid to the Bolshevik idea that socialism could be created in a backward state. If, as Marx thought, socialism can only be created after scarcity has been eliminated, human history to date and all signs for the future surely tell us that it will never come to pass.

* * *

Did the collapse of Soviet communism, then, mean the collapse of Marxism? For neo-Marxists who wish to believe in the Bolshevik variant as a political guide to action, as a justification for a monolithic state to produce socialism with its alleged advantages, the Soviet collapse is a devastating blow. Indeed, for socialists of every stripe, the tragedy of Soviet rule stands as a refutation of the belief that government can, even if it has the will, create well-being for its people. If a state as powerful as the Soviet Union cannot create prosperity in a land as well-endowed with human and natural resources as it was, no state is likely to be able to. Today, with the terrible crimes that occurred under Stalin's rule documented so well that only a very few die-hards any longer dispute them, and the rest of the heritage of Soviet rule becoming obvious as Russia falls deeper into economic ruin, it is hard to believe that the Bolsheviks— and certainly not their successors—ever had the well-being of the Russian people in mind. Idealistic social reformers of the early twentieth century nevertheless believed that the Soviet socialist state would, in fact, elevate Russia and its people to unheard-of standards of living and levels of personal satisfaction. Many of their ideological progeny today seem to believe that it is still possible to create the good society by massive government intervention and control. If there is a redeeming feature of the Soviet experience, it is that it will have taught us the folly of such beliefs.

Unfortunately, history is not encouraging on this score. Ideologies holding out the promise of new societies that are more just or more prosperous or more secure or that have other features that appeal to deep human desires have been used to justify authoritarian or totalitarian regimes that inevitably become vehicles for the cruel suppression of most people in order to satisfy the desires of some ruling elite. We might hope that the experience of communism will lead to a different outcome, but the lesson of history is that there is no sure protection against the ambitions of ideologues driven by visions of an ideal world.

Acknowledgements

The papers in this volume were prepared for a conference cosponsored by the International Institute of George Mason University and the Institute for European, Russian, and Eurasian Studies of the George Washington University. Financial support from the Friedrich Ebert Foundation, the Sarah Scaife Foundation, and the Earhart Foundation is gratefully acknowledged.

List of Contributors

Rudolf Andorka
Budapest University of Economic Science

Anders Åslund
Stockholm School of Economics

James M. Buchanan
George Mason University

Petrus Buwalda
Foreign Service, the Netherlands

Craig Calhoun
University of North Carolina

Daniel Chirot
University of Washington

Randall Collins and

David Waller
University of California

Robert Conquest
Hoover Institution on War, Revolution and Peace, Stanford University

Francis Fukuyama
Rand Corporation

Leonard P. Liggio
George Mason University

Seymour Martin Lipset
George Mason University

John H. Moore
George Mason University

Peter Murrell
University of Maryland

The Collapse in Historical Perspective

Leonard P. Liggio
George Mason University

During the week of August 18, 1991, I was lecturing at a seminar in Hungary, north-east of Budapest. It happened to be a week of unusual excitement as it coincided with a visit of Pope John Paul II to Hungary and with the attempted coup in the Soviet Union. The students were mainly eastern European with western European students and a few from India. Following one of my lectures on European legal and economic history, Ivan, one of the students from Moscow, asked with deep seriousness if I considered Russia to be a European country. Without hesitation, I answered yes.

The United States, Canada, Australia, Argentina, et al., are European countries. They are derived from western European origins which include inheritance from the Roman empire and Germanic settlers, opposition between Church and State, Renaissance, Reformation, Counter-Reformation, and the Eighteenth Century revolutions of individual rights. But, unlike western Europe, the Europeans *l'outre mer* have remained migratory and unsettled, like the Russians. Russians migrated with the decline of the Mongol Golden Horde and its khanates in the Volga valley. There was expansion with the decline of the Swedish Vasa lands along the Baltic, of the Ottoman Sublime Porte and its Khanate of Crimea in the south, and of the Polish-Lithuanian Republic in the west.

Alexis de Tocqueville saw the United States and Russia as similar frontier civilizations, each crossing a continent. Russians and Americans are Europeans migrating and settling continents unlike the stable Europeans. Some Russians, like New England farmers, remain in their old villages ignoring better opportunities, but the bulk of Russians and Americans have been migratory and risk-takers, succeeding to the extent permitted by the legal and political systems.

Indeed, the settlement of North America had its origins in Russia. North America's New France, New England and Virginia, New Netherlands, and New Sweden (Delaware) were established because of the interruption of the trade of Russian furs through cities of the Baltic. The wars of Ivan the Terrible and Successors had disrupted the fur markets and the same investors in London, for example, in the Moscovy and Eastland companies launched the Virginia and Plymouth companies after 1600.

Ivan the Terrible wreaked havoc on the trading city of Novgorod and destroyed the rights of its citizens. *Gospodin Velikiy Novgorod* (Sovereign Great Novgorod) had been part of the culture of Kievan Russia. Great Novgorod's citizens in 997 had received a charter of rights from Prince Yaroslav. For half a millennium Great Novgorod flourished in self-government and was the eastern terminus of the Hanseatic League.

Great Novgorod had a charter of liberties and self-government before almost all of the towns of western Europe. Its charter continued this tradition of liberty into the early modern era when most western European towns also lost their self-government to absolutist monarchies. However, Great Novgorod suffered the massacres of citizens, merchants and clergy, and the destruction of the monasteries carried out by Ivan the Terrible.

North America's New France, New England, New Netherlands, and New Sweden searched the continent's interior to purchase furs. The western Europeans, especially the Quebec *coureurs de bois*, traded for furs westward. With Ivan the Terrible's capture of Kazan and Astrakhan Khanates, Siberia was opened to eastward moving Cossacks. Eventually, the Russian North America Company crossed into Alaska and down the coasts of today's British Columbia, Washington and Oregon to northern California. Like the French, they brought religion, the Russian Orthodox Church, with the fur trade.

Europeans noted the similarity in the American settlement of North America and Russian settlement of Siberia. A decade before de Tocqueville visited North America, American diplomacy was much disturbed by the expansion of the Russian North America Company on the Pacific Coast. The Monroe Doctrine was drafted by Secretary of State (and soon to be president) John Quincy Adams as part of an Anglo-American entente against the Holy Alliance, headed by the Russian Tsar, Alexander. While the Monroe Doctrine included the goal of dissuading France from joining a Spanish return against the independent republics of South America, Russia was the European country in actual possession and expanding its possessions in the Western Hemisphere.

In 1818, Adams had arranged the negotiation with England of the treaty which delineated the northern boundary of the Louisiana Purchase of 1803, extending the boundary along the 49th north latitude to the the Rocky Mountains. From the Rocky Mountains to the Pacific Ocean, the territory was administered as a condominium until James K. Polk's election slogan of "54 degrees, 40 degrees or Fight" led to extending the 49th north latitude to the Pacific Coast. In 1825, Adams' treaty with Russia limited Russia to the current limits of Alaska.

John Quincy Adams (1767–1848) in 1778, accompanied his father, John Adams, to Paris, and in 1781, at age fourteen accompanied Francis Dana, American minister to Russia, as his private secretary. During his father's administration, 1797–1801, Adams was U.S. minister to Berlin. James Madison appointed John Quincy Adams as U.S. minister to St. Petersburg in 1809, where he encouraged Tsar Alexander to act as mediator between England and the U.S. in the War of 1812. Instead, U.S. and English commissioners negotiated the Peace of Ghent (December, 1814). Adams had been one of the peace commissioners and was appointed U.S. minister to England (1815–17). Adams' five years residence in St. Petersburg facilitated the negotiations of the U.S.-Russian Treaty of 1825.

Russia continued to have reasonable relations with the United States through the emancipation of the serfs, the visit of the Russian fleet during the Civil War, and the sale of Alaska to the United States in 1867. President Theodore Roosevelt acted as mediator between Russia and Japan to conclude the Russo-Japanese war by the Treaty of Portsmouth, New Hampshire in 1906. The deep American diplomatic involvement in the February and October revolutions has been fully explored by George Kennan.

The Russian revolution was one of the four European revolutions which were compared in the late Crane Brinton's *Anatomy of Revolution*.[1] Brinton sought to form a model of European revolutions based on his field of expertise: the French Revolution.[2] Brinton, the Harvard historian, compared the four major European revolutions—the mid-17th century English Revolution, which ended in the supremacy of parliament; the late-18th century American Revolution, which led to independence and republicanism; the late-18th century French Revolution, which led to constitutionalism and ultimately, republicanism; and the

1917 Russian Revolution, which ended monarchy and brought a controlled economy. The models of revolutions of Brinton represented his own realism and skepticism in contrast to Robert R. Palmer's emphasis on the constitutional balance of the late-18th century Atlantic Revolutions of America and France, and to Peter Gay's focus on the radical aspects of the Atlantic revolutions. The cycles of Brinton's model of revolutions was a progression to extreme radicalism and the search for stabilization under the rule of Oliver Cromwell, George Washington, Napoleon Bonaparte, and Joseph Stalin.

However, the English, American, and French revolutions witnessed the temporary nature of these stable executives. Cromwell's rule was followed by the Restoration and the Glorious Revolution of 1688. Washington's presidency was followed by the replacement of the Federalists and their repressive Alien and Sedition Acts by Thomas Jefferson's "American Jocobins" who allied with Napoleon's France against England in the War of 1812 (which Tsar Alexander sought to mediate). Napoleon was followed by the Restoration and then the July Monarchy with moderate constitutionalism.

The Russian revolution had gone through Brinton's cycle to bureaucratic stability under Joseph Stalin. After Stalin's death there was a gradual relaxation of repressive rule in Russia. The movement toward normalcy begun by Nikita Khrushchev was stopped by Leonid Brezhnev. The achievement of individual rights, private property and constitutionalism, after long delays, is beginning to open up for the peoples of the former Soviet Union.

The October Russian Revolution was a defining event in the history of the twentieth century. European and American historians, especially before the Russian Revolution, had two dominant developments in their mind's eye. Edward Gibbon's *Decline and Fall of the Roman Empire* re-inforced the existing Latin education. The fall of the Roman Empire was paralleled by the French Revolution, and in particular, the Terror.

The weight of the Roman Empire's military expenditures exhausted the economy and led to collective responsibilities for the payments of taxation. The weight of taxation led to indifference and despair among the population of the Late Roman Empire. Is it any wonder that the most famous economic historian of the Roman Empire was Mikhail Ivanovich Rostovtzeff? From Professor of Ancient History at the University of St. Petersburg, Rostovtzeff became Professor of Ancient History at Yale University.[3]

The Illyrian emperors sought to restore the stability of the bureaucracy and of the collection of taxes. They sought to solve the fiscal problem by depreciation of the currency, and to solve the market's reaction to
inflation by imposition of wage and price controls. Since tax payers sought
to flee from the over-whelming tax burdens, the state imposed collective
tax responsibilities. Since everyone in the collective entity was fully
responsible for the tax payments, they all sought to restrain escape. All
workers, rural or urban, began to be tied to their occupations to assure
that their share of the the taxation would be paid. Rostovtzeff describes
the developments:

> It might be defined as a system of permanent terrorism which from time to
> time assumed acute forms. The most important part in the administration
> was played by countless thousands of policemen of different denominations,
> all of them personal military agents of the emperor. Their duty was to watch
> the people closely both in the cities and in the country, and to arrest those
> who were considered dangerous to the emperor. They were probably
> employed also to quell any troubles and strikes that might arise from the
> heavy pressure of the government on the population in the matter of taxa-
> tion and compulsory work, and to use physical compulsion against those who
> failed to pay their taxes or to discharge the public burdens to which they were
> liable.

> A salient feature of this system of organized terrorism was the further devel-
> opment of the principle of compulsion in all dealing of the government with
> the population, particularly in the sphere of taxation and forced labor. Along
> with taxation, but much more oppressive than it, and no less methodically
> applied, went the system of requisitioning foodstuffs, raw material, man-
> ufactured goods, money, ships, draught cattle, and men for transport pur-
> pose, and so forth....As the success of the system depended on its powers
> easily to reach and keep within call everybody who was subject to compul-
> sion, there was a natural tendency to bind every individual alike to his place
> of residence and to the particular group to which he belonged by birth and by
> profession. A tiller of the soil ought to remain in his domicile, and he ought
> to carry on his work without regard to his desires and inclinations.[4]

Rostovtzeff quotes a Roman contemporary, Herodian:

> But when Maximinus, after reducing most of the distinguished houses to
> penury, found that the spoils were few and paltry and by no means sufficient
> for his purposes, he attacked public property. All the money belonging to the
> cities that was collected by the victualling of the populace or for distribution
> among them, or was devoted to theatres or to religious festivals, he diverted
> to his own use; and the votive offerings set up in temples, the statues of the
> gods, the tributes to heroes, all the adornments of the public buildings,
> everything that served to beautify the cities, even the metal out of which

money could be coined, all were melted down. This conduct greatly grieved the people of the cities.[5]

Rostovtzeff emphasized the role of the depreciation of the coinage in the decline of civilization all over the Mediterranean world:

> One of the most striking phenomena in economic life was the rapid depreciation of the currency and a still more rapid increase in prices. It is not surprising that under such conditions, speculation of the wildest kind was one of the marked features of economic life, especially speculation connected with exchange....The general insecurity of business life led to a fluctuation in the rate of interest, which in the second century had been as stable as prices.[6]

> Closely connected with the reform of the administration was the momentous and pernicious reform of *taxation*. We have often insisted on the fact that the taxation of the early Empire, highly differentiated as it was and based on the traditions prevailing in the various part of the Empire, was not very oppressive. The stress was laid on the indirect taxes and on the income derived by the state and the emperor from the land and other real estate owned by them....The foolish policy of the emperors in systematically depreciating the currency, and the general economic conditions, as well as the system of organized pillage (the Liturgies), produced violent and spasmodic fluctuations of prices which did not keep pace with the steady depreciation of the currency....The most notorious failure was that of Diocletian, both in respect of the currency and in regard to stabilization of prices. His well-known edict of 301, by which fixed prices were established for the various products, was no novelty....As a general measure intended to last, it was certain to do great harm and to cause terrible bloodshed, without bringing any relief. Diocletian shared the pernicious belief which many modern theorists continue to share with him and with it.[7]

> The catastrophe of the third century dealt a severe blow to the prosperity of the Empire and weakened the creative energies of the better part of the population. The reforms of the Diocletian and Constantine, by giving permanence to the policy of organized robbery on the part of the state, made all productive economic activity impossible. But it did not [provide] the formation of large fortunes, rather it contributed to their formation, while altering their character. The foundation of the new fortunes was no longer the creative energy of men, nor the discovery and exploitation of new sources of wealth, nor the improvement and development of commercial, industrial, and agricultural enterprises; it was in the main skillful use of a privileged position in the state to cheat and exploit the state and the people alike. Public officials, both high and low, grew rich on bribery and corruption.[8]

The attempt of the Illyrian emperors to solve the problems of the Roman Empire by structural changes in the administration and in the capture of taxation contributed to the decline. Diocletian sought to de-centralize the administration of the empire by constitutional changes;

but it was not an attempt to de-centralize economically by freeing the people from the depreciation of the currency, the collection of taxes and requisitioning of labor and products. Diocletian divided the empire into two core regions (Greece/Macedonian, and Italy/North Africa) each ruled by an *Augustus*—a pair of senior emperors; and into military frontier regions (Gaul/West Europe; and Asia Minor/Syria/Egypt) each ruled by a *Caeser*—each a future *Augustus*. Diocletian retired as emperor in 305 and lived in his palace at Spalato or Split. Is there not a parallel to Mikhail S. Gorbachev's attempt to solve the crisis of the Soviet system by administrative reforms? At the end, Gorbachev was proposing a new constitutional formula as the answer to the systemic collapse. When Russian society need the oxygen of de-control of the economy to escape the suffocation of state planning, Gorbachev proposed a new re-arrangement of state power in a constitution.

Gorbachev's concentration on government administration and on constitutional changes and reforms parallels the process of the French Revolution. The French Revolution has been an important learning model for classical liberal and Marxian socialist theorists. For the classical liberal, the French Revolution is the model of anti-liberal government programs; for the Marxian socialist, the French Revolution is a model for successful seizure of state power and the means of production.[9]

For classical liberals, the short-lived attempts at reform were destroyed in the French Revolution by the debasement of the money, the confiscations of church and other properties, and the price and wage controls which sought to crush the natural consequences of inflation. One of the most distressing aspects of the French Revolutionary process was a decade which was devoted to seeking to discover the perfect constitution. Having caused major economic disasters, the French revolutionary leaders sought to solve or avoid their self-created problems by ever new constitutional proposals.

For a century and a half after 1789 statesmen and scholars considered the lessons of the French Revolution the great negative reference point for public discourse and public policy formation. The confiscation of the property of the church in 1789 and the issuance of *assignats* created civil war by challenging the peoples' beliefs and expropriating their income through inflation. Until the mid-twentieth century the undermining of French society by the *assignats* was the most important lesson from modern history. The *assignats* were treasury certificates made into compulsory currency by the legislature. The resulting inflation caused the legislature to enact wage and price controls and to empower the committee of Public Safety (*The Twelve Who Ruled*) to carry out the Economic Terror against merchants, artisans, and farmers.[10]

Robert R. Palmer describes the evolution of constitutional thought in Europe, North and South America.[11] The constitutional debate was with reference to the Anglo-American constitutional tradition whereby the constitution might be a means to limit the legislative power in particular, and government power in general, and the French constitutional tradition which did not concentrate on those principles of limitation on the legislative powers. (Recently, there has been a return to these issues with reference to the constitutional court in France, and to the European Court of Justice for the European Community.)

In the coming years, the evolution of a legal tradition, of a court system separate from the government, and a conception of a constitutional limitation on the powers of the executive and the legislature will be important parts of the new societies in the former Soviet Union. Since most of the societies around the world which benefited from eighteenth century debates regarding constitutional limitations on the powers of governments have mostly forgotten the reasons and foundation for the constitutional bases of their progress, the Russian discussion will benefit many other countries.

Perhaps the depth of the emergency for the former Soviet republics is a blessing in disguise. They are unable to try to come up with fresh constitutions before undertaking other activities. The problem which faced the French Revolutionary legislatures and conventions was their concept of writing a constitution *de novo* without reference to the country's previous history, or indeed, in opposition and contrast to the preceding thousand years. The existing administrations in the former Soviet republics can continue to function and confront immense problems, while unofficial thinking and analyses can be made both by professionals and citizens to gain an understanding of limitations on state powers as the principle task for constitutional evolution. If the negative lessons of the seven decades of the reign of the Communist Party can be measured within the thousand years since the formation of Kievan Rus, a perspective regarding a constitutional evolution can emerge. Gorbachev's inability to focus on de-control of the economy and his concentration on government administration structures and constitutional changes parallels the behavior of the legislators of the French Revolution. There was a common fallacy of searching in constitutional arrangements for the problems in the economy. The numerous draft constitutions and constitutions of the French First Republic were an avoidance of solving the high government expenditures paid for by debasement of the currency. Napoleon Bonaparte's success was his recognition that forms of constitutional organization were secondary to the re-establishment of sound monetary foundations. In Revolutionary France, the fiat money, controls and exactions had destroyed all trust. Only the gold standard could revive the economy and substitute for the disappearance of trust.[12]

If the current leaders of the former Soviet republics recognize the secondary importance of constitutions and if they do focus instead on the primary problem of the soundness of the currency, there is some hope of long-term improvement. Whether the Illyrian emperors of the third century or Gorbachev in the late twentieth century, the fantasy of constitutional substitution for monetary soundness led to disaster. But we can go beyond the disaster of the collapse of the Roman empire described by Rostovtzeff to the success of Bonaparte and his successors for a century and a half who kept France on a gold standard and permitted economic growth and political stability.

In the late nineteenth century, Russia, like the United States, Canada, Australia, New Zealand, and Argentina, was an exporter of raw materials, and an importer of European capital. Private investors in America, Canada, Australia, New Zealand, and Argentina borrowed massively from private investors in England and continental Europe. Russia borrowed vast sums from the Paris and Brussels financial markets for state economic entities and state expenditures. America's great progress was due to private borrowing of private European capital. American debtors retired this debt after 1914 when European countries required the sale of the assets by European investors to pay for the costs of the First World War.

America's world political posture was secondary in association with Britain with almost no alliances before 1914. The exception was the Anglo-Japanese Pact of 1902 within which the United States might be said to have sheltered while emphasizing the Open Door and free trade rather than military bases and economic spheres. When Russia collided with the Anglo-Japanese Pact in 1904–1905, the United States sought to extricate Russia from the disaster by mediating the Treaty of Portsmouth, New Hampshire. America's strong interest then in the development of the Manchurian economy through the Open Door seemed more likely under the Anglo-Japanese Pact than Russian control. America's position eroded away from Japan after the Soviet Revolution; the United States pressured Japan to remove its forces that entered Siberia in 1918; and the United States demanded the Open Door in Manchuria, despite Japan's exclusion from American and British markets by the Smoot-Hawley Tariff and Imperial Preference.

During the quarter century before 1914, Russian economic policy was determined by military policies which were based on the attempt of Russia to challenge other major powers regarding parts of Eurasia. Unlike the United States, at that time, Russia sought to act as a major military power with reference to declining empires: the Chinese empire, contesting with Japan; the Persian-Afghan realms, contesting with British India; and the Ottoman Empire in the Balkans, contesting with Austria-Hungary. Before the First World War, Russia was the advancing power, while Japan, Britain, and Austria-Hungary preferred the status quo.

Russian policy of expansion against the established interests of other powers meant that military considerations dominated over economic considerations in government policy making. The Russian state borrowed vast amounts of foreign loans from the Paris and Brussels financial markets for its military goals. The Russian state railway system used these foreign loans to build lines for military objectives, not economic purposes. While many American, English, and European companies built factories in Russia, their expansion was limited by the slow development of the Russian market due to investment in military projects.

With vast natural resources and potential consumer markets, Russia lagged behind other European countries. Being least developed economically, Russia was in advance of European countries in internal crisis. Russia was at the greatest risk in risking war and in undertaking war.

When the Tsar lost the desperate gamble of the mobilization against Germany in August, 1914 by the defeat of the Russian invasion of East Prussia by Paul von Hindenburg and Erich von Ludendorff, the die was cast. Having placed its investments in military objectives, the failure of the military to succeed meant that there was too fragile an economy to sustain the effects of a prolonged war. Unlike the blockaded Central Powers, Russia was able to receive the supplies sent by the Allies, but it did not have sufficient development to adequately utilize the vast supplies which the Allies provided.

The ending of Tsarism removed one of the objections for the United States' associating itself with the Allied coalition in April, 1917. However, the ending of Tsarism did not lead to the ending of Tsarism's heaviest burden on the Russian people, the first world war. In particular, the continuation of the war's eastern front shifted the unspeakable burden on the Russian soldiers. Perhaps, the Soviet Revolution may be seen as a revolt of the soldiers and sailors.

American entry into the war meant the eventual victory of the Allies. The question was how many millions of Russian soldiers would die before a general armistice. The Bolsheviks understood the soldiers' mood best of all.[13]

Once the foreign intervention and the civil war had ended, the Bolsheviks had no reason to fear any military attacks. Yet the Communist Party burdened Russians with a program even more determined by military conceptions. Paul Johnson summarized how General von Ludendorff's war socialism was the model for Soviet economic planning:

> As usual, Lenin thought entirely in terms of control; not of production. He thought that provided he got the system of control right (with the Politburo making all the key decisions), the results would flow inevitably. He was wholly ignorant of the process whereby wealth is created. What he liked were figures; all his life he had an insatiable appetite for bluebooks. One sometimes suspects that inside Lenin there was a bookkeeper genius struggling to get out and bombard the world with ledgers. In all his remarks on economic matters once he achieved power, the phrase which occurs most frequently is "strict accounting and control." To him, statistics were the evidence of success. So the new ministries, and the new state-owned factories, produced statistics in enormous quantities. The output of statistics became, and remains to this day, one of the most impressive characteristics of Soviet industry. But the output of goods was another matter.
>
> By 1917, as we have seen, the Germans had seized upon the state capitalist model of pre-war Russia and married it to their own state, now run by the military. They called it "war socialism." It looked impressive; indeed in many ways it was impressive, and it certainly impressed Lenin. From then on his industrial ideas were all shaped by German practice....When other Bolsheviks objected, Lenin replied with his pamphlet, *On Left Infantilism and the Petty Bourgeois Spirit*: "Yes, learn from the Germans! History proceeds by zigzags and crooked paths. It happens that it is the Germans who now, side by side with bestial imperialism, embody the principle of discipline, of organization, of solidly working together, on the basis of the most modern machinery, of strict accounting and control. And this is precisely what we lack."

German "state capitalism," he said, was a "step forward" to socialism. History had played a "strange trick." It had just given birth to "two separate halves of socialism, side by side, like two chickens in one shell: political revolution in Russia, economic organization in Germany. Both were necessary to socialism. So the new Russia must study the state capitalism of the Germans and adopt it *with all possible strength,* not to spare *dictatorial* methods in order to hasten its adoption of westernism by barbarous Russia, not shrinking from barbarous weapons to fight barbarism."[14]

Ludendorff's organization of war socialism had historical origins in the New Mercantilism which emerged, especially in Germany, in the late nineteenth century as the German Historical School. It is no wonder that the leader of the new generation of the major opponents of the German Historical School, the Austrian School of Economist (based on Carl Menger's Marginalist Revolution of 1870), was Ludwig von Mises.[15]

Mises' initial interests had been primarily historical, and in the end he retained a breadth of historical knowledge rare among theoreticians. But, finally, his dissatisfaction with the manner in which historians and particularly economic historians interpreted their material led him to economic theory. His chief inspiration came from Eugen von Bohm-Bawerk, who had returned to a professorship at the University of Vienna after serving as Austrian Minister of Finance. During the decade before the war, Bohm-Bawerk's seminar became the great center for the discussion of economic theory. Its participants included Mises, Joseph Schumpeter, and the outstanding theoretician of Austrian Marxism, Otto Bauer, whose defense of Marxism long dominated the discussion. Bohm-Bawerk's ideas on socialism during this period appear to have developed a good deal beyond what is shown by the few essays he published before his early death....It must be assumed that he started on *Socialism* only after his release from military duty. He probably wrote most of it between 1919 and 1921—the crucial section on economic calculation under socialism was in fact provoked by a book by Otto Neurath published in 1919, from which Mises quotes.

When *Socialism* first appeared in 1922, its impact was profound. It gradually but fundamentally altered the outlook of many of the young idealists returning to their university studies after World War I. I know for I was one of them. We felt that the civilization in which we had grown up had collapsed. We were determined to build a better world, and it was this desire to reconstruct society that led many of us to the study of economics. Socialism promised to fulfill our hopes for a more rational, more just world. And then came this book. Our hopes were dashed. *Socialism* told us that we had been looking for improvement in the wrong direction. A number of my contemporaries, who later became well known but who were then unknown to each other, went though the same experience: Wilhelm Ropke in Germany and Lionel Robbins in England are but two examples....As students during the early 1920s, many of us were aware of Mises as the somewhat reclusive university lecturer who, a decade or so earlier, had published *Theories des Geldes und der Umlaufsmittel*, known for its successful application of the Austrian marginal utility analysis theory to money—a book Max Weber described as the most acceptable work in the subject. Perhaps we ought to have known that in 1919 he had also published a thoughtful and farseeing study on the wider aspects of social philopsophy, concerning the nation, the state, and economy; *Nation, Staat und Wirtsschaft: Beitrage zur Politik and Geschichte der Zeit.*[16]

Coincidentally, like Carl Menger, Mises had done his earliest work on the peasantry of Galicia from the First Partition of Poland (1772) to the Revolution of 1848. Mises' analysis of the impossibility of calculation under socialist planning was published first as article.[17] Having confronted the institutionalism of the *Verein fur Sozialpolitik* with economic theory, the Austrian school of economists was well prepared to counter the proponents of the institutionalism of Ludendorff's war socialism. Mises' explanation of the failure of socialist economies to calculate provided an immediate and rather widely recognized map among economists of the problems which would be faced by the Soviet Union.

It is important to recognize that theoretical proof of the impossibility of socialist calculation was available in the early 1920s before most of the destructive state planning in the Soviet Union was established. Ultimately, then, socialism was introduced in Russia for reasons of control and domination without any hope of improving the conditions of the Russian people. In the Preface to the second edition of *Socialism*, Mises challenged the pessimism of those who felt that the fallacy of socialism was inevitable:

> And so they will continue to work for Socialism, helping thereby to bring about the inevitable decline of the civilization which the nations of the West have taken thousands of years to build up. And so we must inevitably drift on to the chaos and misery, the darkness of barbarism and annihilation. I do not share this gloomy view. It may happen thus, but it need not happen thus....But new generations grow up with clear eyes and open minds. And they will weigh and examine, will think and act with forethought. It is for them that this book is written.[18]

The Communist Party's adoption of Ludendorff's war socialism permitted political control over society as the price of autarky or minimal economic growth. Unlike war socialism, the Soviet Union pursued central planning as an end itself; foreign policy issues provided external excitement to general popular support for the regime. The separation from the international market ended the discipline on the government of rational policies. For a totalitarian regime a famine can be a positive development within the context of autarky. The Soviet regime was able to carry out the massive annihilation of Russia's human capital once it was protected from the discipline of the international market. The literature on the rational peasant now can increase our understanding of the socialist destruction of Russian agriculture.[19]

The death of Josef Stalin permitted the initiation of a reform perspective by Nikita Khurshchev. But the reform direction was stalled when Khrushchev was replaced by Leonid Brezhvev. Brezhnev assumed power coincidentally with the beginning of a process of change in American polices as the United States began its military escalation in Vietnam. Before the replacement of Khrushchev, Senator Barry Goldwater suggested that contemporary views of a convergence between the Soviet and American economies missed the key point. Goldwater felt that if the process of reform continued in Russia while America turned from the Eisenhower-Kennedy policies, there would not be a convergence between the Soviet and American economies but a by-passing of Russian prosperity with American stagnation.

However, the rise of Brezhnev ended the possibilities of continued Russian reforms. The American economy began its downward spin with the introduction of inflation to tax a tax-shy American electorate to pay for the Vietnam war. The Nixon-Ford-Kissinger period witnessed the continuation of the Vietnam intervention and the continued attraction of inflation to pay for policies the American electorate did not wish to fund from its won pockets directly.

Inflation can give politicians the feeling that they can operate in a new world without the rules of the real world. Inflation masks the economic realities for a period of time; even for a long period of time. Adam Smith noted that there is a lot of ruin in country. A country has often a deep human and moral capital in its citizens as well as financial accumulation from which to draw while pursuing economically damaging policies. Each successive set of politicians takes the innovations of predecessors as a base and introduces new methods of increasing the politicians' financial resources while reducing the resources of the citizenry.

The Nixon-Ford-Kissinger foreign policy viewed the Soviet Union as a difficult player in the world politics if the consequences of its planned economy continued a decline in the Russian standard of living. If Russia was not going to reform its economy, the United States' policy should seek out and subsidize the worst parts of the Soviet economy, such as providing food-stuffs through American loans. The foreign policy of the United States during the 1970s feared a crisis or collapse of the Communist Party of the Soviet Union. The aged leadership of the Soviet Union may have been viewed as insurance against adventurism. The stability of a socialist economy in the Soviet Union provided predictability in foreign relations without the requirement of change in American fiscal and budgetary arrangements which would follow a realistic economic readjustment of the Soviet Union.

For a quarter of a century, the United States not only over-spent on its domestic spending, but also did so in the United States' foreign and military budget. So long as the Soviet Union had the appearance of a major adversary, however hollow its economy really was, the United States spent vast amounts on its military. The Pentagon budget made General Motors, when it was on top of the world market, look like a medium-sized enterprise.

Beyond the military portion of the United States' foreign spending, large amounts were spent during the last quarter century on foreign aid grants, and on loans from the United States government, from American funded international agencies such as the International Monetary Fund and World Bank, and from loans from American money-centered banks to foreign governments. Because the United States government gave formal or informal guarantees or encouragement through American bank loans, these were often the least well utilized investments. The United States government and the international agencies had mechanisms to monitor the loans made to sovereign entities, while the American money-center banks acted as though their debtors were private companies engaged in market activities and, subsequently, did not monitor them. At the least, the U.S. Government and the international agencies knew they had to behave towards foreign governments as they would towards a repeated murderer on parole. When the accounting is made at the year 2000, it will be discovered that the cost of uncollectable Western loans and interest for the past quarter of a century will be many hundreds of billions of dollars. These former savings and investments have not been, and will never be, available to American citizens to provide for their future and future of the economy for their children.

The American electorate's wariness of the existence of a growing financial problem permitted the successful confrontation with inflation. The inflation problem was the principal problem facing the United States and Western countries at the end of the 1970s. Inflation led to the replacement of incumbents as leaders of America, Canada, England, Germany, and France. The successful struggle against inflation by the American Federal Reserve Bank has meant that it is possible to try to solve other economic problems. The other economic problems were not challenged in the 1980s and they have become worse. If the Pentagon and Agricultural Department are seen as among the largest economic entities in the world economy, the increased expenditures for them explain the vast increase during the 1980s of the United States public debt. While the great battle against inflation was successfully won, the secondary battles against the spending of the Pentagon and Agriculture Department are totally lost.

In a sense, the electorate's absolute resistance to paying for government spending by inflation and by taxation was by-passed by Congress through the payment for increased government spending by public debt. While not yet reaching the Italian state debt, which equals the Italian gross national product, the American public debt, resulting from inability to control run-away government spending in the 1980s, has meant that for the foreseeable future the United States must exercise restraint in its foreign aid and loans.

Both the American government and the money-center banks are not in the position to maintain any level of support for foreign aid and loans. American and other western companies. However, due to the success a decade ago in confronting inflation, they will be able to invest in Russia and other countries.

The timing of the collapse of the socialist planned economy is related to the American and Western European crises due to the non-repayability of the loans to Socialist Bloc and Third World countries. The huge over-hang of unpaid and unpayable loans, in many multiples of hundreds of billions of dollars of savings, made it impossible for the present, or for the future, for the United States and other Western countries to sustain through further loans the failure of socialist economies.

One important factor was the Tax Reform Act of 1986. In an attempt to reduce inefficient incentives caused by tax exemptions, an advantageous tax treatment for non-managing partners in commercial real estate, such as office buildings, was abolished. The advantageous treatment in taxation had attracted heavy loans from savings and loan banks increasing the value of office buildings. Once the favorable tax treatment was abolished, the value of American commercial real estate declined strongly, undermining the financial strength of the savings and loan banks, now holding hollow loans. This unintended consequence of the tax reform has meant very high new indebtedness as payments to the failed savings and loan bank depositors escalate. Another consequence is severe short-falls in local and state taxes, as government spending was based on the high assessments of the previously inflated values of commercial real estate. The new realistic assessments mean much lower tax income for the localities and states.

The financial crisis of the overly taxed and overly regulated United States and other Western countries has had the effect of liberating the economies of the former Soviet republics. However difficult the necessary adjustments toward freeing the economies of both east and west may be, all the societies are presented with an opportunity to set the stage for economic growth in each of the economies. It required the less dramatic collapse of the semi-planned economies of the west, of the United States and Western Europe, for the economies of the countries of East-Central Europe and the former Soviet Republic to gain their liberation. Rather than the "End of History" we are faced with a full measure of the unpredictability of history.

Endnotes

1. Brinton, Crane, *Anatomy of Revolution*, Random House, New York, 1965.
2. ————., *Decade of Revolution, 1789–1799*, Harper and Row, New York.
3. In 1926, Rostovtzeff published *The Social and Economic History of the Roman Empire* (2nd edition, 1957, Oxford at the Clarendon Press).
4. Rostovtzeff, *The Social and Economic History of the Roman Empire*, Clarendon Press, Oxford, 1966, pp. 449–50.
5. Ibid., p. 453.
6. Ibid., pp. 470–73.
7. Ibid., pp. 514–16.
8. Ibid., p. 530.
9. The meetings of the International Congress of the Historical Sciences have been graced by the sessions of the Robespierrist Society of the German Democratic Republic. Like Crane Brinton, Robert R. Palmer of Princeton and Yale Universities examined the rule of Robespierre and the Terror in *The Twelve Who Ruled: The Year of the Terror in the French Revolution* (1941).
10. The most recent and best analysis of the economics of the French Revolution is by the Directeur du Centre de tchniques financieres, ESSEC, Paris, Professor Florin Aftalion, *The French Revolution: An Economic Interpretation* (Paris, Editions de la Maison des Sciences de L'Homme, and Cambridge, Cambridge University Press, 1990; translation of *L'Economie de la Revolution Française*, Paris, Hachette, 1987).
11. Palmer, Robert R., *The Age of the Democratic Revolution, 1760–1800*, 2 volumes, Princeton University Press, Princeton, NJ, 1959.

12. ————., *The World of the French Revolution*, Harper and Row, New York, 1971. Translation from *1789: Les Revolutions de la Liberté et de l'Égalité*, Calmann-Levy, Paris, 1967.

13. George Kennan's magisterial study, *Soviet-American Relations, 1917–1920*, Volume 1, *Russia Leaves the War*, 1956; *The Decision to Intervene*, Volume 2, 1958, Princeton University Press, provides us with a sense of the tragedy which the Tsar's decision to mobilize in 1914 caused for Russia, not to mention the rest of Europe.

14. Johnson, Paul, *Modern Times: The World from the Twenties to the Eighties*, Harper and Row, New York, 1983, pp. 89–90.

15. Ibid., p. 237.

16. F. A. Hayek, "Foreward," Ludwig von Mises, *Socialism*, Indianapolis, Liberty Classics, 1981 (New Haven, Ct., Yale University Press, 1951; 1st edition: *Die Gemeinwirtschaft: Untersuchungen uber den Socialismus*, Jena, Gustav Fischer, 1922), pp. xxi, xix–xx.

17. Mises 1920 article on the socialist calculation question was published in English as "Economic Calculation in the Socialist Commonwealth," in F.A. Hayek, ed., *Collectivist Economic Planning*, Routledge and Kegan, London, 1935, pp. 87–130.

18. Mises', *Socialism*, p. 13.

19. Popkin, Samuel L., *The Rational Peasant*, University of California Press, Berkeley, 1979; Powelson, John P., & Stock, Richard, *The Peasant Betrayed, Agriculture and Land Reform in the Third World*, Cato Institute, Washington, D.C., 1990; and Shanin, Teodor, "A Peasant Househould: Russia at the Turn of the Century," in Teodor Shanin, ed., *Peasants and Peasant Societies*, Basil Blackwell, Oxford, 1987.

Causes of the Collapse of the Communist System: Present Situation and Future Prospects in Hungary

Rudolf Andorka
Budapest University of Economic Sciences

Hungary's free multi-party parliamentary election in spring 1990, marks a thoroughgoing change of the political, economic, and social system. It may even be considered a revolution, if revolution is defined as an extremely rapid and very radical change; and if bloodshed is not considered to be an essential element of the definition of a revolution.

Essentially, no social scientist predicted the revolutions that happened around 1990 in Eastern Central Europe. More optimistic social scientists, such as myself, hoped that a slow evolutionary process, beginning with the increased role of the market in the economy and leading finally to some form of a multiparty system, would come to Hungary from Western Europe, and that Hungary would slowly "converge" toward the market-oriented democratic societies. More pessimistic social scientists considered the communist system to be deeply totalitarian — "Asian despotism" — and therefore could never change peacefully, but only through defeat in war or through a bloody revolution.

Contrary to these predictions, the revolutionary changes happened very rapidly and without bloodshed. It is highly interesting to investigate the causes of the changes and to formulate hypotheses on the possible factors of change that were neglected by most social scientists.

Compendiums of social indicators on Hungary[1] and many sociological surveys are available in Hungary for the study of the changes of the society. These data are analyzed within the framework of the three dimensional welfare-theory of Allardt, used in a comparative analyses of Scandinavian countries. The three dimensions of human motivations, needs, or welfare are:

1. having (material living conditions);
2. loving (human relations);
3. being (self-actualization, the opposite being alienation or anomie).[2]

Thus we first analyze how the communist system performed—or how much it failed—in these three dimensions, and how much these failures contributed to the collapse of the system.

Material living conditions

The standard of living, or material living conditions, improved to an important degree during the 45 years following the end of the Second World War. The index of the per capita real personal income of the population increased from 100 in 1950 to 375 in 1990, the index of per capita consumption to 344, and the real wage index to 216. Two remarks ought to be added, however, to these indices:

1. Although it is very difficult to make international comparisons of the level of living and of the per capita GDP, it ought to be stated that according to the comparisons based on a Physical Indicator Model of Ehrlich, the growth rate of the socialist Hungarian economy was somewhat slower than the growth rate of neighboring capitalist Austria: the per capita GDP of Austria was 158 per cent of that of Hungary in 1937, 180 in 1960, 196 in 1970, 191 in 1980 and 209 in 1986.[3]

2. The improvement of the personal income slowed down, indeed almost stopped, after 1978; the real wage index never again attained its highpoint in 1978 and stood at 86 per cent of the level of 1978 in 1990. The real personal income per capita slowly increased after 1978 and almost stagnated in the second half of the 1980s, in consequence of the growing income of the population from the second economy. This extra income from the second economy was attained, however, through increased work-time input, resulting in long total working time of the Hungarian population, as shown by time budget surveys.[4] Thus the improvement of the material living conditions was achieved at the cost of higher efforts than in capitalist countries at similar levels of socioeconomic developments.

It ought to be added, that in contradiction to the official ideology, the income distribution in Hungary was far from equal. In terms of the per capita household income the highest decile obtained 20.2 per of the total personal income in 1962, and 20.9 percent in 1987, the lowest decile obtained 3.9 percent in 1962 and 4.5 percent in 1987. It seems that the income inequality in Hungary was similar to the inequality in the Scandinavian countries.[5]

Of all the material living conditions, housing was the most acutely bottlenecked in previous decades. Most of the extra income of the households, dispensable after satisfying basic needs, was used to build new housing and to improve the existing housing conditions. In consequence, 67 per cent of the housing stock in 1990 was built after 1945 (40 per cent in the 1970s and 1980s). The quality of the housing stock also improved, which might be illustrated by the fact that in 1949 only 13 per cent of the dwellings had a water flush toilet and in 1990 74 per cent had such a toilet.

It ought to be said, however, that in contradiction to earlier ideological promises, the great majority of the new housing was built by private resources, not by the state, and that new housing construction by the state declined strongly in the 1900. Consequently, the difficulties of obtaining housing for newly married couples intensified, and young adults could get a dwelling almost only by building it privately or by buying a dwelling. In order to get an idea of the resources needed to acquire a dwelling, it might be mentioned that in 1990 the cost of construction of a new dwelling of the modest size of 50 square metres was equivalent to more than seven years total average wages.

Human relations

Max Weber observed that in less developed societies, strong solidarity exists within the small face-to-face groups, with every stranger considered to be a potential enemy. Therefore cheating, plundering. and pillaging is permitted against out-group people. In more advanced societies, however, a certain minimum of goodwill and honesty is required among all people cooperating in the society.[6] Lindenberg introduced the concept of "weak solidarity" to describe this cooperative attitude among members of advanced societies needed for the functioning of a market economy and a democratic political system.[7]

All the data indicate that in Hungary strong solidarity within family, kinship, and friendship groups is very widespread. Members of these face-to-face small groups not only have frequent personal contacts, but can also rely on mutual help in case of need. When asked "on whose help can you rely in case of greater work tasks, e.g. building a house?", 83 percent of the interviewed adults mentioned somebody who would provide the help needed, and 70 percent mentioned family members and kin. Thus the present Hungarian situation is reminiscent of the situation in Germany during and after the Second World War, when in conditions of severe hardship and the breakdown of the institutions of the state, the family provided the protection and support necessary for the survival of individuals.[8] It might be hypothesized that in Hungary the family and other primary groups helped the individuals to cope with hardships caused by the communist system.

At the same time, however, survey results pointed to a widespread mistrust and hostility toward strangers, members of the society who do not belong to the face-to-face relations. Utasi explained this lack of trust by the authoritarian character of the regime, in which strangers might be police informers or might use their political influence to do harm to the individual.[9]

Alienation and anomie

It might be assumed that an advanced economy and society is able to function successfully only if the majority of its members are innovative, set prospective goals for themselves, strive to achieve these goals (i.e. have a "Protestant Ethic"), and if the members of the society, with a few exceptions, agree on certain moral norms and the values supporting these norms.[10] In other terms, an advanced society in which alienation and anomie are widespread can not function well.

The definitions of alienation and anomie are far from clear and unanimous in sociology. In consequence, their measurement causes many methodological problems. It is, however, usually assumed in the sociology of deviance that the different types of deviant behavior, which can be measured, are caused by anomie. Certain types of deviance, all of which belong to the "retreatist" type, are very widespread in Hungary and increased strongly since the Second World War.[11]

The suicide rate was 17.7 per 100 thousand population at its lowest point in 1954 (the year of the first I. Nagy Government, which attempted to moderate the totalitarian character of the communist system), and increased to 45.9 in 1984, when it attained its highest point; it leveled off in the following years. Three percent of the Hungarians die as a consequence of suicide. The number of attempted suicides is much higher: according to a survey in 1988, 15.6 per cent of the interviewed persons aged 16 years and up attempted suicide at least once in their life.

The death rate by liver cirrhosis, used as a measure of the frequency of alcoholism, increased from 5.0 per 100 thousand population in 1950 to 51.9 in 1989. It might be estimated that every seventh male becomes an alcoholic during his life.

According to a survey in 1988, three percent of the adult population was seriously depressive, five percent medium-level depressive, and 17 percent showed slight depressive symptoms.[12]

The immediate cause behind these deviant behaviors was, according to the sociological survey, the stressfulness of everyday life. In 1990,

42 percent of the adults complained of sleeping problems, 54 percent of exhaustion, 60 percent of frequent psychological stresses, 46 percent of headaches, and 34 percent of down-heartedness. Twenty-five percent of the adults took sedatives, sleeping pills and/or medication for headaches several times during a week.

It might be hypothesized that deeper causes behind these mental problems were alienation and anomie. Four questions in a survey in 1978, repeated in a survey in 1990, provide the possibility of evaluating not only the state, but also the growth of some dimensions of alienation and anomie (Tables 1–2). Self-estrangement (feeling useless), senselessness of personal life (life has no sense), lack of future prospectives (it is not worth it to formulate perspective plans), and norm and value crisis (one does not know how to live) not only occurred frequently, but increased during the 12 years preceding the collapse of the system.

The fact that the majority of Hungarians considered themselves to be incapable of directing their own life might be at the root of alienation and anomie. In 1990, 30 percent of the interviewed adults considered the statement: "I have the possibility to attain in my life what I desire," to be "not true." The other 41 percent considered it to be "partly true." Eighteen percent considered that the statement; "It depends on my own decisions, how my life turns out," to be "not true," and 42 percent considered it to be "partly true".

Table 1.

Statements on perspective life goals and on life principles, 1978 and 1990

Statement: It is not worth while to make plans to formulate prospective life goals.

Year	Does not Agree	Partly Agrees	Completely Agrees	Total
		percent		
1978	69	17	14	100
1990	17	35	48	100

Statement: Ideals, purposes, principles change so rapidly that one does not know in what to believe and how to live.

Year	Does not Agree	Partly Agrees	Completely Agrees	Total
		percent		
1978	46	33	21	100
1990	13	28	59	100

Table 2.
Statements on the sense of life and on self-confidence,
1978 and 1990

Question: How often do you have the feeling that your life has no sense, no purpose?

Year	Never	Sometimes	Often	Very often	Continuously	Total
			percent			
1978	72	19	4	3	2	100
1990	55	33	6	4	2	100

Question: How often do you lose your faith in yourself, do you have the feeling that you are useless for every purpose?

Year	Never	Sometimes	Often	Very often	Continuously	Total
			percent			
1978	71	22	4	2	1	100
1990	53	38	5	3	1	100

When the degree of influence on the decisions affecting one's own life regarding fields of decision was investigated, (Table 3), it turned out that Hungarians consider themselves to be rather influential in the decisions of their family, much less in decisions at their working place, uninfluential in their local community, and completely powerless on the national level.

It is noticeable that 0.14 per cent of the adults, i.e. an equivalent of about 10 thousand persons in the total population, stated they had a decisive influence on the national level, and another 3 per cent, i.e. an equivalent to about 200 thousand people, stated they had influence on the national level. Ten thousand is not far from the estimated number of the top-power elite, and 200 thousand is not far from the estimated number of "service class" serving as the middle-level power-base of the regime. Thus powerlessness might be considered the deepest cause of alienation and anomie.

Concluding this cursory overview of the performance of the communist system during the past 45 years, it might be hypothesized that within the economic dimension, the system performed worse than the neighboring capitalist economies. Nevertheless, though it achieved a certain level of modernization, the system's performance was much worse in the field of human relations, and most of all in the dimension of

Table 3.
Statement on the influence in decisions affecting one's own life, 1978

Has decisive influence	Has influence	Has little influence	Has no influence	Total
		percent		

Field of the decision:

In the family;

| 42 | 52 | 4 | 2 | 100 |

In the immediate working place, milieu, shop, working group;

| 24 | 56 | 12 | 8 | 100 |

On the working place, on the level of the enterprise, institution;

| 8 | 37 | 27 | 28 | 100 |

In the village, urban district, town where you reside;

| 1 | 12 | 18 | 69 | 100 |

On the national level;

| 0* | 3 | 10 | 87 | 100 |

*0.14 per cent of the interviewed persons stated that they have decisive influence in questions decided on the national level.

alienation and anomie. The greatest harm seems to have been inflicted in the last two dimensions. Just as "weak solidarity" among the members of the society and alienation and anomie might be considered to be serious obstacles for further modernization, the collapse might have been caused by the failures in the "loving" and "being" dimensions of welfare and well-being.

Political opinions

The poor performance of the economy, primarily after 1978, and the harm caused by the communist system in the field of human relations, and in the dimension of alienation and anomie, have to be perceived by an important part of the population in order to generate a will to change the system. Questions on the desirability for change, and of the reform of the economic and of the political system in 1988, proved that the dissatisfaction was very widespread and the wish for some type of change existed in the great majority of the population (Table 4).

Answers to other questions on the same survey indicate that the ideas about the exact form of the desired reforms and changes and the

Table 4
Opinions on the necessity of changes, reforms, 1988

	Very necessary	Necessary	Not necessary	No opinion	Total
		Percent			
Economic system:	76	16	2	6	100
Political system:	40	44	7	9	100

Table 5.
Opinions on societal goals, 1988

Desired Goal:	Very much	Rather	Medium	Rather not	Not at all	No answer	Total
			Percent				
Freedom	45	31	13	5	1	5	100
Democracy	53	31	8	1	0	7	100
National independence	54	31	8	1	1	5	100
Efficient econ. reform	53	28	8	2	1	8	100
Full employment	57	25	9	4	1	4	100
Security of life	74	19	3	0	0	4	100

goals to be achieved were rather vague, sometimes contradictory. A greater role of the market and the privatisation of state-owned enterprises and institutions was desired alongside the wish to avoid unemployment and the growth of income inequalities. Nevertheless, it seems to be clear that aside from "bread-and butter worries," problems of daily livelihood were the greatest concern for most Hungarians. The degradation of moral standards, the visible signs of social inequity, like the advantages enjoyed by party members and the lack of freedom, were also deeply resented. When interviewed about desirable societal goals in 1988, security of life, full employment and an efficient economy proved to be the highest priorities, but national independence, democracy and freedom were also stated to be very desirable (Table 5). Therefore, it is understandable that although economic changes had the greatest support in the population, the great majority also demanded changes in the political system (Table 4).

An intensive debate is going on both in Hungary and throughout the foreign literature regarding the main actors of the regime transition. According to one standpoint, opposition political groups were the main actors because they forced the Communist power elite to abdicate from the monopoly of political power. An opposite standpoint emphasizes that the reformist groups in the power elite itself recognized that the system had to be changed and therefore played the most important role in the transition. The above mentioned data from the survey of 1988, however, permit me to formulate the hypothesis that the main factor in the transition was the mass of the population, which was very much dissatisfied with the socialist system and demanded thoroughgoing changes. The political opposition simply articulated these demands and the power elite in return yielded to the pressure of these demands. This hypothesis does not unduly diminish the role of the opposition and the power elite because the open expression of demands for change were of vital importance, and the willingness of the power elite to accept the regime transition speaks to its intelligence.

The changes in the first two years following the political transition to a democratic political system, 1990–1992

In spring 1990, the political system changed from a one-party dictatorship to a multi-party parliamentary democracy. The Popperian criteria of democracy, namely that the rulers, i.e. the government, can be exchanged peacefully by the population through a free election was met. The parliamentary election of spring 1990, using a rather complicated two-round election, where nearly half of the members of the parliament were elected on party lists and the other half in personal voting districts, resulted in a reasonably balanced parliament. The Hungarian Democrats Smallholders and Christian Democrats emerged with a stable majority, while the the Free Democrats, the Socialists and the Young Democrats provided a strong opposition. No extremist party was able to attain the four percent threshold needed to be represented in the parliament, and no candidate expressing relatively extremist opinions during the election campaign was able to win in any personal voting district.

Positive changes in other domains of the economy and the society were slower to become visible. The GDP, after essentially stagnating in 1988 and 1989, declined by four percent in 1990, and a somewhat greater decline occurred in 1991. However, there is hope that this decline will halt due to the dynamic growth of the small private enterprises. In a spring 1991 survey, 17 per cent of those interviewed stated that they or members of their household are or were engaged in some form of private business. The rate of inflation, significant since the first half of the 1980s, attained 29 per cent in 1990, and 35 per cent in 1991, but began to decline recently. Unemployment approached ten percent in the first months of 1992.

The average per capita income of the population declined, but somewhat less than the GDP. What is more important from the point of view of the social reaction to the changes of the system is the growth of income inequalities. From a survey of 1,000 earners interviewed both in 1989, and in the spring of 1991, the changes of incomes may be speculated:[13]

From April 1989 to April 1991	Percent
The nominal income declined	7
The real income declined	42
The real income stagnated	13
The real income increased slightly	18
The real income increased strongly	15
The real income more than doubled	5
Total	100

Thus half of those interviewed suffered a decline in the real income, but 20 per cent enjoyed a significant increase in their income level. Pensioners, non-skilled workers, and peasants were over-represented among those who suffered losses, and those who became private entrepreneurs and who changed over from employment in the state sector into employment in the private sector usually showed gains. More highly educated sectors of the society (among others, most of the former party and state bureaucracy) were more able to become entrepreneurs and to find jobs in the new private enterprises, including foreign enterprises. The privileged strata of the communist system experienced gains in terms of income. In somewhat simplified terms, the rich became richer and the poor became poorer. Altogether, however, the economic performance of the first two years following the system transition was not entirely bad, and certainly somewhat better than expected by social scientists.

No data are available on the changes in human relations. The growth in the reported crime rate seems, however, a rather unfavorable sign of growing aggressiveness. Impressionistic experiences seem to indicate that aggressive behavior is spreading into in everyday life, e.g. in urban and highway traffic and also in the working places. The political debate in the parliament and in mass communication lacks the tolerance needed in a democracy.

No new survey data are as yet available on alienation and anomie. One fact, however, ought to be stated: the suicide rate, after essentially stagnating from 1984 to 1987, suddenly declined to 41.4 in 1988, and again to 39.9 in 1990. The death rate by liver cirrhosis, the indicator of alcoholism, also did not increase in 1990 as compared to 1989. If the incidence of "retreatism" in these types of deviant behaviors continue to be lower than in the last years of the communist regime, interesting new theories could be developed relevant to their causes.

Future prospects

In view of the failure to predict the changes that happened in Eastern Central Europe around 1989, it would be foolish to make predictions on future development. Some facts, nevertheless, might be mentioned which: 1) justify a cautious optimism concerning the development of the market economy and of a democratic political system in Hungary, and which 2) might endanger it.

The most obvious danger is an eventual long-lasting and very deep depression, which would result in the pauperization of a major part of the society. The disenchantment with the decline in the standard of living is already loud and widespread. The dilemma here is whether it is preferable to have a relatively rapid transition, resulting in a temporary worsening of the standard of living for a significant part of the population, or a slower transition resulting in longer but less shocking decline in the overall level of living. In other words, how far should the segments of the society suffering from the consequences of the transition be protected by social policies which drain part of the economic resources providing a basis for a more rapid economic upswing? The only real political alternative that played a role in the parliamentary election of 1990 (apart from the personal sympathies and antipathies) was that the Hungarian Democrats and the Christian Democrats promised a less rapid transition and more protection for the poorer part of the society than the Free Democrats who at that time were clearly favoring a "shock therapy" and rapid transition. It seemed that the majority of the population preferred the more cautious approach of the parties that after the election.

The appearance of extremist parties—either of the right-wing or of the left-wing type (which, by the way, are usually difficult to distinguish in this part of Europe)—is a more frightful perspective than the economic hardships themselves. The real danger of pauperization is, indeed, that the disenchanted parts of the population might suddenly turn to extremist movements. At present, fortunately, the few extremists and groups (e.g. newspapers) do not seem to have any support in the society.

The greatest danger, however, is the lack of a civil society. This means not simply the markets, societal institutions, and associations which are independent of the state and provide a forum for discussion of public matter,[14] but also civility and self-reliance of the citizens, i.e. their ability and willingness to do things themselves: the tolerance and respect of different opinions.[15]

One of Hungary's important assets in the present period of system transformation are the economic reforms of the centrally planned socialist economic system which were proposed in 1954 and implemented in 1968. Although the path of reform was full of setbacks (it might be best characterized by Lenin's famous dictum: "two steps forward, one step backward") and failures, and though it finally became clear that a market economy cannot work on the basis of a predominance of state ownership of the enterprises, the opening of possibilities of private production for a private market taught the majority of Hungarians the skills of private business behavior. In 1988 only 19 per cent of the adults stated that they did not participate in any form of the second economy, which was in fact a small private sector, tolerated by the government. According to the time budget survey of 1986/1987, 34 per cent of the total working time of Hungarian adults was used in the second economy; i.e. it amounted to about half of the working time input of the first socialist economy.[16] It is more difficult to measure the income generated in the second economy, but it might not be far from reality to estimate that in 1987, at least 20 per cent of the income of households originated from activities in the second economy. Ivan Szalényi[17] predicted already before the system change that an "embourgeoisement" process will develop in Hungary on the basis of the second economy. After the system change, when the policy of the government encourages small-scale private production, this "embourgeoisement" might proceed much more rapidly.

The second important asset of Hungary might be the relatively high education level of the population. Although educational policies in the 1970s and 1980s tended to limit the enrollment in tertiary education and in the gymnasia, which provided general secondary education (as distinguished from specialized secondary educational institutions), the great majority of the Hungarian society might be considered to be well educated, having a rather high level of general cultural knowledge and specialized skills.

In past decades, Western cultural influence has dominated Hungary, despite efforts by the power elite to counterbalance it by the indoctrination of socialist and Soviet culture and ideology. From this point of view, a remarkable indicator of this is that many more Hungarians are speaking Western European languages than Russian.

All this results in the widespread skepticism of most Hungarians toward any demagogy or extremist political movements. Extremist parties were never able to gain more than one quarter of the votes in a fair election: the Hungarian Nazi party obtained 25 percent of the votes in 1939, when they were at the top of their influence in the society, and the Communist Party obtained 22 percent of the votes in 1947.

Fortunately, there is no important national minority in Hungary (with the exception of the Gypsy ethnicity, amounting to about five to six per cent of the population) and therefore no real basis for the development of a "resentful nationalism." The conditions of the Hungarian minorities in the neighboring countries cause concern, but almost everyone agrees that existing frontiers can not be changed in this part of Europe and considers that the way toward the solution of the problems of national minorities comes via the protection of their human rights and finally through the political unification of Europe.

Last, but not least, Victor Pérez-Diaz suggested, on the basis of the experience of the regime change in Spain, that in a new democracy a certain democratic tradition has to be invented.[18] In Hungary, the revolution of 1956 provides an excellent case for such a "reinvention." In 1956, when Hungarian society was heroically fighting for freedom and democracy, all emerging political parties and movements were willing to accept the rules of democracy. Therefore the revolution of 1956 might serve as a reference for all Hungarians who today face the difficulties inherent in the transition to a market economy and to a democratic system.

In conclusion, I wish to express my own—certainly somewhat subjective—feelings concerning the future of the Hungarian economy, society and democratic political system. Dahrendorf,[19] in his reflections on the revolution in Eastern Central European countries, guessed that the formal process of constitutional reform, transforming the authoritarian system into a democratic system, takes at least six months: the general feeling that things are improving as a result of the market-oriented reform is unlikely to spread before six years have passed; but sixty years will be barely enough to lay the foundations of a democratic society, for the civil society to become real. Agreeing with Dahrendorf on the order of magnitude of these three developments, I would dare to be a bit more optimistic: the constitutional transition to democracy is fully achieved, I hope that the first signs of the improvement of the general standard of living will be visible in one to two years, and a really democratic culture and mentality will develop when our grandchildren have grown to adult-hood—in 30 years.

Endnotes

1. Andorka, R., Harcsa, I., "Modernization in Hungary in the Long and Short Run Measured by Social Indicators," *Social Indicators Research*, Vol. 23, No. 1-2, 1990, p. 1-99.

2. Allardt, E., *Dimensions of Welfare in a Comparative Scandinavian Study*, Research Group for Comparative Sociology, University of Helsinki, Research Reports, no. 9, 1975, p. 25.

3. Ehrlich, É., *Országok versenye 1937-1986*, Közgazdasági ás Jogi Könyvkiadó, Budapest, 1991 p. 234.

4. Andorka, R., Falussy, B., "The way of life of the Hungarian Society on the Basis of the Time Budget Survey of 1976-1977". *Social Indicators Research*, Vol. 11, no. 1, 1982, pp. 31-74.

   And: Andorka, R., Harcsa, I., "Economic Development and the Use of Time in Hungary, Poland and Finland," In: *Time Use Studies: Dimensions and Applications*, As, D., Harvey, A.S., WnukLipinski, E., Niemi, I., eds, Helsinki, Central Statistical Office of Finland, 1986, pp. 7-35.

5. Andorka, R., "The Use of Time Series in International Comparison," In: *Comparative Methodology, Theory and Practices in International Social Research*, Oyen, E. ed., Sage, London, 1990. pp. 203-223.

6. Weber, M., *Wirtschaftsgeschichte*, Ducker und Humblot, Berlin, 1958.

7. Lindenberg, S., "Contractual Relations and Weak Solidarity: The Behavioral Basis of Restraints on Gain-Maximization," *Journal of Institutional and Theoretical Econmics*, Vol. 14, pp. 39-58.

8. Schelsky, H., *Wandlungen der deutschen Familis in der Gegenwart*, Enke, Stuttgart, 1960, p. 418.

9. Utasi, A., "Az interperszonális kapcsolatok néhány nemzeti sajátosságáról," In: *Társas kapcsolatok*, Utasi, A. ed., Gondolat, Budapest, 1991, p. 169-193.

10. Hirsch, F., *Social Limits to Growth*, Routledge and Kegan Paul, London, 1977, p. 208.

11. Merton, R.K., "Social Structure and Anomie," *American Sociological Review*, Vol. 3, 1938, pp. 672–682.

12. Kopp, M., Skrabski, A., *Munkaképesség csökkenés – pszichológiai és szociális háttértényezök – népességi rétegek szerint*, Vol. 1–2, PxKft, Budapest, 1989, pp. 176–156.

13. Kolosi, T., Róbert, P., *A rendszerváltás társadalmi hatásai*, TÅRKI, Budapest, 1991, p. 35.

14. Pérez-Diaz, V., *Civil Society and the State: The Rise and Fall of the State as the Bearer of a Moral Project*, Instituto Juan March de Estudios e Investigationes Working Paper 1992/3, Madrid, 1992, p. 27.

15. Dahrendorf, R., *Reflections on the Revolution in Europe*, Chatto and Windus, London, 1990, p. 154.

16. Falussy, B., A magyar társadalom életmódjának változásai az 1976–77, évi és az 1986–87, évi idômérleg felvételek alapján, KSH, Budapest, 1990, p. 350.

17. Szelényi, I., *Socialist Entrepreneurs. Embourgeoisement in Rural Hungary*, University of Wisconsin Press, Madison, 1988, p. 255.

18. Pérez-Diaz, V., *The Emergence of a Democratic Spain and the "Invention" of a Democratic Tradition*, Instituto Juan March de Estudios e Investigaciones Working Paper 1990/1, Madrid, 1990, p. 46.

19. Dahrendorf, Ralf, *Reflections on the Revolution in Europe*, Chatto, London, 1990.

Varieties of Russian Nationalism

*Francis Fukuyama**

The worshipping of one's own people as the chosen vessel of the universal truth; then the worshipping of one's own people as an elemental force, independent of its relationship to the universal truth, finally the worshipping of the historical anomalies and the national particularism which separates one's people form civilized mankind, i.e., the worshipping of one's own people of the basis of a denial of the universal truth; these are the three stages of our nationalism.

Vladimir Solovev

I. The Significance of Russian Nationalism after August 1991

The failure of the August 19, 1991 coup attempt in Moscow accelerated the process of democratization and hastened the disintegration of the Union, but it also paradoxically increased the chances that a hostile, anti-Western Russian nationalist regime will one day emerge on Russian soil. Indeed, after the coup it is safe to say that Russian nationalism is virtually the only mobilizational ideology that could serve as the basis for the re-emergence of a significant military threat to the West from the territory of the former USSR.

The failure of the August 19, 1991 coup was important for Russian nationalism because it spelled the demise of Russian nationalism's some-time partner, sometime rival, communism. The abortive coup confirmed what has been increasingly evident for the past year or two, namely, that anti-communism is one of the most potent political forces in Russia today. It also revealed the tremendous weaknesses of the Soviet communist party and undermined the latter's ability to operate as a coherent political force in the post-coup environment. Up until the coup itself, a great many conservative Russian nationalists had been locked in a tight alliance with communist fundamentalists and other hardliners in the

---

*The views expressed here are the author's alone and do not reflect those of the Rand Corporation or its sponsors.

police and army. That alliance went down to a crashing defeat, and it should be evident now to many nationalists that their ties to the communist party—which were for many merely a matter of tactics—were much more of a liability than an advantage. The state is now set for the emergence of a purer form of Russian nationalism, unhobbled by ties to an illegitimate and discredited CPSU.

The coup improved the prospects for Russian nationalism in a second way as well. With the old Soviet Union no longer in existence and its constituent republics moving quickly toward independence, some 25–30 million ethnic Russians will now find themselves stranded in what have become foreign countries. While some will find homes in this new order, many will, like the French colonists in Algeria, make their way home to Russian, while others will likely be objects of persecution by intolerant nationalisms in their new "host countries." Just as in the case of the Serbs living in Croatia and Bosnia, this group of extra-territorial Russians will constitute the major bone of contention between Russia and the other republics, and will guarantee that the breakup of the Union will not be accomplished painlessly. Their plight, as well as that of those who have returned to Russia, will become a major preoccupation for Russian nationalist of all stripes in the months and years ahead. When coupled with the economic collapse that the entire country is undergoing, it is easy to see why the current situation has been compared to that of Weimar Germany in the 1920s. At a minimum, the new Russia promises to be unstable; at a maximum, we cannot rule out the eventual emergence of a fascist Russia.

And yet, it is important to recognize that while a fascist Russia is the most threatening to us, it is just one of several possible outcomes of the current political turmoil in the USSR. There are a variety of forms that Russian nationalism can take, and at the moment the dominant one, represented by Russian president Boris Yeltsin, is remarkably moderate, tolerant, and non-expansionist. Over the coming months and years, it will be important for policy makers to learn to distinguish between legitimate expression of national interest and those that threaten regional or world order or otherwise contradict fundamental Western values. They must understand the need to make careful distinctions between various forms of nationalism, encouraging moderate ones and being vigilant against the emergence of virulent and pathological forms.

II. 19th Century Slavophilism and Pan-Slavism

Contemporary Russian nationalism has a very long and rich intellectual heritage, and many of the themes expressed by modern nationalists echo those voiced by Slavophiles over a century and a half ago. What is important to recognize about historical Slavophilism is that it, like contemporary Russian nationalism, was not a monolithic phenomenon, but contained within it a variety of forms. We generally remember pan-Slavism as an intolerant, xenophobic, anti-Western doctrine that served as the basis for Russian imperial expansion up to the time of the First World War. Such elements were undeniably present, but there was also a cosmopolitan and relatively tolerant side to Slavophilism that is less often noted.

The first generation of Slavophiles, writers like A.S. Khomyakov, Ivan Kire'evskiy, Konstantin and Ivan Aksakov, and the like, were all well-educated people familiar with the culture and traditions of Europe. Most accepted the universalism of Christianity and were not haters of the 'world civilization' created in the West; what they sought was to define Russia's place in world history, and the specific contributions it could make to a larger whole.[1] Indeed, many of these writers were more religious than nationalistic in their orientation. Most of the early Slavophiles, moreover, were strongly opposed to the doctrine of official *narodnost'*, or nationality, initially promulgated in he 1830s by S.S. Uvarov, which asserted the primacy of "orthodoxy, autocracy, and nationality."[2] In contrast to the proponents of official nationality, who advocated unlimited obedience to autocracy, many early Slavophiles were defenders of free speech and highly critical of many aspects of their own society. They strongly supported the reforms of Aleksandr II, such as abolition of serfdom and reform of the judiciary, and admired aspects of the English political system.

This early generation of Slavophiles should be contrasted with those of the last third of the nineteenth century, who, in conditions of growing competition with a unified Germany, took an increasingly chauvinistic, xenophobic, and imperialist line. The early Slavophiles were interested in defining Russian's cultural uniqueness and paid little attention to external affairs; and later generation, by contrast, was quite explicit in justifying an expansionist foreign policy based on pan-slavism. For example, Nikolay Danilevskiy rejected the Christian universalism of Chaadaev or Khomyakov, in favor of Spenglerian view of a world dominated by distinct and self-regarding civilizations.[3] He believed that Western culture was in a terminal decline, locked in a struggle with that of the Slavs: "[this period] will decide whether the Salves are powerful...by their significance, whether they are an equal member in the family of Aryan nations, called to play a role of a world power like their older brothers and to form one of the original cultural types of world history—or whether they are destined to be only vassals, ethnographic material serving as nourishment to its proud rulers."[4] Danilevskiy argued for the creation of a pan-Slav empire that included roughly the territory ruled by Stalin by 1945. The poet Fedor Tyutchev, cited by Boris Yeltsin as his personal favorite,[5] argued the need to conquer Constantinople as the capital of a new Slav empire. His famous poem, "Russian Geography," contains the lines: "Moscow, Peter's city, and Constantine's city—these are the sacred capitals of the Russian empire. But where are its limits? Where are its boundaries?...The future is destined to discover it. Seven inland seas and seven great rivers.... From the Nile to the Neva, from the Elbe to China, from the Volga to the Euphrates, from the Ganges to the Danube, behold the Russian realm, and never will it end, as the Spirit forewarned and Daniel foretold."[6]

In the second half of the 19th century, Slavophilism began to merge with or develop into pan-Slavism, which had a more overt foreign policy focus. The initial impetus behind pan-Slavism came from the Western or Southern Slavs who sought Russian help in liberating themselves from Ottoman or Austrian rule. The Russians, however, understood pan-Slavism more as a kind of pan-Russianism, where the Slavs outside of Russia would be used as spearheads for Russian imperial influence; they had little interest in promoting other Slavic cultures as such and ruthlessly Russified those Slav peoples already within the empire, the Poles and Ukrainians. The writings of general R.A. Fada'ev exemplified this point of view.[7] Despite constant assertions by Russian nationalists of Russian's peaceful intentions and the non-military character of the empire, pan-Slavism became the ideological underpinning for expansionism in the late 19th and early 20th centuries.

While recognizing differences among different 19th century Slavophiles, there were a number of themes that have remained prominent in Russian thought, and are evident in the writings of contemporary Russian nationalists like Aleksandr Solzhenitsyn.[8] One is the distrust of the universalism of Western liberal thought, and the belief that Russia constituted a separate civilization with its own unique virtues, or *samobytnost'* ("uniqueness"). At the same time, many people have noted the messianism of such Russian nationalist: even as they believed that Russian represented a separate civilization, they also argued that it has a potentially universal significance for all of mankind. Consistent with

their Christian beliefs, many Slavophiles stressed the superior spirituality of the Russian people, a spirituality that was in their view made
greater as a result of the Russian's lack of external freedom.[9] According
to Konstantin Aksakov; "In the West...they kill souls and replace them by
the perfecting of political forms and the establishment of good order and
by political action. Conscience is replaced by law; regulations become a
substitute for the inward impulse; even charity is turned into a mechanical business in the West; all anxiety is for political forms."[10] Many Slavophiles expressed hostility to Western parliamentary institutions on the
grounds that there was a higher and less divisive form of democracy. Ivan
Kire'evskiy argued that while Western political development had proceeded through a process of force and conflict, Russian society had developed on the basis of peaceful consensus based on Orthodox *sobornost'*, or
community. The strife between government and opposition characteristic of Western parliamentary government was made unnecessary by the
patriarchal Russian state; Russians, consequently, had no need for Western constitutional safeguards.[11] Davilevskiy argued that Russian, as
opposed to Western, political history had progressed peacefully and
organically, and that there was therefore no need for political parties or
an opposition in Russian.[12]

Many if not all of these themes can be found in Aleksandr Solzhenitsyn's political writings. Solzhenitsyn's criticisms of a Western civilization built on the basis of a rational humanism, and the spiritual vacuity
that exists in contemporary Western societies, are well known. Like
Aksakov, Solzhenitsyn distinguishes between inner and outer freedom,
arguing that the former is far more important: "External, or social, freedom is very desirable for the sake of undistorted growth, but it is no more
than a condition, a medium, and to regard it as the object of our existence
in nonsense. We can firmly assert our inner freedom even in external
conditions of unfreedom."[13] Even under the communist dictatorship
which he spent a lifetime opposing, Russians have maintained a certain
greater inner freedom:

> A fact which cannot be disputed is the weakening of human personali-
> ty in the West while in the East it has become firmer and stronger. Six
> decades for our people and three decades for the people of Eastern
> Europe; during that time we have been through a spiritual training far
> in advance of Western experience. The complex and daily crush of life
> has produced stronger, deeper, and more interesting personalities
> than those generated by standardized Western well-being...it is also
> demeaning for [society] to stay on such a soulless and smooth place of

legalism, as in the case of yours. After the suffering decades of violence and oppression, the human soul longs for things higher, warmer, and purer than those offered by than today's mass living habits, introduced as by a calling card by the revolting invasion of commercial advertising, by TV stupor, and by intolerable music.[14]

It has been argued that Solzhenitsyn moderated his views on Western democracy since his writings in the 1970s, but there is in fact a great deal of continuity to his thought.[15] For example, Solzhenitsyn's most recent programmatic political treatise, published in 1990 in *Komsomolskaya Pravda* and *Literaturnaya Gezeta*, notes that "it is not mandatory to respect the individual only in the form of a parliamentary system."[16] His continuing hostility to Western-style political parties, reminiscent of Danilevskiy, is also evident: "'A party' means a part. Splitting into parties means that we split into parts. As a part of the people who does a party oppose? Obviously, the rest of the people who have not followed it. Every party works primarily for itself and its own rather than for the entire nation...The rivalry of parties distorts the will of the people....No fundamental resolution of the fate of the state is found on the part of parties or may be entrusted to the parties."[17] Indeed, there is a certain sense in which Solzhenitsyn is less liberal than the Slavophiles of the 1830s and 1840s, and has more in common with those of the 1870s who were less tolerant, for example in his criticisms of unbridled freedom of speech and his annoyance with the Western press.[18]

III. Russian Nationalism in the Pre-Gorbachev Era

Despite the overtly internationalist perspective of Marxism-Leninism, the Soviet regime has always made use of Russian nationalist themes as an alternative source of legitimation. National Bolshevism was a term used to describe a group of nationalists in the 1920s who did not believe in communism, but who for tactical reasons aligned themselves with the Bolsheviks on the grounds that Bolshevism was the best available means of building a strong centralized state and keeping the empire together.[19] Stalin made use of nationalist themes as a mobilizational tool, particularly during the darkest days of World War II, and had himself at times been labeled a National Bloshevik.[20] The distinction between a National Bolshevik and Stalinist (or today, a neo-Stalinist) is a subtle but important one, however identical their programs are in many respects. A National Bolshevik is a nationalist first and a Bolshevik by convenience, whereas the loyalties are reversed in the case of the Stalinists, a difference that is important in post-Gorbachev Russia as nationalists break more overtly with the communists.

In the postwar period, however, Russian nationalism became a visible and significant force only in the mid-to-late 1960s, with the emergence of what Aleksandr Yanov has characterized as the "New Russian Right." It was, in many respects, the only form of non-conformity tolerated after the ending of the thaw. The rebirth of Russian nationalism was evident in two separate forms. One was overtly political in nature, with the publication of a series of articles by writers like Sergei Semanov, Mikhail Lobanov, and Viktor Chalmaev in the journal *Molodaya Gvardiya*, the organ of the Komsomol Central Committee. These authors inveighed against the growth of Western bourgeois influence and consumerism in the Soviet Union—in Lobanov's phrase, Russia was being turned into a nation of "educated shopkeepers"—and argued that there was a distinct "Russian spirit" threatened by it. They glorified the pre-Bolshevik Russian past, saw a continuity between Russia's pre-revolutionary national traditions and the Soviet present, and sought to resurrect Russian national heroes normally deemed "reactionary" or even anti-communist by the regime. Lobanov, furthermore, indirectly suggested that the Jews were the source of contemporary problems.[21]

The second manifestation of resurgent Russian nationalism was more cultural in nature. The 1960s saw a sudden growth of interest in Russia's rapidly disappearing rural life and traditions, as described by a group of writers collectively know as the *derevenshchiki*, or "village prose" school. These writers viewed with some dismay the disappearance of the countryside in the face of economic modernization, and attacked the decline in traditional values associated with the peasant village that occurred as a result. The writers of this school were quite varied in their political outlook, and included such authors and Vladimir Soloukhin, Efrim Dorosh, Sergei Zalygin, Fedor Abramov, Boris Mozhaev, Viktor Likhonosov, Valentin Rasputin, Aleksandr Solzhenitsyn, and Vasiliy Belov. Many of these authors wrote for the "liberal" *Novyy Mir* while it was under the stewardship of Aleksandr Tvardovskiy, but a large number of village prose writers migrated to the journal *Nash Sovremennik* after Sergei Vikulov was appointed editor in 1968. Especially after Tvardovskiy's removal from the editorship of *Novyy Mir* in 1970 and the purge of its editorial board, *Nash Sovremennik* emerged as the premier platform for a wide range of nationalist authors, both liberal and conservative.[22]

Russian nationalism was expressed during the Brezhnev era through the promotion of a number of issues whose advocacy was more or less tolerated by the communist authorities. The first, already noted, was a concern over the decline in the traditional moral values associated with the peasant village, the disintegration of the family, and the rise of a host of vices associated with modern urban life like promiscuity, corruption, drug use, and the like. This concern over moral values frequently had a Christian religious basis, as in the case of Solzhenitsyn or Vladimir Osipov, founder of the All-Russian Social-Christian Union for the Liberation of the People (VKSON) and editor of the samizdat national journal *Veche*. As a general phenomenon, nationalism is a concomitant of industrialization. The transition to a modern, impersonal urban society from the courtryside with its stable bonds of community is a traumatic one, which nationalists in all countries experiencing it have decried; and in this respect contemporary Russian nationalists are not different from their French or German counterparts in the 19th and early 20th centuries.

The second issue of broad concern to Russian nationalists in the Brezhnev years was preservation of cultural and historical monuments, as well as the written record of pre-revolutionary times. The communist regime had recklessly destroyed large numbers of monuments—in particular, churches—first under Stalin, and then in Khurshchev's time. One of the largest Soviet voluntary societies in Brezhnev's time was the All-Russian Society for the Preservation of Historical and Cultural Monuments (VOOPIK), founded in 1966. Although officially sponsored by the state, VOOPIK attracted considerable spontaneous support across Russia.[23] This society was quite active in the following decade collecting money for the rehabilitation of churches and other historical sites. Even in as innocuous as area as cultural preservation, however, the intolerant side of Russian nationalism was evident in the frequently-heard charge that Jewish communists bore special responsibility for the destruction of Russian monuments.[24]

A third common nationalist concern was environmental protection in Russia. Indeed, the chief nationalist issue on the policy agenda as Gorbachev came to power was the effort to conceal *Minvodkhoz's* (Ministry of Water Resources) massive plan to divert the waters of several northward-flowing Siberian rivers southward into the deserts of Central Asia, through an expensive and complex series of canals.[25] Saving Lake Baikal and other Siberian lakes and rivers also became a common rallying cry for both liberal and conservative nationalists, uniting the likes of

Sergey Zalygin and Valentin Rasputin. For many Russian nationalists, criticism of government policy on specific projects was only the opening wedge of a much broader critique of the Soviet penchant for rapid industrialization and mindless gigantism. At times, environmentalism reflected a conservative nostalgia for the agrarian Russia being destroyed by industrialization; in other cases it more resembled the modern anti-technologism of Western environmental movements that never experienced that world. Rasputin's words could have been spoken by a European or American Green: "In the twentieth century the path chosen by mankind is quite unacceptable...the ecological crash can only be postponed but not avoided....I am convinced that mankind must change over to an absolutely different way of life. We must reject the consumer mentality and moderate our appetites. We do not need the quantity of everything we produce today."[26]

A final concern of the nationalists, which might be subsumed under the category of moral decline noted above, was with alcoholism. Many considered the prevalence of alcoholism among ethnic Russians to be not just a health problem, but a moral plague that sapped the strength of the Russian people, and a few were not above spinning conspiracy theories as to who was responsible for addicting the Russian population to drink.[27]

From the time of their re-emergence in the 1960s, the Russian nationalists had a highly checkered, love-hate relationship with the Soviet regime. On the one hand, the nationalists' emphasis on pre-revolutionary themes, traditions, and heroes, did not sit very well with orthodox communist teachings that held, essentially, that nothing good had happened in Russia until Lenin. Indeed, much of the praise for pre-Bolshevik personalities and practices could be understood as indirect but pointed criticism of the communist regime. On the other hand, many people in the upper reaches of the CPSU believed that use of nationalist theses could build legitimacy for a party whose ideology appeared to be running out of steam,[28] and a good number of them felt personally sympathetic to the nationalist cause. Nationalism was sufficiently strong within the Soviet elite, in any event, that the regime felt there was a real cost in offending the "Russian Party." This schizophrenic attitude toward the nationalists helps explain the various ups and downs in relations between the two groups.

Thus, for example, the series of nationalist articles appearing in *Molodaya Gvardiya* in the late 1960s engendered an at times furious counterattack from orthodox Marxists, including a lengthy rebuttal by

Aleksandr Dement'ev in *Novyy Mir* that appeared in 1969, and culminating in a definitive rebuke published in the CPSU theoretical journal *Kommunist* in 1970. *Molodaya Gvardiya's* editor-in-chief, Anatolyy Nikonov, was sacked and replaced by Anatolyy Ivanov.[29] On the other hand, the nationalists soon had their revenge: the whole editorial board of the liberal *Novyy Mir* was purged, including the venerable Tvardovskiy, reportedly for having published Dement'ev,[30] while Dement'ev was himself attacked by the leading nationalists in an open letter to *Ogonek*. The nationalists' power and influence in high places was further demonstrated two years later when Aleksandr Yakovlev, then acting chief of the CPSU Central Committee Propaganda Department, published a long attack on Russian nationalism in *Literaturnaya Gazeta* from an orthodox Marxist point of view. This shot across the bow led to Yakovlev's removal from the secretariat and his prolonged exile as ambassador to Canada.[31]

A similar round of attack and retreat occurred in the early 1980s. This time, it was *Nash Sovremennik* that published a series of articles by Russian nationalists like Vladimir Shubkin, the village prose writer Vladimir Soloukhin, and Vadim Kozhinov, on the occasion of the centennial of Dostoevskiy's death. These articles were bolder than those appearing in *Molodaya Gvardiya* a decade earlier, containing overtly religious themes and veiled criticisms of the Brezhnev regime. John Dunlop speculates that *Nash Sovremennik's* patron was the party's chief ideologist, Mikhail Suslov; and when Suslov died in January 1982, a flood of criticism poured down on Soloukhin, Kozhinov, and the other recently published nationalist authors.[32] Yuriy Andropov, who succeeded Brezhnev later that year, was overtly hostile to Russian nationalism, and during his brief tenure launched a crackdown both on official and unofficial nationalists. Andropov brought Yakovlev, now notorious in nationalist circles, home from Ottawa and made him an institute director, and publicly endorsed the concept of *sliianie*, the merger of the different Soviet nationalities. Konstantin Chernenko appeared to be continuing the anti-nationalist stance of his immediate predecessor when he took power in 1983, but by the end of his tenure permitted the rehabilitation of some of the nationalists attacked under the Andropov regime.[33]

IV. Gorbachev and the Nationalists

The uncertain relationship that existed between the Russian nationalists and the communist regime persisted for the first year or two of Mikhail Gorbachev's tenure as General Secretary, as many nationalists took a "wait and see" attitude. Many nationalists were aware that there were serious problems with the Stalinist system that needed urgent, if not radical, reform. Indeed, there were a number of signs early on that Gorbachev would be significantly more sympathetic to implementation of the anti-alcohol campaign in May 1985, whose chief proponent within the new Gorbachev team was the "second" secretary, Yegor Ligachev. Temperance had, of course, been a nationalist *cause célèbre*, and the Gorbachev regime went about the project with considerable vigor. The second was cancellation by the Politburo of the Siberian river diversion project, after a prolonged lobbying on the part of *Nash Sovremennik* and a host of individual nationalist writers and publicists like Valentin Rasputin.[34] Ligachev had manifested concern over the pollution of Lake Baikal and other Russian environmental concerns, so here again his influence was evident in putting nationalist issues on the Gorbachev Politburo's agenda.[35] Finally, Gorbachev at times used certain codewords implying sympathy for the nationalist cause, for example, when he spoke of "Russia" rather than the "Soviet Union" when speaking in the Ukraine.

This initial honeymoon between Gorbachev and the nationalists rapidly began to break down, however, beginning in late 1986 and early 1987. The conservative nationalists were dismayed by the meteoric rise of Aleksandr Yakovlev, who became party secretary responsible for culture after the 27th CPSU Congress in March 1986, candidate member of the Politburo in January 1987, and full member by June 1987. Since the 1972 *Literaturnaya Gzeta* article, Yakovlev had been tagged as a staunch anti-nationalist, and in his position a culture secretary he began to act out the worst nightmares of the conservative nationalists. Under the general heading of the policy of *glasnost'* Yakovlev replaced the editors of a series of conservative or nondescript Soviet newspapers and journals with Westernizing liberals like *Moskovskie Novosti's* Yegor Yakovlev, *Ogonek's* Vitalyy Korotich, *Znamya's* Grigoryy Baklanov, and *Sovetskaya Kultura's* Albert Belyaev. Yakovlev was able to purge the leaderships of the Filmmakers and Theater Workers Unions (though he had much less success with the Writers Union), and placed the liberal nationalist Sergey Zalygin at the editorship of *Novyy Mir*. These liberal intellectuals proceeded to use their new platforms to open up critical discussion of the Soviet Union's Stalinist past, and to permit discussion of a range of cultural issues previously forbidden.[36]

Gorbachev's policies had the effect of splitting nationalists into liberal and conservative camps. There is a common tendency to identify Russian nationalism with its conservative manifestation, but while the latter may in in some sense represent its mainstream, there has always been a liberal variant present from the early 19th century to the present. The liberal nationalists included writers like academician Dmityy Likhachev, a historian with impeccable nationalist and preservationist credentials, who sided with Gorbachev and eventually ended up on the barricades with Anatolyy Sobchak during the abortive August 1991 coup; Sergey Zalygin, who had been active in the campaign against the Siberian river diversion and other Russian environmental causes; the village prose writer Boris Mozhaev; and the Christian nativist Alla Latynina, who served on the editorial board of *Literaturnaya Gazeta*. By 1988, almost all of these writers stopped publishing in *Nash Sovremennik*. The journey of writer Viktor Astaf'ev, whose works from the mid-1980s had unmistakable anti-Semitic overtones, took longer, but by August 1991, he had moved to Yeltsin's side of the barricades.

The conservative nationalists, on the other hand, became increasingly hostile to Gorbachev and found themselves at odds with their former liberal nationalist allies. The reaction of writers like Valentin Rasputin, Vasilyy Belov, Yurily Bondarev, Vadim Kozhinov, and Aleksandr Prokhanov to Gorbachev's cultural policies was one of outrage and dismay, though their reasons for unhappiness were somewhat more nuanced than some have suggested. Most shared a hatred for the Western cultural influences being introduced into the Soviet Union, from liberal economic theory to avant garde art, rock and roll, the publication of formerly banned books, discussion of the dark side of Soviet history, as well as drugs, pornography, and the like. They also disliked the very atmosphere of cultural pluralism being created, and feared that its effect would be corruption of the Soviet youth and an undermining of their belief in their country. As Rasputin put it in a 1990 interview:

> Satan, who until quite recently preferred to remain in the shadows, who did not appear out in the open, and did not speak in lofty phrases, has simply turned into a hero. And all his rules and devices, which contradict not only Christian but also any other human morality, are being professed openly. Well, when can there be such a thing when people speak seriously about a pluralism of moralities?! There can be no pluralism in morality—it is either there or it is not. We are now sinking to the extreme depths of moral decline. I have in mind what is being propagandized on the pages of newspapers and the screens of television

sets. Such things do not exist anywhere in the civilized world. No capitalist country, even on that has experienced a sexual revolution, has reached this point.[37]

But while most were made very uneasy about criticisms being aired publicly of the Stalinist past, reasons for this differed depending on whether one tended more towards neo-Stalinism or National Bolshevism. The former wanted to preserve Lenin's legacy intact, indeed, to preserve what they believed were the positive aspects of Stalin's legacy, and saw in the continuing revelations of Stalinist crimes a poorly-veiled attack on the Soviet system as a whole. The National Bolsheviks, by contrast, were not entirely unsympathetic to an airing of the crimes of the communist past. Indeed, Russian nationalists leaning to the National Bolshevik state like Vadim Kozhinov and Vladimir Soloukhin attacked liberal or reformist communists like Anatolyy Rybakov and Mikhail Shatrov for trying to foist the entire blame for the crimes of the thirties on the shoulders of a single individual, rather than seeing it as a natural outgrowth of communism itself, which they regarded as a foreign ideology imposed on the country by Lenin.[38] But like the neo-Stalinists, the National Bolsheviks were very much concerned that the attack on authority as such, justified or not, would destroy the great Soviet state and lead to the growth of foreign, Western, Jewish, or other malign influences.

From 1987 on, the conservative Russian nationalists became the core of the "right-wing" intellectual opposition to Gorbachev, commanding far greater respect than outright neo-Stalinists like Nina Andreeva. The road to their emergence as the chief "opposition party" outside the CPSU was marked by a number of advances, retreats, and skirmishes. One of the first public expressions of conservative criticism of Gorbachev's polices was voiced in March 1987, by the leadership of the RSFSR Writer's Union, whose deputy chairman, Yuryy Bondarev, sharply criticized liberalizing tendencies in his speech a the 19th party conference in June 1988. A plenum of the Union's board was held in Moscow in December 1988, and became the occasion for virulent attacks on the leading liberal lights of *perestroika*.[39] Gorbachev and Yakovlev were completely stymied in their attempts to liberalize the leadership of the USSR Writers Union,[40] which remained a bastion of conservative opposition. *Nash Sovremennik* stopped publishing liberal nationalists altogether, and with *Molodaya Gvardiya* and *Moskva* became the focus for conservative nationalist opposition to Gorbachev's policies. *Literaturnaya Rossiya* (the organ of the RSFSR Writers Union), *Nash Sovremennik*, and *Oktyabr'* all saw their leadership pass to hardline (or more hardline) Russian nationalists in 1989.[41]

In addition to these developments in the literary profession, the conservative nationalists created a number of political organizations opposed to the process of liberalization. In March 1989, the Union for the Spiritual Revival of the Fatherland (know as *Otchestvo* for short) was founded under the sponsorship of a number of "patriotic" organizations like VOOPIK and the *Sovetskaya Rossiya* and *Molodaya Gvardiya* publishing houses. *Otchestvo* was headed by Mikhail Antonov, a member of the extremist Fetisov group in the 1960s and the formulator of a non-Marxist, non-liberal economic doctrine, who was once jailed in a psychiatric hospital for his nationalist activities during the Brezhnev era.[42] One of *Otchestvo's* most notable early members was Aleksandr Rutskoy, whom Yeltsin later picked his running mate in the June 1991 election for the Russian presidency. And in June 1990, the All Russian Association of Lovers of Russian Letters and Culture, "Unity" (*Edinstvo*) was founded with Yuriy Bondarev as its first president.[43]

In addition to organizations like *Otchestvo* and *Edinstvo* that represented the mainstream of the conservative nationalists, the late 1980s saw the appearance of a number of fringe organizations that were much more openly fascist, violent, and anti-Semitic, the most notorious of which was *Pamyat'*. *Pamyat'* itself encompassed a number of extremist right-wing strands from neo-Stalinists to monarchists, and suffered a number of splits and schisms during its short history.[44] Most members of *Pamyat'* were, however, convinced that Russia was in the grips of a Jewish-Masonic conspiracy that threatened to destroy its culture and moral character. In addition, *glasnost'* permitted the emergence of various neo-Nazi, skinhead, and other openly racist groups.[45] While a great deal of Western press attention was focused on *Pamyat'*, it is not clear that this organization, whose members total no more than a few hundred, was more than a very marginal political actor. These groups were interesting in that they provided a window onto the right-wing Russian "street," representing as they did a less-educated and lower-income social stratum than the established conservative nationalist writers. Moreover, *Pamyat'* constituted an important bellwether of nationalist belief: while no mainstream conservative nationalist admitted to being a member of *Pamyat'*, many expressed sympathy with some of its aims and attacked those attacking it, just as liberals in Western societies have sought to protect leftist radicals from persecution even as they distanced themselves personally from their cause.[46] There is some evidence that one of *Pamyat'*'s secret sympathizers was Yegor Ligachev, and that he protected the group's activities while he was ideology secretary.[47] Boris Yeltsin met with members of *Pamyat'* while Moscow's Gorkom chief and has said some surprisingly sympathetic things about them, but obviously does not have deeper ties to this organization.

The conservative Russian nationalist press responded with growing alarm to all aspects of the changes taking place in the Soviet Union of the late 1980s, political, economic, social, and cultural. But their underlying complaint concerned the fact that ethnic Russians were themselves the biggest victims of their recent history, while at the same time being blamed as the chief victimizers. The more moderate nationalists made the point that the Russians as much as any other nationality had suffered under communism, but a depressing number of mainstream conservative nationalists attributed this victimization to a pervasive "Russophobia" by a worldwide conspiracy of outsiders, the ringleaders of which were almost inevitably Jewish. This was the theme of a now famous article by the same title by Igor Shafarevich, Solzhenitsyn's former collaborator,[48] and is illustrated by the following passage from a "Letter from the Writers of Russia," signed by leading conservatives Rasputin, Kunyaev, Lobanov, Prokhanov, Kozhinov, Shafarevich, Petr Prokkurin, Yuriy Kuzentsov, Karem Rash, and the like:

> Concentrated hounding, vilification and persecution that are unparalleled in the entire history of mankind are being directed against the representatives of the country's indigenous population....Russia's entire historical past, pre-revolutionary and post revolutionary, is being subjected to a regular racist abuse....The distinguishing characteristic of our own revilers and slanderers is that they deny the true nature of their activity—they deny the indisputable fact of Soviet *Russophobia*, and they refuse to acknowledge that what they are doing constitutes a crime against Russia and the Russian people.[49]

In a curious reversal of causality, the letter claims that charges of Russian fascism are being used as an excuse for discrimination against Russia, and it asks "Isn't it a noteworthy fact, in and of itself, that the fabrication of the myth of 'Russian fascism' is taking place against the backdrop of the headlong rehabilitation and reckless idealization of Zionist ideology?"[50]

For all of their strength within certain literary association, the conservative nationalists did not fare at all well when put to the test in the first reasonably free elections held in the USSR in 1990–1991. For example, in the local elections held in the spring of 1990, supporters of the liberal Democratic Russia won 57 of 65 seats assigned to Moscow in the Russian parliament; of the 70 "patriotic" nationalist or neo-Stalinist candidates running in those same constituencies, only two were elected.

Moreover, in contrast to the large number of liberal journalists and writers elected as people's deputies, many prominent nationalist failed to win election, including the painter Ilya Glazunov, *Nash Sovremennik's* editor Stanislav Kunyaev, writers Vladimir Bondarenko, Anatolyy Salutskiy, and Eduard Volodin. This occurred in spite of relatively heavy media coverage of nationalist candidates. It is therefore not surprising that the defeated nationalist candidates appealed to the Soviet authorities to annul the election results.[51]

By the end of the 1980s it was quite clear that the conservative Russian nationalists would never come to power or reverse the liberalizing policies they found so distasteful playing by the newly created democratic rules. Nationalist themes had little electoral appeal in 1990–1991, and the conservative nationalists themselves, for all their anti-intellectualism, were for the most part a group of chattering *litterateurs*, inexperienced in and unprepared for pure political struggle. Many of them were, on the other hand, extremely well connected in the Soviet establishment, with friends and sympathizers scattered throughout the Central Committee, General Staff, and KGB. It was against this background that many of the leading conservative nationalists made a fateful decision in the late 1980s to align themselves with neo-Stalinist conservatives in the party, police, and army, and to call for a state of emergency or coup d'etat that would end the period of reform initiated by Gorbachev.[52] The long tradition of national Bolshevism in the Soviet Union, and an overarching hatred of a common enemy—the Westernizing, liberal intelligentsia— led the conservative nationalists to overlook the fact that the Communist Party was quickly becoming one of the most politically unpopular organizations in the USSR, not just on the part of liberal intellectuals and non-Russian nationalists, but among rank-and-file working class Russians who should have been the nationalists' natural constituency. Alliance with party and army/police conservatives seemed to be not a liability but a shortcut to power, since a coup by the existing service institutions would obviate the necessity for the long and painful process of building a political organization and struggling for some form of popular support.

The communist conservatives in the party, police, and army for their part welcomed this overture from the nationalists. The Communist Party of course had a long history of manipulating Russian nationalist symbols and themes for its own purposes, and appeared to believe that nationalism would be a more effective mobilizing ideology at the present moment than Marxism-Leninism. Conservatives in the party (possibly including Yegor Ligachev), following in the tradition of Suslov, were themselves sympathetic to the nationalist cause. The nationalist agenda coincided with the professional interests of the police and army, whose careers were tied to the continued existence of the Soviet Union as political and military superpower. The Gorbachev era had meant a sharp downsizing of the Soviet military, withdrawal from Eastern Europe, and continuing attacks against the military establishment of the part of the liberal intelligentsia, all of which gave many officers common cause with the nationalists.[53]

As the old Union began to fracture under the pressure of various nationalism—peripheral as well as Russian—in 1990–1991, the focus of the conservative alliance between Russian nationalists and neo-Stalinists began to change from opposition to domestic social and political reform to preservation of the internal empire. And as the drives for independence in the Baltic states, Moldavia, and other like republics began to pick up steam, a new nationalist issue arose that previously had not been seen as a problem: the fate of the ethnic Russians living outside of the Russian federation, who would be trapped in *de facto* foreign countries should the Union break apart. According to the last official census (1989), the number of Russians in this situation totaled almost 25 million, 44 percent of whom were located in the Ukraine (see Table I).[54]

Table I
Ethnic Russians Outside of Russia

State	total population	number of Russians	Russians as % of local population	as % of all Russians out of Russia
Russia	147,400,537	119,807,165	81.3	N/A
Ukraine	51,706,742	11,340,250	21.9	44.9
Belarus	10,199,709	1,341,055	13.1	5.3
Moldova	4,337,592	560,423	12.9	2.2
Armenia	3,287,677	51,553	1.6	0.2
Georgia	5,443,359	338,645	6.2	1.3
Azerbaijan	7,037,867	392,303	5.6	1.6
Kazakhstan	16,536,511	6,226,400	37.7	24.6
Kyrgyzstan	4,290,442	916,543	21.4	3.6
Uzbekistan	19,905,156	1,652,179	8.3	6.5
Turkmenistan	3,533,925	334,477	9.5	1.3
Tajikistan	5,108,576	386,630	7.6	1.5
Estonia	1,572,916	474,815	30.2	1.9
Latvia	2,680,029	905,515	33.8	3.6
Lithuania	3,689,779	343,597	9.3	1.4
Tot. excl. Russia	139,330,280	25,264,385	N/A	N/A

It is very hard to tell the degree to which these Russians were in fact facing persecution in 1990–1991. Certainly, the non-Russian nationalist popular fronts were hostile to Russians in many ways: Lithuania, for example, drafted very tough laws on citizenship and language requirements that would have disenfranchised the many Russians who live there, and Soviet military forces stationed in the Baltics, whose members were predominantly Russian, were the objects of active protest. Russians were certainly the victims of individual instances of violence throughout the Soviet Union. Nonetheless, the movements that sprang up to defend the rights of Russians in the republics like the intermovements in the Baltics and the so-called left-bank Dniester SSR in Moldavia were in large measure creations of the local communist party apparatuses and the all-Union KGB and MVD. Much of the hostility directed against Russians in the Baltics arose less from their ethnicity *per se* than from the fact that they were being used by the center to thwart independence, or because of the fact that as soldiers they were visible symbols of Moscow's power.

Soviet conservatives hoping to preserve the union saw the situation of Russians outside Russia as a threat, but also as an opportunity to turn these indigenous Russian populations into fifth columns that could oppose independence in the breakaway republics. As nationalist agitation spread in the Baltics and elsewhere, the conservative central Soviet press began to harp more and more on discrimination faced by indigenous Russian communities. The most visible spokesmen for the interests of the Russians outside Russia were not the long-time conservative nationalist writers, but members of the "Soyuz" group who claimed the adherence of 561 deputies in the all-Union Congress of People's Deputies.[55] The so-called "black colonels" Viktor Alksnis and Nikolay Petrushenko united in their own personas both the interests of the professional military (as political officers, they were members of the group most threatened by reform within the Soviet military), and those of the Russians living in the Baltics and other republics seeking independence from the USSR (Alksnis was a Russified Latvian serving in Latvia, while Petrushenko served in Central Asia). Alksnis, for one, claimed not be attached to socialist ideology, but was primarily interested in the cause of preservation of the Union.[56]

By December 1990, the conservative alliance had hounded communist party liberals Bakatin, Yakovlev, and Shevardnadze out of their positions of power, and were openly calling for a state of emergency that would reverse the democratic reforms of the recent past. As in the case of many of the shadowy groups that emerged in the wake of the abolition of article 6 of the Soviet constitution (e.g., the Liberal Democratic Party or the United Front of Workers), it is not clear whether the Soyuz phenomenon was a spontaneous one, or whether it was really a child of the CPSU or KGB.[57] Just as the grievances of the Russians in the Baltic States or Moldavia were being artificially fanned by communists there and in the center, so too their "representatives" in the Soviet parliament appeared to have patrons within the apparatus that explained their sudden and disproportionate influence in Soviet politics.

The logical culmination of the alliance between conservative nationalist and neo-Stalinists within the party, army, and police was the attempted coup of August 19, 1991. While the full extent of the involvement of individual Russian nationalists in the plotting is not yet clear, many of them certainly supported the effort politically. In retrospect, one of the clearest harbingers of the coup was the hysterical "word to the people" published in *Sovetskaya Rossiya* on July 23, calling on the Soviet people to unite "in order to halt the chain of reaction of the ruinous disintegration of the state." The letter was signed by Vasilyy Starodubtsev and Aleksandr Tizyakov who would the following month become members of the "State Committee for the State of Emergency" (GKChP), but also by the conservative nationalist writers Yuryy Bondarev, Eduard Volodin, Valentin Rasputin, and Aleksandr Prokhanov.[58] The initial communique of the GKChP justified the state of emergency on entirely nationalist rather than Marxist-Leninist grounds, making numerous references to the fact that the "motherland" was in danger and that the union had to be preserved, but never once mentioning socialism as a goal.

The coup's rapid demise—almost laughable in retrospect—demonstrated the degree of the conservative nationalists' miscalculation. Alliance with communist conservatives was not a shortcut to power, but rather a political liability which left the nationalists vulnerable to the charge that they were fellow-travelers hoping to bring back the old discredited Stalinist system. Their message about the need to protect the greatness of Russia was lost because the very membership of the GKChP made clear to everyone that the coup was being masterminded by the old, entrenched communist party apparatus.

Moreover, the ability of the GKChP to appeal to Russian pride and national awareness was gravely undermined by prior development, that is, the capturing of certain key Russian nationalist themes by their liberal archenemy, Russian president Boris Yeltsin, after his election as Russian president in the spring of 1990. It is fair to say that Yeltsin had few Russian nationalist credentials prior to 1990. Apart from a single meeting with representatives of *Pamyat'* which occurred when he was Moscow Gorkom chief in 1987, Yeltsin has no past history of association with nationalist organizations or leaders. Perusal of his autobiography does not reveal any early interest in nationalist issues like environmentalism, religion, alcoholism, or cultural preservation (indeed, he was the Sverdlovsk party chief who implemented orders to tear down the Ipat'ev house in which the Romanov family had been shot in 1918, the site of which has become something of a national shrine). He explained his decision to run for Russian president in purely tactical terms, arguing that if he and his allies couldn't bring democracy to the whole of the USSR, then perhaps they could do so in a part of the country. An interview given by Yeltsin on his decision to run for the RSFSR presidency is revealing. When the interviewer, who noted that she had very little personal sense of Russian national identity, asked whether it was the same for him, Yeltsin replied:

> I used to have the same feelings as you. I saw myself as a citizen of the country and not Russia, and well also a patriot of Sverdlovsk Oblast since that is where I worked. And the concept of "Russia" was so conventional for me that in my daily work as first secretary of the Sverdlovsk party obkom most of the time I did not even go through the Russian authorities.[59]

Nonetheless, when Yeltsin started his campaign for Russian president, he skillfully exploited the most powerful nationalist theme, namely, that of Russian victimization. While he did not use the term "Russophobia," he did portray Russia as the object of exploitation by the old system. His words from a speech during the 1990 presidential campaign are typical:

> The center is for Russia today the cruel exploiter, the miserly benefactor, and the favorite who does not think about the future. We must put an end to the injustice of these relations....The economic sovereignty of Russia is possible only on condition that republican ownership is formed, whose basis must be the land, the soil beneath and the air above, forests, water and other natural resources, enterprises, all produced output and its scientific-technical and intellectual potential. It is necessary to guarantee in law that they are used exclusively in the interests of Russia.[60]

Yeltsin made the powerful case that Russians above all had suffered during the seventy years of communism, and needed to set up their own institutions in order to be able to defend themselves from the center in the future. Yeltsin's words should be compared to the election platform of the conservative nationalist "bloc of patriotic Russian movements" (including *Edinstvo, Otchestvo*, the VOOPIK, the "Russia Club" of people's deputies, and other groups), which called for "Soviet Russia" to "re-establish or create from scratch its own administrative and economic administration, which will end interference in the republic's affairs by Union agencies," and "to discontinue the discreditable practice of turning over to the Union budget tens of billions of rubles that go for subsidies and the artificial elevation of the standard of living in other union republics, something not derived from their own labor."[61]

The "patriotic bloc" and other conservative Russian nationalists differed sharply from Yeltsin, of course, insofar as they went on to attack the dismantling of the centralized command-administrative economic system, private property, "profiteers" (i.e., the cooperatives), the "mass media," critics of the military, and the like, thereby demonstrating to all their ties to the existing communist establishment. What Yeltsin did was to present a central Russian nationalist theme shorn of any communist baggage—indeed, he combined nationalism with strident attacks on the entrenched party apparatus—and linked the establishment of Russian sovereignty to liberal policies like greater democracy and market-oriented economic reform. This formula proved extremely attractive to many people, and propelled him in the first instance to his narrow victory as Russian president in May 1990.

The power of the nationalist theme was evident in the fact that it was immediately adopted by Yeltsin's opponents. For example, Aleksandr Vlasov, the former RSFSR premier who was Gorbachev's last minute choice to head off Yeltsin's candidacy for the Russian presidency, himself began to use the same nationalist themes in his campaign rhetoric. This career communist bureaucrat argued before the Russian parliament that "it was Russia more than others that suffered from the rigorous centralized administrative and bureaucratic system, which essentially nullified the republic's political sovereignty..."[62] Like Yeltsin, Vlasov based his candidacy on the need for Russia to reclaim its sovereignty in economic affairs and to stop subsidizing the other republics.[63] Similarly, while demands on the part of conservatives within the CPSU in the spring of 1990 to establish a Russian communist party were part of an ideological struggle with Gorbachev for control over the All-Union party itself, it also reflected a nationalist demand for the creation of specifically Russian institutions.

The alliance between Russian nationalists and conservatives in the party, army, and police failed, then, for two related reasons. In the first place, the nationalists tainted themselves by their association with the entrenched communist bureaucracy. Those who might otherwise have been sympathetic to the Russian cause and in favor of an authoritarian solution to its problems were deterred from supporting the coup because they saw in it a reassertion of the same old communist institutions handed down from Stalin. Indeed, the distinction between nationalist and communist "patriot" was probably blurred for many, given the party conservatives' cynical use of nationalist themes over the years. On the other hand, much of the nationalist agenda— resentment of victimization and the belief that Russia should look to its own interests before those of the Union—had suddenly been usurped by Boris Yeltsin, who managed to give the quest for Russian sovereignty a progressive and liberal cast. The failure of the August 19 coup led to the routing of communists throughout the former Union, and a purge of the institutions that had been their power base. There was no short-cut to power via military takeover, and the nationalist-communist alliance arrived at a dead end. This did not mean that Russian nationalism was spent as a force—quite the contrary, Yeltsin's successful exploitation of this cause demonstrated its very great and growing power. But the conservative nationalists would henceforth have to go it alone. This liberation from their former communist allies could yet prove to be a blessing is disguise.

V. Divisions Within the Nationalist Camp

In considering how Russian nationalism will play in future Russian politics, it is necessary to begin by noting that the nationalists are a divided and rather heterogeneous group.[64] A number of attempts have been made to classify them, but the problem with many existing taxonomies is that the different varieties cannot be arrayed along a single continuum that proceeds, for example, from left to right. They are divided by a number of cross-cutting cleavages that require a two-or higher dimensional matrix to capture all the different possible combinations of belief. Some of the major divisions are outlined below.

On Democracy and Authoritarianism

With the exception of a few monarchists, most nationalists in the USSR claim to believe in some sense in "democracy," that is, in the primacy of the interests of the Russian *narod* or people.[65] What divides liberals from conservatives or the left from the right is whether they believe these interests are best served by Western parliamentary institutions and legal protections, or by some form of authoritarian government. There is now a significant group of what might be called "liberal nationalists" in the Soviet Union, that is, people who believe that there is a distinct Russian national identity worth protecting, but who nonetheless feel that this identity is perfectly compatible with Western liberal institutions. In recent years, one of the most visible spokesmen for this point of view has been Academician Likhachev, who has drawn a distinction between "patriotism," which is tolerant, and "nationalism," which is not.[66] Yeltsin and many of the so-called "democrats" in his camp would fall into this category, seeking a Russian revival *through* the establishment of true parliamentary democracy there.

On the other hand, many long-time Russian nationalists in the former USSR are clearly authoritarians. For some, belief in authoritarianism is derivative of their desire to maintain the empire, or a strong central state, which they rightly feel cannot be held together through democratic means. For others, including Solzhenitsyn, the essence of Russian *samobytnost'* lies in the superior inner spirituality of the Russians, whose realization does not require external legal and institutional guarantees and which is actually damaged by Western consumerism and politics.[67]

On Communism

Among the conservative or authoritarian nationalists, there is a spectrum of views regarding communism.[68] Some, like Solzhenitsyn, are categorically and vocally opposed to communism in all its aspects, and believe that Marxism-Leninism was an alien Western doctrine imposed upon a Russian people whose inclinations were quite otherwise. Other authoritarian nationalists—the National Bolsheviks—have been supportive of the communist state for tactical reasons, while others—the neo-Stalinists—are Marxist-Leninists first and nationalists for tactical or sentimental reasons.

The distinction between the National Bolsheviks and neo-Stalinists might at first appear to be a hair-splitting one, since both groups have effectively supported identical policy agendas over the past few years—that is, both have advocated a CPSU/military/police grab for power that would turn the clock back to the days of Brezhnev, if not Stalin. Both have come close to worshipping power for its own sake, and have included notorious anti-Semites in their ranks. Nonetheless, the difference between the two groups is critical and will become all the more so in the future. The infamous Nina Andreeva, for example, is a neo-Stalinist; the "principles" that she refuses to give up are Marxist-Leninist ones. In her famous letter published in *Sovetskaya Rossiya* in 1987, she criticized the Russian nationalists as a deviation, though one admittedly less harmful to her cause than the liberal heresy. Yuriy Bondarev, Aleksandr Prokhanov, or Valentin Rasputin, by contrast are better characterized as National Bolsheviks. Prokhanov has enunciated a neo-fascist doctrine that owes little to communism; indeed he has praised the Soviet army for its hardness and discipline over and against the communist party, which he regards as corrupt and ineffective.[69] Prokhanov openly blames Bolshevism for having overturned the centralist Tsarist state, only to re-establish it at the cost of 60 million lives.[70] He will accept whatever ideology is enunciated by the Soviet military, as long as it is successful in building a powerful centralized state. Vadim Kozhinov has criticized virtually the entire communist legacy beginning with Lenin, and has aimed his fire at figures like Bukharin who at one time were heroes for the reform communists.

In Valentin Rasputin's fiction (as in the case of other village prose writers), there is an implicit but powerful anti-communism that runs as a constant theme throughout many of his works. His novel *Farewell to Matera*, for example, concerns a small village on the Angara river is Siberia that is threatened with extinction as a result of a large hydroelectric project planned by the communist authorities. In some sense he could be protesting industrial development *per se*, but he emphasizes the particular mindless gigantism and bureaucratic ruthlessness with which the communist authorities have overrun both Russian village life and the Russian natural environment. His short story *The Fire* is similarly set in a Siberian logging town that was recently established when the traditional village was flooded by a hydroelectric dam. In fighting a fire that consumes the town's warehouses, the morally upright residents of the older village find themselves confronted with a group of crude and violent seasonal laborers referred to as *akharovtsy*. The latter wander from camp to camp and have no permanent roots in their community. It is believed by many of Rasputin's readers that the *akharovets*[71] is a symbol for the communist, the "rootless cosmopolitan" who imposed himself on traditional Russian society and modernized it at the expense of Russia's traditional values. It seems reasonably clear that while Rasputin was willing to make common cause with the communists, there is in him a tremendous hostility to communism just under the surface. The latent anti-communism of many National Bolsheviks is what distinguishes them from the neo-Stalinists: in the post-August 19 political atmosphere, it is possible to envision a Rasputin or Prokhanov jumping on the anti-communist bandwagon were a credible nationalist-authoritarian alternative to present itself, whereas it is not possible to imagine this happening in the case of a Nina Andreeva.

On the Territorial Issue

Cross-cutting the issues of liberal versus conservative and National Bolshevik versus neo-Stalinist is the question of how large the nationalist want or hope Russia to be. As recently as the 1970s, most Russian nationalists were firm believers in Russia's right or duty to rule over non-Russians—certainly those who found themselves within the bounds of the Tsarist empire, as well as those added to the empire by Stalin in 1945. But one of the more remarkable developments of the past decade is the increasing legitimacy among nationalists of a "small Russia" concept—that is, that Russia should let the peripheral republics (the Baltics, Central Asia, and the Transcaucasus) go their own way, and concentrate on restoring a Russian identity on the territory of the Russian republic, or else within a union of Eastern Slavs that would include the Ukraine and Belorussia as well.

The earliest and most consistent advocate of a "small Russia" concept was, of course, Aleksandr Solzhenitsyn.[72] In line with his cultural understanding of Russian nationalism, he argued over the years that ruling non-Russians sapped Russian energies and diverted Russians from the real work of reclaiming their own identity. His position was restated forcefully in his brochure, "How Shall We Re-construct Russia?" published in *Komsomolskaya Pravda* and *Literaturnaya Gazeta* in September 1990, where he stated:

> He should immediately proclaim loudly and clearly: The three Baltic republics, the three Transcusausian republics, the four Central Asian republics, and also Moldavia, if it is drawn more to Romania, these eleven—indeed!—definitely should be separated for good....I am alarmed to see that the awakening Russian national self-awareness in many of its parts cannot free itself from the expansionist-great power thinking and imperial befuddlement, and has borrowed from the communists the inflated "Soviet patriotism" which has never existed.

Even Solzhenitsyn, however, found himself being overtaken by the pace of events: denying that there was such a thing as a separate Ukrainian nation stretching back to the ninth century, he called for a "pan-Russian" union of the three Slavic republics. If the Ukraine or Belorussia insisted on going their own ways, Solzhenitsyn argued that there should be an oblast-by-oblast referendum to determine whether the local populations wished to join the new state or to remain with Russia.

The growing acceptance of the "small Russia" idea was evident in the relatively relaxed response that Solzhenitsyn's article engendered in the Soviet Union. Whereas he earlier would have been (and was) denounced for his "anti-patriotic" views, his loudest critics in the USSR of 1990 were Ukrainian and Kazakh nationalists who found his views on their respective nationalities insulting and smacking of great-Russian chauvinism.[73] While he was criticized by Gorbachev and other like-minded "internationalist" reform communists, he found support throughout the liberal intelligentsia; from people like Yuriy Karyakin, Galina Starovoitova, Alla Latynina, Father Gleb Yakunin, and others. Something like the Solzhenitsyn program was implicit in Boris Yeltsin's drive for Russian sovereignty and renegotiation of the Union treaty on a looser basis, and it is not surprising that Yeltsin spoke favorably about the article. It is fair to say that most Russian liberals initially hoped that the USSR could somehow be liberalized and democratized while remaining a unitary (albeit voluntary) union. By the spring of 1990 they were beginning to come to grips with the fact that democratization and union were fundamentally incompatible, a view that was fully accepted in the minds of most only after Gorbachev's turn to the right in November 1990, and the ensuing crackdown in the Baltics and elsewhere.[74]

But while it is perhaps not surprising that the liberals should come to accept a "small Russia" concept, it is even more remarkable that a number of conservative or authoritarian nationalists have arrived at a similar conclusion. Like the liberals, few of them regarded the breakup of the Union with any pleasure, and they were loath to grant the legitimacy of the nationalist demands of the baltic states and other republics. Yet grudging as their position may be, they were increasingly prepared to envisage a Russia cut loose from the internal empire. The views of the conservative nationalist Eduard Volodin, for example, are revealing. Noting that "It is painful and difficult" to discuss the topic of the Union's breakup, he nonetheless asserts that "the existing state of affairs cannot continue because it is unnatural. Could the union of countries of the block be long and durable if it has been ideologized through and through and its economy based on subsidies?"[75] Apart from the evils of Russian economic subsidies to the other republics, Volodin foresaw a positive program in the sloughing off of empire:

> We have hard work ahead of us for restoring the all-Russian economic ties and the market and the revival of the peasantry. We need a national program for the development of Central Russia. Life is being renewed here, Russia is being renewed, and the destiny of the homeland will be decided in this historical center of Russia.[76]

He ends by saying that in taking back her own name, "Russia is taking back her dignity and her own historical purpose."

A similar theme was taken up by the "nightingale of the General Staff," Aleksandr Prokhanov. In an article written in January 1990, he warned about the horrendous consequences of the second effort to destroy Russian centralism in this century (the first being the overthrow of the Tsarist monarchy in 1917), and castigated liberals for bringing this situation about.[77] But when he published the second part of the article in May he made a rather different argument. He implicitly criticized the "traditional" centralists who believed that dissolution of the Union was unthinkable because it would lead to a colossal and violent explosion, and put forward a different view, with which he seemed to associate himself:

> The Russian "scparatism" that has become tired from the insults directed at Russia, that feels bitterly every Russian death, every wound in inter-ethnic conflicts that are increasing everywhere...feels "Russia's goal is Russia!" The Utopia of international world revolution and the imperial "Moscow is the third Rome" cosmogony have sucked the Russian ethnic group dry and have drained its blood, and while that ethnic group is listed among the great peoples of the earth it is finally time to stop expending its forces and its vital juices to satisfy international mythologies.[78]

Prokhanov noted that Russia on its own had everything it needed to remain a great power. In a situation where the non-Russian nationalities were highly mobilized, he asserted that few Russians were willing "to lay down even a single shaved Russian head [i.e., a Russian soldier]" for the sake of keeping the empire together by force, even among those "indignant concerning the liberal appeasement of the national extremists." He invites the Balts and the Transcaucasian republics to leave the Union, ungraciously suggesting that they will get what they deserve.

Besides the kinds of articles just cited, there is evidence that quite a number of conservative nationalists have reluctantly accepted the idea of a "small Russia."[79] That many in this camp were only half-hearted believers in empire is suggested by the defections that have occurred from the imperialist camp: as noted earlier, Viktor Astaf'yev broke with the authors of the July 23 appeal before the coup, while Yuriy Bondarev jumped aboard Yeltsin's small Russian bandwagon thereafter.

It is difficult to interpret "small Russia" pronouncements coming from the pens of nationalists like Volodin and Prokhanov, since they are obviously quite upset about the prospect of the Union's breakup. Both, as noted earlier, were signers of the July 23, 1991, *Sovetskaya Rossiya* "appeal to the people" calling for a coup, and both clearly backed the coup of August 19, whose major ostensible purpose was to block signature of a new Union treaty. Their various actions can perhaps be reconciled with one another if we assume that they are reluctant acquiescers in a "small Russia," who would prefer maintenance of a Union (which would in any case be the consequence of the authoritarian restoration they desire), but who would accept an independent Russia if this were the condition for a Russian national revival and the ending of liberal reforms at home.

It should be noted that almost all of the the conservative nationalists who have spoken of a "small Russia," from Solzhenitsyn to Prokhanov, have advocated border adjustments in the event the Union dissolves, and some have suggested forceful intervention to protect the lives of Russians outside of Russia. Few show sympathy for the national aspirations of the non-Russian peoples of the USSR, often characterizing them as "Russophobes" or "racists" bent on discriminating against Russians. For example, Eduard Volodin noted that; "Only Russia, by applying political *and other* means, is capable of creating its representations in the national union republics and not allowing nationalists to raise the racist theory to the level of a political doctrine which is degrading to their own people."[80] Aleksandr Prokhanov is even more explicit: if Russia "leaves the dance floor....Not a single hair must fall from a Russian head. Not a single tear must be shed. The Russian population will not be used as hostages in national or political games. Russia will arise with all its great-power might to defend them, to defend its compatriots, and will put their interests in the center of its state interests."[81]

It should be clear from the above that territorial preferences do not necessarily correlate with political ones. Just as there can be conservative (i.e., authoritarian) nationalist proponents of a "small Russia," so too can there be liberal or reformist nationalist advocates of a large Russia.[82] The latter is far from a null set. Many "democrats" who eventually flocked to Yeltsin favored, as Yeltsin himself did, a continued Union, and were surprised and dismayed when the Ukrainians, Belorussians, and others announced they wanted no part of it.[83] Nikolay Travkin's Democratic Party of Russia, for example, has distinguished itself from other democratic groups by its strong support for a continued union, and for the protection of the rights of Russians outside Russia. After the August 19 coup, Travkin appeared before audiences in the so-called "Dniester republic" of Moldavia and told them in language reminiscent of the Russian "patriots" that Russia would never forget them. The Russian Popular Front of Valeriy Skurlatov has a program that combines centralizing Russian imperialism with support for free-market economics, with Abraham Lincoln and the Tsarist reformer Petr Stolypin among the group's heroes.[84] Roman Szporluk refers to a group of Westernizing, liberal democratic "empire savers" who would like to turn Russia and the former USSR into what they imagine the United States to be, that is, a multi-ethnic society in which ethnicity is divorced from territory, and in which the center could play a progressive role in protecting the rights of individuals and minorities against local authoritarianisms.[85] It is not obvious that liberal nationalists will be any less eager than their conservative counterparts to champion the rights of Russians facing persecution abroad, though presumably they would be somewhat less quick to resort to forceful methods to do so.

On Economic Questions

Russian nationalists are also divided on economic questions. The liberal nationalists, of course, almost universally support some form of free market economics, though some might characterize themselves as more social-democratic in orientation. Apart from a few hard-line national Bolsheviks who approve the whole of the Stalin legacy, most conservative nationalists favor some sort of free agriculture and policies designed to re-establish a strong and independent peasantry. This is not surprising, since the initial concern of many of the cultural nationalists and *derevenshchiki* was the destruction of the Russian countryside and the loss of the moral life of the traditional village. Solzhenitsyn is very firm in his belief that it is necessary to restore private property to the peasantry, which he notes is "part of the notion of individuality."

On the question of private ownership of large industrial enterprises, there is a much wider range of views. Many conservative nationalists share with their Bolshevik allies a strong distaste for private capital and free markets, and for the consumerism, foreign investment, and inequality that goes with it. Indeed, Mikhail Antonov, head of *Otchestovo*, has formulated an economic doctrine reminiscent of mercantilist or even medieval Christian "just price" theories that manage to be at the same time anti-capitalist and non-Marxist. Antonov, who is sometimes regarded as an economic spokesman for the conservative nationalists, sharply criticizes advocates of free-market economics like Nikolay Shmelov or Tatyana Zaslavskaya, argues against free trade zones and joint ventures, and would clearly oppose broader Russian integration into the world economy.[86]

On the other hand, other conservative nationalists are more open to the free market. Soyuz's Col. Alksnis, for example, has stated that he personally favors some kind of free-market authoritarianism: "All economic activity should be based on market relations. Forcefully, if need be....Believe me, the Army wants a single state, which is neither capitalist nor socialist. It wants no dogmas."[87] Noting that Catherine the Great forced peasants to grow potatoes, Alksnis has suggested that Chile or South Korea might be acceptable models for the Soviet transition to the market.[88] On the other hand, Soyuz is not united on economic questions; co-chairman Yuryy Blokhin stated that he still favored a socialist path of development, and asserted that eighty percent of Soyuz's membership did as well.[89]

Were a conservative nationalist government to come to power, it would probably advocate a mixed economy, combining relatively free agriculture with state supervision of large-scale industry. The state would heavily regulate wages, prices, investment, and the like, and the economy would remain largely closed to the outside world. There are many earlier precedents for such a semi-mercantilist, semi-socialist economy, including those of Peronist Argentina or Mexico in the heyday of economic nationalism. The frequently disastrous performance of such economies suggests that the nationalists in the long run will not be able to provide any better an answer to Russia's economic crisis than the communists did.

On Foreign Policy

The clash between proponents of either a large or small Russia suggests that there are also major differences among them on questions of foreign policy. The nationalists have debated domestic issues much more intensively than foreign policy, so it is harder to delineate separate camps on the latter issue. "Small Russia" nationalists, whether of a liberal or conservative bent, are primarily concerned with rebuilding Russia and therefore tend to be relatively isolationist; the conservatives would probably extend that isolation to economic relations while the liberals would favor integration into the global economy.

Members of Soyuz and other "big Russia" neo-imperialists, on the other hand, have been very vocal in their denunciations of "new thinking" and the strategic retreat from Eastern Europe, which they felt undermined the Soviet Union's position as a great power and exposed it to grave threats from Germany and the West. Indeed, it was former foreign minister Eduard Sheverdnadze's support for American policy during the build up to the Persian Gulf war that brought forth the sharpest criticisms form Soyuz that ultimately led to his resignation in December 1990. The "big Russia" nationalists have almost universally favored Iraq, not for the ideological reasons put forward by the Brezhnev regime (i.e., that Iraq was a progressive "liberated country"), but simply as a matter of reflexive anti-Westernism and anti-Semitism. Indeed, perhaps as a result of their anti-Semitism, many conservative nationalists appear much more preoccupied with the Middle East than with Moscow's traditional sphere of influence in Eastern Europe, and were more visibly upset by Soviet policy in the Gulf than by the retreat from Europe.

Other than to say that they will be hostile to the United States, it is very difficult to predict the foreign policy of conservative nationalist Russia. One is inclined to think that such a regime will remain quite preoccupied with the former internal empire, and will be economically hard pressed to afford a more expansionist foreign policy. Beyond this, nationalists have shown particular interest primarily in countries on the former USSR's immediate periphery (i.e., Eastern Europe, China, the Middle East, etc.), rather than with far-flung former Soviet clients like Cuba and Vietnam which are both expensive and of interest only for outdated ideological reasons.

On Culture and Politics

A final distinction between types of Russian nationalists concerns whether they are more interested in cultural or political matters, roughly corresponding to the distinction John Dunlop draws between the National Bolsheviks and those he labels *vozrozhdentsy*, or "revivalists." Many of those who became nationalists in the 1960s or 1970s, including the *derevenshchiki* and the contributors to *Nash Sovermennik*, were primarily preoccupied with moral and cultural problems. They sought to define Russian *samobytnost'* in largely spiritual, rather than political or territorial terms. The more vocal "big Russia" nationalists of the early 1990s are largely military officers or party members whose interest in the question is almost entirely political and professional. Viktor Alksnis and Yuriy Blokhin have never shown the slightest interest in traditional Slavophile concerns like the question of "inner freedom" or Orthodoxy. Some writers like Rasputin or Prokhanov have tried to bridge both worlds, writing on cultural issues while also seeking to play a role in contemporary Russian politics.

VI. The Future of Russian Nationalism

As suggested above, the conservative nationalists made a grave tactical mistake in aligning themselves with conservatives in the party, army, and police. But the coup's failure and the discrediting of those nationalists who had supported it do not by any means signal the end of the "Russian idea" in Russian politics. Indeed, Russian nationalism is today more powerful than ever, as are the nationalisms of the former USSR's constituent republics. But in Russia, nationalism has for the moment been captured by Boris Yeltsin and the "democrats." The West, indeed, owes Yeltsin a considerable debt for taking the nationalist issue and giving it a moderate and liberal face, thereby naturalizing an ideology that might otherwise have taken an aggressive and intolerant turn.

But the liberal nationalism that has for the moment emerged as the dominant form may not survive the economic and political turbulence sure to come in the years ahead. Yeltsin's ability to speak in a moderate way for Russia and Russian nationalism is by no means a permanent state of affairs, or else Yeltsin himself may someday evolve into the nationalist demagogue that his numerous detractors frequently accuse him of being. The process of making the transition to a market economy will be much longer and more painful than the already long and slow processes taking place in Eastern Europe, and it will be much complicated by the continuing fallout of the breakup of the Union and the establishment of a series of independent states on the territory of the former USSR. Both of these conditions will provide sources of acute discontent throughout Russia, and will pose grave challenges to Yeltsin and the democrats now holding political power in Russia.

The failure of the August 19 coup may, paradoxically, set the stage for the appearance of a far more powerful form of nationalism by potentially liberating conservative Russian nationalism from its debilitating alliance with the communist party. The obvious lesson for a conservative nationalist to draw from the events of August is that association with the old communist apparatus is an utter liability in contemporary Russia, and that nationalists would do much better to go it alone—indeed, to combine conservative nationalism with a kind of demagogic anti-communism, and a demand for the protection of the rights of Russians outside of Russia. None of the traditional Russian nationalists has thus far moved in this direction.[90]

The only figure to have experimented to date with such a combination of views is the Liberal Democratic Party's Vladimir Zhirinovskiy. The latter came in third and won eight percent of the vote in the June 1991 election for Russian president, beating both the liberal communist Vadim Bakatin and the neo-Stalinist Albert Makashov. Most pollsters indicated that Zhirinovskiy's support was rapidly growing at the time of the election, and he would have received a much higher vote had the election campaign lasted longer than two weeks. Zhirinovskiy campaigned on an openly non-nationalist position like the unlimited production of cheap vodka and the renting out of the Soviet army to the United Nations. He appealed directly to those Russians living in the Baltics and other republics, playing on their fears of persecution:

> I would like to address again the Russians and Russian-speakers. To date, Russians are the most humiliated and insulted nation. I do not want to raise Russians above other peoples; I am an opponent of nationalism....But today, 155 million Russians are suffering, and I, as future president of Russia, if the election allows me to do this, will definitely protect all Russians, all Russian-speakers.[91]

He argued that the Soviet Union ought to abolish republican borders and replace them with administrative ones, and that he would make Col. Alksnis governor of the new Baltic region.[92] At the same time he emphasized that he was not a communist and had nothing in common with the party nomenklatura.[93]

It is questionable whether Zhirinovskiy will ever play more than a marginal role in Soviet politics. He speaks poorly, he has taken utterly eccentric positions on a wide variety of issues, his Liberal Democratic Party is widely believed to have been established with help from the KGB, and he is a great Russian chauvinist commonly thought to be half-Jewish. But if it is not Zhirinovskiy himself who is able to exploit the Russian nationalist/anti-communist combination, then his degree of success in June 1991 suggests that it is a position with explosive potential. The fact that Zhirinovskiy could rise from total obscurity to win eight percent of the Russian vote further suggests that the person who eventually does put together a broadly popular Russian nationalist platform need not necessarily come from the ranks of the long-time conservative nationalists. Indeed, the Rasputins, Belovs, Prokhanovs, and the like are primarily scribblers with little taste for rough-and-ready politics; in the future, it may be some previously unknown businessmen, colonel, or even a former communist, who will ride the nationalist issue to power. The way that such an individual comes to power may be violent, but it could also be through a free and fair election, just as Hitler was elected by a plurality of the German people in 1933.

VII. Policy Issues for the United States

It should be clear from the above that Russian nationalism is not a monolithic or simple phenomenon. There is a widespread tendency in the West to see nationalism as an alternative to democracy, and then to assume further that all nationalisms ultimately take on intolerant and aggressive forms. But this legacy of the two world wars and Nazism is misleading because it is based on a selective reading of the way in which nationalisms developed in this century. While German fascism did indeed take the downward spiral just described, Spanish fascism remained isolated and inward-looking. Turkish nationalism became explicitly anti-imperialistic, and was the basis for the devolution of the remaining parts of the Ottoman empire in the 1920s. All modern Western European nationalisms, having passed through the crucible of the world wars, have evolved in a reasonably tolerant and liberal direction. To be French or Italian has a real meaning for inhabitants of those countries, but a meaning that is expressed primarily in the cultural area; national identity in such cases has been made compatible with liberal democracy and has lost any association with military imperialism.

There is, as we have seen, a wide variety of types of Russian nationalism, ranging from Boris Yeltsin's relatively liberal "small Russia" variety, to the "big Russia," imperialist visions of Soyuz, or the neo-fascist, intolerant, and anti-Semitic program of *Pamyat'*. Many people have assumed that a Russian nationalist regime would automatically adopt the program of the latter organization, but *Pamyat'* represents only the most extreme fringe of the nationalist spectrum. Even among the conservative nationalists there are significant differences on the territorial question, foreign policy, and economics; it is entirely possible to imagine a brutal, authoritarian Russia that was nonetheless passive and isolationist in foreign policy, or a liberal Russia that was both imperialist and interventionist. Clearly, it matters very much to the United States what form a Russian nationalist government takes, since there are some we can work with, and some that would present a major military threat. We must not assume ahead of time that any particular form will predominate, and U.S. policymakers should make careful distinctions between the two such that the best does not become the enemy of the good.

The view that Russian nationalism inevitably degenerates into its most aggressive and intolerant from in the absence of foreign intervention is most closely associated with the early work of Aleksandr Yanov. Yanov based this view of his reading of Russian history: he noted that there have been no fewer than eight previous periods of reform, each of which engendered a powerful counter-reform that washed away earlier gains and re-established a new sort of tyranny. He argued that the more intolerant forms of nationalism can always outbid the more moderate ones, particularly when they start appealing to the Russian "street."

While Yanov's historical pessimism is well-founded, he is perhaps a bit too deterministic in seeing massive foreign intervention as the only force that can effectively break this cycle. For the Russian political system and society have not remained static between cycles. In particular, there has been a steady evolution over the past hundred years towards the kind of "middle class society" that Yanov himself sees as crucial in sustaining liberal democracy in North America and Europe. Other countries with authoritarian historical traditions and weak civil societies have made successful transitions to democracy in the past, and there is no obvious reason why the Russians should be unable to do so as well eventually, even if the transition does not occur in this generation.

American policymakers should not believe that they have a choice as to whether to be pro or con Russian nationalism, or indeed any other nationalism in the former Soviet Union. All post-communist governments in this region are going to be nationalist to one degree or another. Mikhail Gorbachev's brand of reform communism was the last gasp of an "internationalist" order based on socialist ideology rather than the nation, but it has no abiding political constituency and, as in Eastern Europe, is proving to be a transitional stage. Much as we can be grateful to Gorbachev for the historical role he has played, and much as some may regret to waning of his influence, his internationalism is no longer a realistic alternative.

The question for the U.S. is what kind of nationalist government we deal with in Russia, and whether U.S. influence can be brought to bear to make it compatible with the greatest degree of democracy and liberal rights. Just as in the case of the old Soviet Union, we will have to set standards of conditionality regarding acceptable and unacceptable behavior, beginning first with foreign policy, and then concerning the dominant national group's treatment of its own ethnic minorities. This is a standard that needs to be applied toward Russia, but also toward other republics that may become guilty of mistreatment of Russians living among them.

In defining acceptable standards of behavior, we perhaps need to draw a distinction between nationalism and national interest. That is to say, not every instance in which a country asserts its national interest is an instance of an unacceptable and potentially dangerous nationalism. Russia, like Germany, suffers from a (self-inflicted) historical legacy of distrust on the part of its immediate neighbors, who interpret virtually everything its government does as great Russian chauvinism. This distrust is heightened by Russia's preponderant size. It was quite evident the week after the August 19 coup, when the Russian government announced that it would have to consider border adjustments in the event that the other republics with Russian populations declared independence. This statement was immediately interpreted as an instance of Russian chauvinism and an effort to restore the Russian empire. Such interpretations were rampant not only in Kiev and Alma-Ata, but in Washington and Paris as well.

But all countries have legitimate national interests, and indeed their governments become de-legitimized domestically if they do not appear to be promoting those national interests vigorously. The international community invites trouble when it demands that certain countries atone for past sins by restraining even their most reasonably national interests for a prolonged period of time, as Germany was forced to do after World War II. And the most neuralgic national issue for Russia is likely to be the question of those 25 million Russians living outside Russia. It is hard to imagine any legitimate Russian government being indifferent to what happens to them, as "democrats" like Yeltsin and Travkin have made clear. Americans in particular should remember the extraordinary lengths to which the American government went to secure the release of a mere handful of American citizens held hostage first in Iran, and then in Lebanon. And Americans cannot content themselves with a policy that says that concern over Russians abroad is legitimate, but that forceful means to protect them are not. The U.S. invasion of Grenada was justified on the grounds of a threat to the lives of a group of American medical students, while the invasion of Panama was at least in part explained because the wife of an American soldier had been sexually accosted by a member of the Panamanian National Guard. France and other European countries have repeatedly violated the sovereignty of various African countries to protect the lives of their nationals there. American policymakers may soon be faced with a decision on how to react to military intervention on the part of a democratic Russia against, say, a repressive, non-democratic Kazakhstan to protect the interests of the Russian half of that republic's population. Is this a case of unacceptable imperialistic nationalism, or legitimate national self-interest? Many people will immediately make the former case, arguing that Hitler's expansion started with legitimate German claims on behalf of the Sudeten Germans and Danzig, and they may well be right. Russia's sheer size makes any kind of military intervention troublesome. On the other hand, would we expect any other "normal" liberal democracy to act differently?

A further question that will have to be addressed is how an aggressive Russian nationalism might be expected to arise. One obvious way is by another coup d'etat against Yeltsin and the democrats currently ruling Russia, a coup that avoided the childish mistakes of the one in August 1991. Alternatively, a nationalist demagogue could come to power by entirely constitutional means, exploiting the electorate's dissatisfaction with the economy and the status of Russians. But a third alternative is also possible, that Boris Yeltsin himself could metamorphose from a democrat into a dictator in the way that many of his detractors expect. Serbia's Slobodan Milosevic underwent a similar transformation from forward-looking technocrat to rabble-rousing nationalist as he sought a formula for staying in power.

Yeltsin's record to date gives one grounds for hope. While he has exploited Russian nationalist themes, he has always avoided quite scrupulously the intolerant and xenophobic ones that are unfortunately so much part of the nationalist legacy. He has, for example, consistently declined the temptation that even Lech Walesa was unable to resist, of falling back on anti-semitism to build his popularity. Shortly after being elected president of Russia in May 1990, he began touring the RSFSR, assuring the smaller nationalities that they would be permitted the degree of autonomy or even independence that Gorbachev was at that time denying to the Union republics. While it is true that Yeltsin's spokesman referred to the need for border adjusiments in the chaotic week following the August coup, this statement appears in retrospect to have been a calculated effort to slow down the process of headlong disintegration and force the different republics back into a negotiation on their future relationship. (It was, moreover, a calculation that had its intended effect.)

Nonetheless, we must recognize that whatever Yeltsin's present intentions, he and the other democrats will come under strong pressure to assert Russian national interests in ways that will make his Western supporters quite uncomfortable. He has already begun ruling by decree and overriding the decisions of locally elected bodies in ways that have given rise to charges of authoritarianism. And as noted above, it is not clear that any legitimate government of Russia will be able to resist pressures to take measures, even forceful measures, to protect the interests of Russians outside of Russia. The concept of a "small Russia" is probably one that looks better in the abstract than in the concrete. For while it may seem like a noble project to rebuild central Russia, attention will necessarily be focused on the plight of Russians suddenly finding themselves without a home or rights in Azerbaijan or Kazakhstan. Sobchak's solution to this problem—that they should come home to Russia—begs the question of where they will live once they return, and how the atrocities that characterized partition of the Indian subcontinent in 1948 will not be duplicated during the movement of such large populations.

Indeed, these objective pressures to defend Russian national interests may make a number of former friends seem something less than friendly in the future. Aleksandr Solzhenitsyn, for example, has been rightly admired for this monumental courage in standing up to the Soviet regime, and to its apologists in the West. But he is by no means a Western liberal, and it is entirely possible that he will play a less than helpful role in building democratic institutions when he returns to Russia.

Problematic as the positions of Yeltsin or Solzhenitsyn may one day become for us, we have to remember that there are many conservative Russian nationalists who do not want Russia to be a liberal democracy, who hope to re-establish the empire, certainly the former USSR and perhaps its acquisitions in Eastern Europe as well, who worship military power, and who have scant regard for the rights and liberties of their own citizens. It would be foolish for the United States to look only at threats from a revived communism, and to discount entirely the potential for an aggressive fascism to arise on Russian soil. Democracy is still quite new and fragile, and will undergo severe tests as the economy deteriorates and ethnic tensions rise. Conservative Russian nationalism is one of the few systematic ideological alternatives to liberal democracy left in the world today, and the only one with sufficient dynamism and adherents to fill the vacuum left by discredited democracy.

Endnotes

1. See Nikolai Berdyaev, *The Russian Idea*, Greenwood Press, 1979, p.44. Aleksandr Yanov, not normally a friend of Russian nationalism, says of the Slavophiles: "Whatever one may think of [Slavophilism], the nobility of its scheme and the purity of its intentions cannot be denied. Essentially, Slavophilism was an opposition movement. Although its first advocates were themselves nationalists, they hated official nationalism, the ideology of Nicholas I's dictatorship. They passionately opposed human oppression in all its forms, whether serfdom, censorship or official lies. They called upon people not to live by lies. Moreover, although they claimed Russia's spiritual, cultural and potential political superiority over the West, this superiority was not to be used to harm the West. The Slavophiles wished merely to open the West's eyes to the ultimate truth, and in the spirit of generosity to extend a helping hand." Aleksandr Yanov, *The Russian Challenge and the Year 2000*, Basil Blackwell, Oxford, 1987, pp. 25.26.

2. On the theory of official nationality, see Sergi V. Utechine, *Russian Political Thought: A Concise History*, Praeger, New York, 1963, p. 72.

3. On Sanilevskiy, see Utechine, 1963 (op. cit., note 2), p.86; Yanov, 1987 (op. cit., note 1), p. 34; Berdyaev, 1979 (op. cit., note 1), p. 65.

4. Hans Kohn, *Pan-Slavism, Its History and Ideology*, 2nd Edition, Vintage Books, New York, 1960, p.199.

5. Yeltsin's citing of Tyutchev has been taken as an ominous sign by some of a lurking imperialist frame of mind, but it should be kept in mind that Tyutchev is considered by many to be the greatest Russian lyrical poet since Pushkin, who himself was given to rather chauvinistic utterances on the question of Russia.

6. Quoted in Kohn, 1960 (op. cit., note 4), pp 157–158.

7. Thus at the second pan-Slav conference held in Moscow in 1867, the Russian spokesman (to the dismay of the non-Russians attending) argued in favor of the spread of the Russian language among Slavs and other forms of Russification. See Kohn, 1960 (op. cit., note 4).

8. See Richard Pipes, *Russia Under the Old Regime*, Weidenfeld and Nicolson, London, 1974, pp. 266–268.

9. The idea is also in Berdyaev, who argues that there is a greater spirit of freedom in Orthodoxy than in Catholicism; see Berdyaev, 1979 (op. cit., note 1), p. 43.

10. Quoted in Berdyaev, 1979 (op. cit., note 1), p. 43.

11. Kohn, 1960 (op. cit., note 4), pp. 148–149.

12. Ibid., pp. 185–196.

13. From the 1973 postscript to "As Breathing and Consciousness Return," in Aleksandr Solzhenitsyn, *From Under the Bible*, Little Brown and Co., Boston, 1974. p. 22.

14. Aleksandr Solzhenitsyn, *A World Split Apart: Commencement Address Delivered at Harvard University*, Harper and Row, New York, 1978, p. 15.

15. See, for example, John B. Dunlop, "Russian Reactions to Solzhenitsyn's Brochure," *Radio Liberty Research Bulletin*, December 14, 1990, pp. 3–8.

16. Aleksandr Solzhenitsyn, "How Are We to Structure Russia?—A Modest Contribution," *Komsomolskaya Pravda*, September 8, 1990, :3–6; and *Literaturnaya Gazeta*, no. 38, September 18, 1990.

17. Ibid. This passage echoes one written twenty years earlier: "Do we not discern in the multiparty system yet another idol, but this time one to which the whole world bows down? 'Partia' means a part. Every party known to history has always defended the interests of this one part against—whom? Against the rest of the people...cant we not, we wonder, rise above the two-party or multiparty parliamentary system? Are there no *extraparty* or strictly *nonparty* paths of national development?" Solzhenitsyn, 1974 (op. cit., note 13), p. 19.

18. For a critique of Solzhenitsyn's Harvard commencement address and a tracing of the intellectual roots of many of his ideas, see Richard Pipes, "Solzhenitsyn and the Russian Intellectual Tradition." *Encounter*, June, 1979, 52 no. 6: 52–56.

19. On the National Bolsheviks, see Mikhail Agursky, *The Third Rome: National Bolshevism in the USSR*, Westview Press, Boulder, CO, 1987.

20. On Soviet nationalism in this period, see Frederick C. Barghoorn, *Soviet Russian Nationalism*, Oxford University Press, New York, 1956.

21. On *Molodaya Gvardiya* in the 1960s, see Yanov, 1987 (op. cit., note 1), pp. 103–113; John B. Dunlop, *The Faces of Contemporary Russian Nationalism*, Princeton University Press, Princeton, NJ, 1983, pp. 217–221.

22. See Yitzhak M. Brudny, "The Heralds of Opposition to Perestroika," *Soviet Economy*, 5 no.2: 162–200.

23. Dunlop, 1983 (op. cit., note 21), pp. 66–87.

24. Ibid., pp. 81–83.

25. On the water-division project, see Nikolai N. Petro, "The Project of the Century: A Case Study of Russian National Dissent," *Studies in Comparative Communism*, 20 nos. 3–4, Autumn-Winter, 1987: 235–252.

26. Rasputin interview with Ilya Tolstoy in *Dialog*, March 4, 1990: 106–112.

27. See Dunlop, 1983 (op. cit., note 21), pp. 103–105.

28. This of course is an observation that is easier to make with the hindsight provided by the Gorbachev period, but Aleksandr Yanov reports a speech by a high foreign ministry official back in the late 1960s who noted that Marxism-Leninism was for all practical purposes dead in the Soviet Union, and needed to be replaced by Russian nationalism as a mobilizational ideology. See Aleksandr Yanov, *The Russian New Right: Right Wing Ideologies in the Contemporary USSR*, Institute of International Studies, University of California, Berkeley, 1978.

29. On this incident, see Dunlop, 1983 (op. cit., note 21), pp. 221–224; Brudny, 1989 (op. cit., note 22), p. 166.

30. See Dunlop, 1983 (op. cit., note 21), p. 221. Note that while the whole of *Novyy Mir's* editorial board was sacked, thereby ending its role as a herald of liberal thought in the USSR, only the editor-in-chief of *Molodaya Gvardiya* was removed and the journal survived the indecent more or less unscathed.

31. Ibid., pp. 227–233; and Yanov, 1987 (op. cit., note 1), pp. 120–123.

32. John B. Dunlop, *The New Russian Nationalism*, Praeger, New York, 1985, pp. 9–25.

33. Ibid., pp. 26–35.

34. Nikolai N. Petro, "The Project of the Century: A Case Study of Russian National Dissent," *Studies in Comparative Communism*, 20 no. 3–4, Autumn-Winter, 1987, p. 238. Valentin Rasputin's cautious reactions to the Gorbachev regime's environmental policies is evident in the interview he gave to *Der Speigel*, no. 15, April 6, 1987: 177–186.

35. On Ligachev's relationship wit the conservative nationalists, see Julia Wishnevsky, "Ligachev, Pamyat', and Conservative Writers," *Radio Liberty Research Bulletin Report on the USSR*, March 10, 1989: 12–15.

36. On these changes, see John B. Dunlop, "Soviet Cultural Politics," *Problems of Communism*, 36, no. 6, November-December, 1987: 34–56.

37. Rasputin's interview with Ilya Tolstoy in *Dialog*, March 4, 1990: 106–112. One wonders what kind of sheltered experiences Rasputin must have had during his visit to the Midwest and Great Plains when he was the guest of the University of Kansas in 1985.

38. For this interpretation of Kozhivov's essay "Pravda i Istina," see Dimitry Pospielovsky, "Russian Nationalism: An Update," *Radio Liberty Report on the USSR*, February 9, 1990: 8–17.

39. See Julia Wishnevsky, *"Nas Sovremennik* Provides Focus of 'Opposition Party'," *Radio Liberty Research Bulletin*, January 20, 1989: 1–6.

40. Dunlop, 1987 (op. cit., note 36), pp. 40–43.

41. Thus Anatolyy Anan'ycv was removed as editor of *Oktyabr'*, Mikhail Kolosov replaced by Erst Safonov at *Literaturnaya Rossiya*, and Sergy Vikulov by Stanislav Kunyaev at *Nash Sovremennik*. The conservative nationalist also managed to isolate the liberal *Aprel'* committee of the Leningrad Writers Union. See Robert Otto, "Contemporary Russian Nationalism," *Problems of Communism*, November-December, 1990: 96–105.

42. See Douglas Smith, "Formation of a New Russian Nationalist Group Announced," *Radio Liberty Research Bulletin*, July 7, 1989: 5–8.

43. See John B. Dunlop, "New National Bolshevik Organization Formed," *Radio Liberty Research Bulletin*, September 14, 1990: 7–9.

44. See Julia Wishnevsky, "A Second Pamyat' Emerges," *Radio Liberty Research Bulletin*, November 6, 1987; "Soviet Media sound Alarm over Anti-Semitism," *Radio Liberty Research Bulletin*, March 3, 1989: 7–9; John B. Dunlop, "A Conversation with Dmitrii Vasil'ev, the Leader of Pamyat'," *Radio Liberty Research Bulletin*, December 15, 1989: 12–16. See also the discussion on *Pamyat'* in Darrel Hammer, *"Glasnost'* and the 'Russian Idea'," *Radio Liberty Research Bulletin* special edition on *Russian Nationalism Today* December 19, 1988, pp. 19–20.

45. See Valeryy Konovalov, "Neo-Nazi in the USSR" From 'Mindless Childish Games to a Program of Action," *Radio Liberty Research Bulletin*, June 16, 1989: 10–13.

46. Thus, the "Letter from the Writers of Russia" noted that "While screaming hysterically about the threat presented to mankind and to all the peoples of the USSR by the odious characters in *Pamyat'*, the central press keeps persistently toning down or shamelessly whitewashing the ideological essence of

Zionism." *Literaturnaya Rossiya*, no. 9, March 2, 1990: 2–4. This letter was also reprinted in *Nash dovremennik, Molodaya Gvardiya*, and *Moskva*. Otto, 1990 (op. cit., note 41) p. 104, notes that in subsequent version of the letter, the phrase "odious characters" was removed, and replaced by, "and, in essence, from any patriotic organization."

47. See Wishnevsky, "Ligachev", 1989.
48. Igor Shafarevich, "Russophobia," *Nash Sovremennik*, June, 1989: 167–192. Also see the discussion for the nationalists' preoccupation with Russophobia in Walter LaSueur, "From Russia with Hate," *The New Republic*, February 5, 1990: 21–25.
49. Ibid.
50. Ibid.
51. Julia Wishnevsky, "Patriots Urge Annulment of RSFSR Elections," *Radio Liberty Research Bulletin*, April 6, 1990: 18–21.
52. On this alliance, see John B. Dunlop, "Moscow Report: Russia's Surprising Reactionary Alliance," *Orbis*, 34 no. 3, Summer 1991: 423–426.
53. On Prokhanov and Rash as nationalist-militarist ideologists, see Galeotti, Mark, "The Soviet Army's new Interest in Imperial Traditions," *Radio Liberty Research Bulletin*, December 28, 1990: 8–10.
54. Gosudarstvennyy Komitet po Statistike, *Itogi Vsesoyuznoy Perepisi Naselenie 1989 goda. Tom I. Chislennost' i Razmeschchenie Naseleniya SSSR. Chast 1* (Moscow: 1992).
55. See Elizabeth Teague, "The 'Soyuz' Group," *Radio Liberty Research Bulletin*, May 17, 1991: 16–21.
56. In various of his numerous interviews, Alksnis has asserted quite forcefully that he and Soyuz were not committed to either socialism or to the CPSU: "First, the elimination of all parties. THe CPSU and the rest. Then the announcement of a state of emergency and the introduction of censorship....To salvage the Union and introduce a market economy by force." (*Le Nouvel Observatuer*, March 21–27, 1991.) Soyuz "represents a wide range of opinions, from social democrats to communists. Yet, for the time being we all support out main objective, which is the preservation of the unity of our state." Interview is *Der Morgen*, May 6, 1991.
57. For an analysis of the origins of Soyuz, see Aleksey Kiva, "Union of Obsessives: Political Portrait of a Deputies Group Aspiring to a Serious Social Role," *Izvestiya*, May 12, 1990.
58. The letter was also signed by one of the leaders of *Soyuz*, Yuryy Blokhin, and by generals Valetin Varennikov and Boris Gromov. This letter was preceded by one sent to Gorbachev in December 1990 urging that he "take immediate measures against separatism, subversive antistate activities, instigation, and interethnic strife." (*Sovetskaya Rossiya*, December 22, 1990). This letter was signed by nationalists Yuryy Bondarev, Vasilyy Belov, and Aleksandr Prokhanov, as well as by the August conspirators Tizyakov and Oleg Baklanov.
59. *Soyuz*, no. 38, September, 1990.
60. Moscow television, May 22, 1990, as reported in *FBIS* Soviet Union Daily Report, May 23, 1990, pp. 96–97.
61. *Literaturnaya Rossiya*, December 29, 1989.
62. Moscow television, as reported in *FBIS Soviet Union Daily Report*, May 21, 1990, p. 99.

63. Vlasov also emphasized a nationalist issue relatively untouched by Yeltsin, that is, the need to revitalize the countryside and to protect small villages and hamlets in central Russia: "Regrettably, these days it is recalled less and less that from time immemorial [the countryside] not only fed Rus', but was also guarantor of our spiritual well-being and keeper of our folk wisdom and work ethic." Ibid., p. 102.

64. On taxonomies of nationalists, see Dunlop, 1983 (op. cit., note 21), pp. 242–273; and "The Contemporary russian Nationalist Spectrum," and Darrell P. Hammer, "Glasnost' and the 'Russian Idea'," in *Radio Liberty Research Bulletin*, special edition on *Russian Nationalism Today*, December, 19, 1988, pp 1–10 and 11–24.

65. There has been a widespread revival of interest in the Russian monarchy in Russia since 1985, which does not necessarily translate into support for restoration of the institution. Among the contemporary supporters of some form of monarch are elements of *Pamyat'*, Valdimir Osipov's "Christian Renaissance" organization, and an extremist group called the Orthodox-Monarchist-Union-Order (*PRAMOS*). See John B. Dunlop, "Monarchist Sentiment in Present-Day Russia," *Radio Liberty Research Bulletin*, August 2, 1991, p. 27–30.

66. *Le Nouvel Observateur*, May 8–14, 1987.

67. In *From Under the Rubble*, Solzhenitsyn states: "Let us note that in the long history of mankind there have not been so very many democratic republics, yet people lived for centuries without them and were not always worse off. They even experienced that 'happiness' we are forever hearing about, which was sometimes called pastoral or patriarchal....They preserved the physical health of the nation....They preserved its moral health, too...a level of moral health incomparably higher than that expressed today in simian radio music, pop songs and insulting advertisements....Many of these state systems were authoritarian, that is to say, based on subordination to forms of centuries under various forms of authoritarian rule. Russia too preserved itself and its health, did not experience episodes of self-destruction like those of the twentieth century, and for ten centuries millions of our peasant forebearers died feeling their lives had not been too unbearable." Solzhenitsyn, 1974, p. 23.

68. In theory the liberal nationalists could be divided into camps depending on their attitude toward communism, but most liberal nationalists have moved into the non or anti-communist Yeltsin Democratic Russia camp. The category of liberal (or reformist) Communist-nationalist is, to this author's knowledge, an empty one.

69. See, for example, his article "Thoughts on the Polish Army," *Krasnaya Zvezda* (July 10, 1988), in which he praises the Polish army over the Polish communist party, and implicitly calls on the Soviet armed forces to seize power.

70. See "The Tragedy of Centralism," *Literaturnaya Rossiya*, no. 1, January 5, 1990.

71. The word *Akharovets* comes from one Akharov who was a police official in 19th century Moscow.

72. Solzhenitsyn, 1990. Also see John D. Dunlop, "Solzhenitsyn Calls for the Dismemberment of the Soviet Union," Vera Tolz, "Solzhenitsyn Proposes a Plan for the Reconstruction of Russia," and Ann Sheehy, "Solzhenitsyn's Concept of a Future Russian Union: The Nationalities Angle," *Radio Liberty Research Bulletin*, October 5, 1990: 9–16.

73. For an overview of reactions to the Solzhenitsyn article, see John B. Dunlop, "Russian Reactions to Solzhenitsyn's Brochure," *Radio Liberty Research Bulletin*, December , 1990: 3-8.

74. For examples of the painful rethinking of the question of the union on the part of Russian liberals, see for example the interview with Vasilyi Selunin where he notes that "I would be glad if the Union did not break up. However, reality is such that the empire has perished, and nothing will save it now. We should be thinking about post-imperial development....It is us in Russia who are second-class citizens." (*Ekho Litvy*, April 26, 1990.) Marina Sal'ye noted in a similar vein "The truth actually consists in the fact that a nation that oppresses other nations cannot be free...I am convinced that the 'God-chosen' status of the Russian nation proved to be too costly for it and that it was tormented and it suffered just as much as the other nations in our country...the Russian nation, possible to a greater extent than other nations, has has an interruption in the enthnocultual tradition." *Raduga*, no. 5, May 1990. See also Vera Tolz, "Democrats Start Their Own Discussion of Russian National Problems," *Radio Liberty Research Bulletin*, March 30, 1990.

75. "The New Russia in a Changing World," *Literaturnaya Rossiya*, no. 4, January 26, 1990a. Also see John B. Dunlop, "Ethnic Russians on Possible Breakup of the USSR," *Radio Liberty Research Bulletin*, March 2, 1990.

76. In the tradition of earlier Slavophiles, Volodin asserts that "Russia and her people have created a culture and acquired spiritual experience so that they have gone beyond the national framework and become world historical phenomena."

77. "The Tragedy of Centralism," *Literaturnaya Rossiya*, no. 1, January 5, 1990; see also Prokhanov's comments in the roundtable published in *Pravda*, June 24, 1990; and Vera Tolz and Elizabeth Teague, "Prokhanov Warms of Collapse of Soviet Empire," *Radio Liberty Research Bulletin*, February 9, 1990.

78. "Essay and Current Affairs: Notes of a Conservative," *Nash Sovremennik*, no. 5, May, 1990b.

79. Dimitry Pospielosvksy (1990, p.8) reports that during a trip to the Soviet Union, "most of the Russian nationalists I encountered expressed a nationally motivated preference for the separation of Central Asia and were ready to accept secession of the Baltic republics (though without enthusiasm).

80. Emphasis added. Volodin, 1990.

81. Prokhanov, 1990b.

82. John Dunlop characterizes Aleksandr Solzhenitsyn as a liberal nationalist on the ground that he favors breakup of the empire and liberation of its constituent nationalities. I would characterize him rather as a moderate conservative who also happens to favor a "small Russia."

83. This Dimitry Pospielovsky (1990, p. 9) quotes Sergey Stankevich as saying of Baltic secession, "I should hate to see this...but absolutely nobody should be held to us by force.."

84. Skurlatov and the Russian Popular Front, like Valdimir Zhirinovskiy's Liberal Democratic Party and Vladimir Voronin's so-called "Andrey Sakharov Union of Democratic Forces," which were together aligned in the so-called "Centrist Bloc" in 1990, is a rather questionable organization possibly set up with help from the KGB and CPSU. Skurlatov made a name for himself in the 1960s as a quasi-fascist, and his Popular Front has advocated a radical, even violent democratization program which has been used by the

CPSU to discredit more genuine democrats. See John B. Dunlop, "Leadership of the Centrist Bloc," *Radio Liberty Research Bulletin*, February 8, 1991: 4–6.

85. In this context, Szporluk cites the newly appointed head of the Ethnography Institute of the USSR Academy of Sciences, Valeriy Tishkov. See his "Dilemmas of Russian Nationalism," *Problems of Communism* (July–August 1989), pp. 15–35.

86. On Antonov, see Otto (1990), pp. 98–100; and Geoffery Hosking, *The Awakening of the Soviet Union*, Harvard University Press, Cambridge, MA, 1900, p. 109.

87. *Kosmsomolskaya Pravda*, February 26, 1991.

88. Alksnis seems to enjoy the idea of the forceful means to be used to introduce the market as much as the final result itself. Interview in *Der Morgen*, May 6, 1991.

89. *Soyuz*, no. 52, December 1990.

90. As one early indicator of such a shift, *Pamyat'*, which earlier asserted that liberal reformers like Gorbachev, Yakovlev, and Shevardnadze were really Jews with names like Liberman and Esptein, have now attributed Jewish genealogies to the makers of the August 19 coup.

91. Moscow television, June 11, 1991, as reported in *FBIS Soviet Union Daily Report*, June 12, 1991, p. 65.

92. Zhirinovksiy has also staked out a rather expansionist foreign policy, questioning the national independence of Finland and suggesting that the Middle East would be a natural sphere of influence for the Soviet Union.

93. During the campaign, Zhirinovksiy stated: "All of my rivals belong to the party nomenklatura, which made a career along the state line or in administrative service. They reached the ceiling....In this sense, I am again sharply different from them. I relate to the middle strata of the population, which receives a salary of 200 rubles, has a two-room apartment, and does not have any privileges." From an interview in *Krasnaya Zveda*, May 30, 1991. Elsewhere, Zhirinovksiy has claimed that his professional progress was blocked by the communist party.

Nationalism, Civil Society and Democracy

Craig Calhoun
University of North Carolina, Chapel Hill

In 1989, the self-declared "free world" reveled in the collapse of communism. Capitalism and democracy seemed simply and obviously triumphant. The cold war was over. Everyone would live happily ever after.

Of course, there would be "transitional problems." Word came of fighting in Nagorno-Karabak. It crossed some minds that many residents of Soviet Central Asia might find fundamentalist Islam more appealing than American capitalism. Enthusiasm for Lithuanian nationalism was occasionally dimmed by memories of Lithuanian fascism and anti-semitism. But in an efflorescence of faith in progress not seen since the 19th century, most Western politicians and intellectuals confidently saw "excesses" of nationalism as at most minor detours on the road to capitalist democracy. Even thinkers on the left joined the enthusiasm and, embarrassed by seeming association with the losing side, hastened to forget the lessons of history and the need for serious analysis.

But 1989 imperceptibly gave way to 1992, and anxiety began to regain a little intellectual respectability. Still, it took quite dramatic events, from Ethiopia to the former Soviet Union and especially Yugoslavia, to focus attention on the relationship of nationalism to democracy. As late as the spring of 1990, a committee of respected American sociologists could conclude that nationalism was "passé," and not of major sociological importance.[1] Even now, nationalism appears in discussions of democracy and civil society more as a hazard to be avoided than as a central dimension of the subject. As a result, the entire discourse about democracy and civil society has tended to neglect the problem of deciding what political units are relevant to claims for "self-determination." This theoretical failing leaves democrats poorly prepared to address current problems in Eastern Europe and the former Soviet Union, where nationalism appears centrally and seemingly almost inescapably as a successor ideology to communism.

The present paper is not a detailed analysis of nationalism or a specific study of any of the former communist countries. It is, rather, an attempt to situate problems of nationalism within the theoretical discourses of civil society and democracy. The first section briefly distinguishes dimensions of civil society, calling attention especially to the theme of how societal integration is accomplished. I turn then to the general nature of the discourse of nationalism (as it has been mobilized in a variety of settings), to the reasons why nationalism figures as a successor ideology to communism and finally to some implications of nationalism for democracy.

Civil Society

In the 1980s, the work of Hungarian and other East European intellectuals was responsible for a renewal of attention to one of the core concepts of modern Western history, the idea of civil society. The events of 1989 catapulted this concern from academic circles to the broader public discourse. The phrase is now on the lips of foundation executives, business leaders and politicians; it seems as though every university has set up a study group on civil society and the phrase finds its way into every dissertation in political sociology. None of this has, of course, helped to sort out whether civil society means Milton Friedman's capitalist market policies or social movements like Solidarity or the sort of "political society" or "public sphere" beloved of thinkers from Montesquieu to Tocqueville and Habermas, and once thought to exist mainly in cafes and coffee houses.[2]

The issue is basic, not just to practical politics but to our very conception of society. For what is signaled by the ambiguities in the use of civil society is the basic question of societal integration: how is society held together? Is society constituted by the rule of a state, or in the language of older political theory, by sovereignty? Is society held together by the seemingly self-organizing system of capitalist economic relations? Or is society organized, at least in part, through the voluntary social relations and actions of its members? Too easy use of the notion of civil society obscures the distinction between the latter two of these possibilities, the two which share the claim to organize social life outside the immediate control of the state.

Capitalist ideology sometimes suggests that capitalist economic life *is* precisely the realm of free social relations. But these are relations only among buyers and sellers, seen quintessentially as the owner-operators of small businesses and individual consumers. The same capitalist ideology negates its proffered freedom by reference to the immutable "laws" of the market, and the implicit recognition that the key to capitalist economic life is its systematicity, its capacity to achieve self-regulation outside the control of any central (or dispersed) planning agency. This much is granted by the ideology itself, even when it refuses to recognize the salient distinctions between giant corporations and human individuals, or the inevitable dependence and mutuality between capitalist economics and certain forms of state support. What this means is that capitalism, however important, cannot be a full answer to the question of societal integration. Most especially, capitalism is not the dimension of modern social life which offers the greatest possibility for the free and voluntary organization of human society. It is a realm in which social relations present themselves as external to human construction; this is the essential meaning of reification.[3] It is crucial to look beyond capitalism (and more generally beyond the narrow realm of the economy as a putatively self-sufficient and self-regulating system) to seek (a) the extent to which societal integration can be accomplished through webs of interpersonal relations, and (b) the extent to which both these social relations and the more abstract ones of the economy can be organized voluntarily through public discourse. Only when these possibilities are addressed do we have a conception of societal integration which can serve as foundation to a theory of democracy.

Nonetheless, capitalism *did* historically and can still play a special and crucial role in the growth of a civil society. The early growth of capitalist business relations provided essential support to the development of a sphere of political discourse outside the realm of state control. This is not to say that businessmen were the primary protagonists of the bourgeois public sphere. On the contrary, various state employees from ministerial clerks through university professors, and dependents of aristocratic sponsors played far more central roles in the 18th century "golden age" of the public sphere.[4] But the development of a public discourse in which private persons addressed public issues was made possible, in part, by both the policy issues posed by the growth of the non-state dominated market activity, and the creation of settings for such discourse in coffee houses, journals and other forums operated as businesses.

It is crucial not to accept capitalist ideology uncritically, and therefore to imagine that capitalism is somehow by itself an adequate support for democracy or a viable alternative to state power. It is equally crucial not to ignore the role of certain kinds of at least quasi-autonomous business institutions in facilitating the development of a sphere of public discourse outside the immediate control of the state. But we must not forget the importance of sociable relations governed by neither economy nor state. In other words, from the point of view of democracy, it is essential to retain in the notion of civil society some idea of a social realm which is neither dominated by state power nor simply responsive to the systemic features of capitalism. Civil society cannot be simply a realm in which representatives of state authority vie for attention with economists claiming to predict the economy like the weather on the basis of its reified laws. It must include an institutionally organized and substantial capacity for people to enter as citizens into public discourse about the nature and course of their life together. This capacity depends not just on formal institutions, but on civil society as a realm of sociability.

In this conceptualization, civil society must also be a realm of intermediate associations. Communities, movements and organizations (from churches to political parties and mutual aid societies) are all potentially important. Though the nationalist impulse is sometimes to condemn these as intrinsically "partial," this needs to be affirmed as one of their major virtues. For it is precisely in such partial social units that people find both the capacity for collective voice and the possibility of differentiated, directly interpersonal relations. Such intermediate associations are also the crucial defenses of both distinctive identities imperiled by the normalization of the mass and of democracy against oligarchy.

Hidden in this discourse—in two centuries of public discourse as well as in the last few paragraphs—is the problem of identifying "the people" who may be members of a discursive public or a civil society. From its earliest instanciations, from classical Athens through revolutionary America or Enlightenment Europe, the democratic public sphere has been marred by exclusionary tendencies. Not just slaves, but non-natives, propertyless men and all women have been excluded at various points from both direct political participation (e.g. voting) and from participation in the discourse of the public sphere. Some other exclusions seem more justifiable, though the theoretical status of the justifications is complex: the participation of children, criminals and the mentally incompetent is almost universally restricted. In short, "the people" have not all been citizens.

That democracy has always been restrictive has certainly been noticed. But there is an equally basic version of the question "who are the people?" which is less often posed. When we say, for example in relation to the break-up of Yugoslavia, that we believe in the right of "self-determination," just what self is involved? The notion of self-determination is basic to democracy and yet both neglected by democratic theory and shrouded in illusions of primordiality. The problem of self-determination is that for every socially relevant self we can see internal divisions and vital links to others. There is no single, definite and fixed "peoplehood" which can be assumed in advance of political discussion. As "no man is an island unto himself," no nation exists alone.[5] Each is defined in relation to others and exists within a web of social relationships which traverse its boundaries. Supposed historical autarky was never complete, and modern attempts to close borders have had only partial and temporary success. Conversely, claims to indivisibility are always at least partially tendentious and often (as in the United States pledge of allegiance) recognitions of the successful application of force to preserve unity. In short, do we speak of Macedonians, Croats and Serbs, of Yugoslavians, of Slavs, of Christians and Muslims, or of Europeans? The answers are obvious only from particular and partisan vantage points. Too often it is only forcible repression which makes us sure we see a true national identity. We lack a theory of the constitution of social selves which will give descriptive foundation to the prescriptive notion of self-determination. We are poorly prepared to talk about national identity or nationalism.

Nationality and Nationalism

Ideologists of nationhood almost always claim it as a "primordial" identity, an inheritance rather than a contemporary construct. This is one of the bases for the widespread illusion that somehow earlier traditions and identities can just be picked up and the communist era treated as an inconsequential interregnum. In Russia, for example—and in a good deal of Western discussion of Russia—the idea is current that the "real" Russia is that of the Czars. To some this means an ancient spiritual identity, preserved through long travails and waiting to flower again as beacon to all Slavs. To others, this means a political and cultural development, moving forward rapidly in the late 19th and early 20th centuries, when Russia could aspire to European leadership. Protagonists of each interpretation imagine that somehow when the pall of communism is lifted, the Russians of the late 20th century will begin to write like Tolstoy, and pick up the torch of an interrupted political development. In this remembered history, the struggles against Orthodox religion, against Czarist rule and rural landlords, and between narodniki, bourgeois democrats and various stripes of socialists are somehow submerged and communism becomes something both alien and accidental, not an outgrowth of national history.

In Hungary, it is easier to make the case that communism was something imposed from outside, but it is still not obvious that the nation can simply go forward in 1991 as a direct extension of that of 1945 (or 1921). Is national identity simply ancient and timeless? Or has it been forged and remade in centuries of struggle? What is the relationship between the Hungary which struggled against Hapsburg rule—and flowered under it, the Hungary which struggled to maintain independence and build a modern state in the early twentieth century, that of Nazi rule and resistance to it, that of communism, both domestic and imported, that of the Georg Lukacs who lived in Budapest and the one who lived in Moscow, that of 1919, 1956 and 1989? Different answers to these questions flow from different visions of what it means to be Hungarian. There are similar questions in every country's history, and they are central to the reasons why nationalism is always caught in an intimate but ambiguous relationship with history. Nationalist movements always revere martyrs and cherish sacred dates; they always give nations a history. But as Ernest Renan wrote in perhaps the most famous essay ever written on the subject, "Forgetting, I would even go so far as to say historical error, is a crucial factor in the creation of a nation, which is why progress in historical studies often constitutes a danger for [the principle of] nationality. Indeed, historical enquiry brings to light deeds of violence which took place at the origin of all political formations, even those whose consequences have been altogether beneficial. Unity is always effected by means of brutality..."[6]

The issue goes further. History is problematic for nationalism and the tacit assumption of national identity because it always shows nationality to be constructed not primordial. The history which nationalism would write of itself begins with the existence of national identity, continues through acts of heroism and sometimes struggles against oppression, and unites all living members of the nation with the great cultural accomplishments of its past. It is usually not a sociological history, of diversity forged into unity, of oppression of some members of the nation by others, of migration and immigration, and so forth. Precisely because it is not a sociological history, it allows all present day Russians to identify with 19th century novelists, and for the Westernizing efforts of Peter the Great to make him now a nationalist hero. And even in cosmopolitan Budapest it encourages some Hungarian patriots to identify with Magyar horsemen, accept centuries of international influences, and yet think of Hungarian Jews as members of an alien nation.

So nationality is not primordial but constructed. It is, moreover, a construction specific to the modern era and to the emergence of a modern world system in which claims to statehood became crucial bases for standing in world affairs, and potentially for autonomy, and in which claims to statehood can be justified most readily by professions of nationhood. This does not make nationality or the sentiments of nationhood any less real. But by the same token, nationality is not *more* real than many other identities which people may claim, or feel, or reproduce in their social relations. The nationalist claim is that national identity is categorical and fixed, and that somehow it trumps all other sorts of identities, from gender to region, class to political preference, occupation to artistic taste. This is a very problematic claim.

It is not easy to define nationalism. There are important variations where different cultures are at issue, where conquest has subordinated one group of people to another, where older ethnic groupings are being recast in terms of the idea of nation, and where an attempt is being made to forge a new unity out of previous diversity. It is better to see nationalisms in terms of family resemblances (following Wittgenstein) rather than to search for an essentialist definition of nationalism. When we speak of nationalism, thus, we speak of a somewhat arbitrary subset of claims to identity and autonomy on the part of populations claiming the size and capacity to be self-sustaining. For the purpose of any specific analysis we may want to include, say, the religious and political struggles in Northern Ireland or keep them distinct; there is no perfect boundary, no criterion of selecting nationalisms which includes all the familiar cases we are sure we want to consider without also including a variety of dubious outliers.

With more confidence, we can address the underlying factors which gave rise to nationalism and made it a major genus of identity-claim and source of political mobilization in the modern era. Indeed, by noting these underlying factors we can see why in a strong sense only the modern era has produced nationalism. People have always been joined in groups. These groups have derived their solidarity from kinship and other forms of social (including economic) interconnection, from a common structure of political power, from shared language and culture. But in the modern era, cultural and social structural factors have converged to create and disseminate the notion of national identity and make it central.

Culturally, the most decisive idea behind nationalism (or national identity) is the modern notion of the individual. The idea that human beings can be understood in themselves as at least potentially self-sufficient, self-contained and self-moving is vital. It is no accident that Fichte is crucial to the histories of both individualism and nationalism. For Fichte's notion of self-recognition, of the person who seemingly confronts himself (or herself) in a mirror and says "I am I" is inextricably tied to the notion of the nation as itself an individual. Just as persons are understood as unitary in prototypical modern thought so are nations held to be integral. As Benedict Anderson has indicated this involves a special sense of time as the history through which the nation as perduring and unitary being passes rather than as a differentiable internal history of the nation.[7] The process of individuation is important not just metaphorically, but as the basis for the central notion that individuals are directly members of the nation, that it marks each of them as an intrinsic identity and they commune with it immediately and as a whole. In ideology, at least, the individual does not require the mediations of family, community, region, or class to be a member of the nation. This is a profound reversal of the weight of competing loyalties from the premodern era (and much of the rest of the world). In this we see the sharp difference of nationalism from the ideology of honor of the lineage, and the chilling potential for children to inform on their parents' infraction's against the nation.[8]

Nineteenth century ideologists of nationalism emphasized a world-historical (or evolutionary) process of individuation in which the world's peoples took on their distinctive characters, missions and destinies. Or at least the world's "historical nations" did so; others lacked sufficient vigor or national character; they were destined to be failures and consigned to the backwaters of history. Not surprisingly, this is typically how dominant or majority populations thought of minorities and others subordinated within their dominions. This was another conceptualization, in effect, of the Springtime of Nations. It was the period when

France took on its "mission civilatrix," Germany found its historical destiny and Poles crystallized their Romantic conception of the martyr-nation.[9] Each nation had a distinct experience and character, something special to offer the world and something special to express for itself. "Nations are individualities with particular talents and the possibilities of exploiting those talents."[10]

It is no accident, thus, that philosophers like Fichte emphasized simultaneously the individuation of the person and of the nation. The two notions remain inextricably linked.[11] This very linkage, however, could create tensions. The great cultural geniuses of a nation's history were widely celebrated in the 19th century; the proliferation of individual geniuses was proof, especially for the Romantics, of the greatness of the nation. Though Norway had but recently gained an independent cultural status (and was not yet independent politically) her production of geniuses in the late 19th century, from Munch to Grieg to Ibsen, was proof enough of her standing even for the German intellectuals of the period. But being cast as the bearer of national identity was not always entirely comfortable for geniuses (or others) with their own individual identities. Writing to Ibsen on his 70th birthday in 1898, the Norwegian poet Nils Kjoer tried to recover something of the autonomy of the person from the demand for representation of national character:

> "But a people's individuality is manysided, sufficient to explain any peculiarity of the mind and therefore it explains nothing."[12]

If recognized geniuses could feel a tension with the demand that they serve as icons of the nation, there is apt to be even more pressure on cultural deviants and minorities. And indeed, though nations are ideologically composed of individuals, they are not generally promoters of individual distinctiveness. In the formative phases of nationalism, heroic individuals—cultural as well as military and political heroes—figure prominently, but often in the established nation, conformity to the common culture becomes a central value. The character of nationalism is changed as it shifts from insurgent movement to dominant ideology, though even insurgents can be sharply intolerant of diversity. It is easier to admire heroes from afar, and easiest to claim them when they are dead.

The key structural change which makes it possible to conceive of the nation as unitary is the rise of the modern state. Previous political forms neither demarcated clear boundaries nor fostered internal integration and homogenization. Cities dominated hinterlands; sometimes particularly powerful cities dominated networks of others together with their hinterlands. The various kinds of military (and sometimes religious) elites we call 'feudal' controlled substantial territories but with a minimum of centralization of power and limited ability to remake everyday life. Though empires could call on subject peoples for tribute and sometimes foster substantial interaction among diverse subjects, they posed few demands for cultural homogenization. Yet the rise of the modern state involved remarkable administrative integration of previously quasi-autonomous regions and localities. Eventually, state power could be exercised at the farthest point of a realm as effectively as in the capital. Not only could taxes be collected, but roads could be built, schools run, and mass communications systems created. Linguistic standardization is a common measure of national integration, and historical research reminds us how recent such standardization was in most European countries. Most Frenchmen did not speak French before the second half of the 19th century.[13] Even demographic behavior—fertility rates, for example—which once varied from locality to locality, become strikingly uniform within 19th and 20th century European nation-states.[14]

The capacity of states to administer distant territories with growing intensity was largely due to improvements in transportation and communications infrastructure, on the one hand, and bureaucracy and related information management on the other. It was part of a general growth in large scale social relations. More and more of social life took place through forms of mediation—markets, communications technologies, bureaucracies—which removed relationships from the realm of direct, face-to-face interaction. In addition to facilitating state power, this growth in "indirect" and large-scale relationships directly facilitated nationalism. It encouraged, for example, increasing reliance on categorical identities rather than webs of relational identities.[15] This transformation was closely related to the growth of capitalism. In the first place, a growing division of labor and intensification of trade relations knit localities and regions together in relations of mutual dependence. Capitalism continually drove its agents out beyond local markets, established competitive pressures around the globe, and demanded coordination of ever-growing supplies of labor and raw materials—even before the generation of increasing consumer demand became an obsession. Capitalism thus both depended on and continually increased the capacity for large scale and indirect social relations. Because more and more of the activity on which lives and livelihoods depended was taking place at a distance from immediate locales, attempts to conceptualize the commonalities and connections among locales were increasingly important. Beyond this, connections established only through markets and the commodity form were especially prone to reification and representation in categorical terms. The nation became the domestic market, other nations international competitors or clients. A relatively benign though potentially problematic aspect of nationalism in Eastern Europe and the former U.S.S.R. is the intentional deintegration of markets and division of labor. Rather than enhancing their cross-border relations, most formerly communist countries seem bent on developing their own individual relations with the West and their own autonomous development plans. Economic integration seems to be experienced as a lack of national freedom, but this both forfeits comparative advantages in economic exchange and makes future conflicts more likely.

Partly (though not entirely) under pressure of capitalist expansion, the entire world was divided into bounded territories. Every inch of land was declared the province of one state on another. No longer were there hinterlands in which people could follow their ways of life relatively undisturbed by pressures to conform to one or another state's dominant culture. Attempts to preserve local tradition now required active resistance. Where empires demanded mainly political loyalty, states imposed pressures for multifarious forms of cultural loyalty and participation. The opportunity for a people to be self-organizing was increasingly limited to those who could mount a successful claim to state sovereignty. Whatever the actual form of government claimants anticipated, from the moment that sovereignty came to be a claim from below, by the people, rather than from the rulers above, the modern ideal of the nation-state was born. Even Hobbes, in justifying the absolute sovereignty of kings, required first a body of citizens—a nation—capable of granting the right to rule in explicit or implicit social contract. And these citizens were, perforce, basically interchangeable as members of the nation.

This is a crucial contrast between the empire and the nation-state, or, as Weintraub has shrewdly noted, between the cosmopolitan city and the polis. The creation of a political community called for a new kind of interrelationships, and something more than a "live and let live" urbanity. In the cosmopolis or empire, since "heterogeneous multitudes were not called upon to be citizens, they could remain in apolitical coexistence, and each could do as he wished without the occasion to deliberate with his neighbors."[16] In both the polis and the modern nation-state, membership in a common polity requires more than tolerance and common subjection to an external sovereign. It requires mutual communication. This poses an impetus for erasure of differences among the citizens. One of the crucial questions of the modern era is whether meaningful, politically efficacious public discourse can be achieved without this erasure.

The claim to be a nation was a claim to be entitled to a state (or at the very least, to special recognition in the constitution of a state). Though the reciprocal claim was not logically entailed, it was common. By the 19th century it was thought not only that every nation deserved a state, but that each state should represent one nation. Nationalism, as Ernest Gellner writes, held that nations and states "were destined for each other; that either without the other is incomplete, and constitutes a tragedy."[17] One of the features of this new way of conceptualizing sovereignty was that it treated all nation-states as formally equivalent, whatever their size or power. It was no longer possible to conceive of derogated levels of partial or subordinate sovereignty—kings and dukes below emperors, autonomous cities under the protection of prices, etc. Either Burgundy was part of France or it was an alien state; if part of France, it was merely part and not nation in itself. In the mid-19th century United States, extreme claims to "states' rights" in a weak confederacy of strong subsidiary parts were not so much the claims of one or more alternative nationalisms as claims against nationalism itself. The "country" to which Confederate soldiers owed a duty was conceived from the immediate family and community outward (and largely through a hierarchy of aristocratic connections, not laterally). It was not conceived primarily as a categorical identity, coterminous with a single polity and culture.[18]

Just as the spread of capitalism created a world system in which only capitalist competition could be effective, so the division of the world into states created a continuing pressure for the production of nationalisms. Claims for greater autonomy or greater unity could gain legitimacy primarily as claims to create a nation-state, that is, to create a new state to match a pre-existing nation. This is why the single term nationalism encompasses both fissiparous or secessionist movements and unificationist or "pan-"nationalist movements. Croatian or Ukrainian nationalism and pan-Slavic nationalism are dimensions of the same process. Programs for the unification of Europe draw on new histories which emphasize the commonality of the European experience and identity; the specificity of Europe is counterposed to the rest of the world, rather than the specificity of France being counterposed to Britain or the

Netherlands. At the same time, fringe nationalist movements (and claims for regional autonomy) flourish within the European Community. And on Europe's eastern border, Yugoslavia and perhaps other countries seem set to splinter into tiny nation states. Indeed, nationalist struggles in Eastern Europe reveal the continuing relevance of nationalism in a Western Europe whose publicists had claimed it had moved beyond it. Divergent visions of the European Community and divergent interests have been brought out not just by German unification, but by fighting in Yugoslavia and appeals from Poland, Czechoslovakia and Hungary for community membership. Not least of all, East to West migration both results from nationalist strife (and nationalist protectionism which creates economic strife) and contributes to xenophobic nationalist responses.

Contrary to some over-glib journalism, there is no global reason for nationalism to be more integrating or disintegrating. The same rhetoric can as readily be deployed to claim unity across separate states (all Slavs or all Arabs) as to demand autonomy for a region of one (e.g. Slovakia or Ruthenia). But there are global reasons why nationalism remains the central form of identity in which people pose their claims to sovereignty. The most important of these is simply the creation of the world system as a system of states. Though some analysts predict the dissolution of such states in a postmodern welter of local identities and global corporations, the states do not yet seem to have given up the ghost. Nationalism remains important in part because claims to state sovereignty do matter—not least of all because states remain the central organizational frameworks within which democracy can be pursued.

Of course, as state administrative power was growing, and the world was divided into bounded territories, not all potential nationalisms thrived.[19] A variety of factors helped. One was simply the history and development of nationalist discourse itself. As Anderson points out, nationalist discourse was not simply a product of simultaneous invention around the globe. It was, at least in part, diffused from certain colonial experiences to Western Europe and thence re-exported.[20] The nationalist discourse has grown during the last three hundred or so years; more is available as resource to late-comers. Within any putative nation as well, there may be greater or lesser history of nationalist discourse. There may be richer and more evocative discourses on national history and culture to provide particular content to nationalist aspirations. Specific experiences of external challenge or oppression may help to promote national consciousness, providing a clear and significant other for self-identification by contrast. It may be more or less possible to frame other discontents within the nationalist idiom. And other organizing bases, class above all, but also religious organizations, may be either absent, or congruent and supportive rather than competitive.

By the same token, not all nationalisms take the same form. They are shaped in different international contexts and from different domestic experiences. Some grow in response to histories of direct colonialism, others in response to present weakness in the world system without any specific colonial antagonist to shape them.[21] Some are elite, others democratic. Some seem to absorb an entire culture, claiming everything from language and literature through political practices and agricultural methods as specific to the nation. Others are more narrowly political movements, recognizing common participation in a broader culture. And last but not least, nationalist movements are shaped by the periods of their flowering: it was easier to believe in a happy fellowship of nations in the 1840s than it is today.

Nationalism as Successor Ideology

As recently as the early Gorbachev years of the mid-1980s, the leadership of the Soviet Union was still propounding a modified vision of the happy fellowship of nations. The condition of this fellowship was the elimination of the social antagonisms which set capitalist nations against each other and made nationalist conflicts an attractive distraction from class struggle. As a book in Novosti's series on "the Soviet Experience" put it, "as social antagonisms disappeared under socialism, so did national strife and racial inequality and oppression in every form. ... The socialist multinational culture has been enriched through an intensive exchange of cultural and intellectual values. The socialist nations that have emerged in the USSR have formed a new historical community of people—the Soviet people. ... Today it would be no exaggeration to say that a feeling of being members of one family prevails among Soviet people."[22] On the one hand, such lines from a work entitled *How the Soviet Union Solved the Nationalities Question* seem laughably divorced from reality. On the other hand, a moment's reflection of the rapid return of nationalist conflict to what was once the Soviet sphere of influence reminds us why for so long Soviet ideology claimed the resolution of "the nationalities question" as one of the central accomplishments of communism.

Nationalism enters contemporary politics most strikingly in the wake of communist crisis and retreat. As obviously in Ethiopia as in Eastern Europe, this has much to do with conditions which preceded (and sometimes coincided with) communism. Contemporary nationalism is, in part, a direct continuation of old struggles for autonomy from neighbors and stature among nations. This is accentuated in much of Eastern Europe (and western or central Asia) by the extent to which communism appeared in the guise of Russian domination. But Russian nationalism is also resurgent, so this cannot be the whole story. Similarly, communism was in many cases imposed on people who had not made a commitment to it through struggles of their own. This too has probably made nationalism more likely as a successor ideology, but its effects should not be exaggerated, for the countries in which communism had most indigenous strength before becoming a Soviet supported state ideology do not seem markedly less prone to nationalism than those for which communism was more clearly an external imposition.

Communist regimes were perfectly prepared to try to mobilize nationalist sentiments to bolster their legitimacy. The Romanian state made a massive enterprise of reproducing folklore in ways it could both claim and control.[23] The reconstruction of historical buildings was a major part of postwar rebuilding in both Poland and Hungary. Enormous resources and prestige were invested in production of international athletic successes. At the same time, communist states acted in ways which highlighted national identities in arenas where they officially denied or minimized their significance. Thus, Stalin sought to build "socialism in one country," and his Chinese counterparts still pursue "communism with Chinese characteristics."[24] Russia imposed its language as primary in the Soviet Union and secondary throughout the Warsaw pact. In Yugoslavia, the very stratagem of holding the country together by balancing national groups (and even making sure each nationally defined state contained regions with substantial members of other nationalities) reaffirmed infra-Yugoslavian national identities at the same time that it temporarily held nationalist rivalries in check.[25] Not least of all, the Soviet Army's occupation of much of Eastern Europe could hardly fail to stir some nationalist resentment, especially when coupled with political interference.

Indeed, the most basic reasons for nationalism to flourish in the wake of communism have to do with political repression not socialist—or statist—economics. Communist states repressed most forms of subsidiary identities and discourses on alternative political arrangements. Faced with pressures or opportunities for collective action, people were thrown back on pre-existing bases for identification and collective action. This worked in two ways. First, when people chafed under centralized misrule their national identities were the most readily available ways to understand and respond to abuse. Second, when communism collapsed, nationalism was available to take its place. The latter was true especially where communism collapsed without the development of strong indigenous movements of resistance and counter-culture. In Poland, Solidarity offered an alternative arena of cultural production and discourse—though of course Solidarity had a strong nationalist current of its own. In varying degrees other Eastern European countries had both opportunities for cultural creativity and public discourse, and movements which both challenged the existing order and offered an alternative cultural discourse. In much of the Soviet Union, by contrast, repression was more severe, and insurgency from below less developed. One result was that in many settings—the Transcaucasus, for example—nationalism could emerge as the primary form of identity and the basic medium through which people expressed their aspirations for a better life.[26]

Communist states did not encourage the cultural creativity and free flow of discourse which could have both knit them together and opened a variety of bases of identity. This had several effects. It meant that in large and heterogeneous countries like the Soviet Union, only state-sponsored cultural productivity could work to unify the country as a whole. When the state lost its credibility, so did much of the cultural basis for unity at the largest level. Behind this suggestion is the general postulate that for populations to achieve some unity as citizenries, they need to be knit together by a common discourse. This does not mean that they are knit together simply by similarity of ideology. On the contrary, mere ideological similarity is a fairly brittle and easily fractured form of cultural unity, particularly when confronted with problems outside its familiar range. A shared discourse of problem solving provides a stronger foundation for confronting new challenges. More generally, culture is a stronger source of unity when it is open to rich and varied forms of creation and discussion. When discussion and creativity are foreclosed in order to maintain ideological conformity, it becomes difficult to achieve the manifold continuous cultural adjustments which are essential to both legitimation processes and sense of common membership in a political community. So, ironically, the very attempt to maintain complete conformity undermined identification with the whole, left it superficial and easily forgotten.

At the same time, the absence of an open cultural sphere or political discourse meant that the development of multiple bases for individual identity was impeded. Outside the range of authoritarian rule and strong nationalism, it is common for people to gain their identities from a range of cross-cutting group affiliations (as Simmel suggested), and from membership in a variety of different salient cultural categories. Thus a woman in the United States may feel a strong sense of identity stemming from her occupation, her gender, her family, her community, her political activity, and her religion as well as and partially in competition with her nation. Though national identity may be a source of inspiration or pride, or of a sense of obligation to help others by pursuing the common good of the United States ahead of the general good of humanity, it is unlikely to be an identity which "trumps" all others. Of course, it is an open question how long this would last if the U.S. ever came under severe external pressure, or wars were again fought on American soil.

In the face of such pressure—and its immediate memory, as in Eastern Europe—liberalism may seem a fairly thin ideology. Liberal capitalism is, however, the main ideological option offered by the West today. There is of course the Catholic church, with its resurgent conservatism on the one hand (abetted by a Polish Pope) and the remnants of liberation theology on the other. The left remains relevant mainly by pursuing a variety of ameliorative reforms within the framework of welfare state capitalism, and defending various special interests of subordinated groups. But it is in disarray overall and no longer seems to offer a very compelling or positive vision to complement its critique of liberal capitalism. Indeed, the Western left's failure of vision is directly related to the resurgence of nationalism in Eastern Europe, as the left was not able to make much significant connection with advocates of a "third way" or a more robust notion of civil society. Westerners "on the left" found East Germany's "New Forum" group appealing, thus, but were unable to connect with it in very deep or sustaining ways which would help to provide a viable electoral alternative to the vision of unity promoted by the Christian Democrats (largely because their own social democratic vision had been narrowed to a series of ameliorations of capitalist ills). The weakness of the Western left (not least its defensive posture in the U.S.) helped to open the way to a discourse in which liberal capitalism and versions of nationalism are the main contenders for succession to communism. These contenders, as the German example reveals, are not as antithetical as has sometimes been thought. Many forms of nationalism can thrive quite happily on a capitalist foundation and put forward their claims in the rhetoric of liberalism. Indeed, liberalism's strengths run to the enunciation and preservation of certain liberties, not to the constitution of strong social or cultural identities. Nationalism can be its complement—rooted in the same individualism—as readily as it can be dissolved by liberalism's advocacy of the individual as the basic unit of analysis.

Nationalism and Democracy

Nationalism is not an intrinsically "bad" ideology. It has been and remains an important source of inspiration. Any account of the political problems attendant on nationalism which does not recognize the achievements of poets, painters, and composers who were moved by nationalist sentiments misses an important part of the story.[27] Any account which imagines that citizens or human beings could be rational actors unmoved by cultural commitments and pre-rational identities loses touch with reality. In the political realm itself, nationalism is not intrinsically pernicious or anti-democratic. In the first place, there needs to be some culturally constructed identity behind the word "self" in the idea of self-determination. It is worth recalling too that in the 1840s nationalism often appeared as a progressive, liberal ideology in which a domestic push for democratic expression was coupled with a respect for other nations. Even more than respect, Romantics of the early 19th century were sufficiently inspired by heroic nationalist struggles to offer their own lives on behalf of alien nations. Yet even this phrase reveals a tension. To the strong Romantic humanist—to Byron, say—there were no alien nations, only many expressions of a common humanity striving for freedom and creative voice. Yet in extremes Romanticism (like its current postmodernist successors) had as much trouble making sense of difference as Enlightenment rationalism; neither grappled well with the problem of incommensurable practices, with the reasons why differences become hostilities.[28] And the exclusivity implied by the word alien is more common in the rhetoric of nationalism. Nationalism is all too often the enemy of democracy rooted in civil society.

In the first place, nationalism in power is very different from nationalist resistance to alien rule. Not unlike authoritarian regimes as I described them above, nationalists too often tend to promote the pseudo-democracy of sameness instead of the recognition and respect of difference. Ironically like communism, nationalism often stifles cultural discourse—not in the name of the state or even necessarily by the imposition of state power; it can work by a closure of the mind. Nationalism in power is often a repressive ideology demanding strict adherence to the authority of the official embodiments of national tradition—and very unlike nationalism in opposition which is generally a strong stimulus to cultural productivity. The problems arise with the assertion that there is only one right way for any individual to be a Pole, or a Russian, an Azeri or an American.

Repression is wielded not just against diversity of cultural expression but against the variety of alternative bases for personal identity which might compete with the nation. Thus the common antagonism of nationalists to autonomy and equality for women is not just a continuation of sexist traditions. Nationalism encourages this sexism by internal (and I think non-essential) cultural traditions—e.g. valuing the family as the source of the nation's continuity in time, and seeing men as potential martyrs, women as mothers. Beyond this, however, nationalists resist women's movements because accepting the domination of male interests and perceptions merely perpetuates a taken-for-granted, monolithic view of the nation, while encouraging women to identify their distinctive interests and views opens claims that gender has autonomous status as a basis for personal identity which does not pale into insignificance before the commonalties of (male-dominated) nationhood.

In this sense, nationalism has totalitarian potential. It can be treated as a categorical identity more fundamental than other personal identities, even able to override them, and as fixed in both biographical and historical time. This is what I mean by saying that nationalism is used to "trump" other identities or values.[29] Nationalists often want the sentiment or sense of national identity to go beyond the feeling of being more at home in one place than another, beyond placing a special value on the traditions with which one grew up, beyond focusing one's attention more on one subset of humanity than on the whole. In its extreme forms, nationalism, like religious fundamentalism, often involves claims to monopolize the sources of legitimate identity.

The decisive question about nationalism, therefore, is whether its proponents can open the nation to competing conceptualizations, diverse identities and a rich public discourse about controversial issues. The long history of anti-semitism can serve as an index of the difficulty many have had in doing so. These issues were faced in France in the late

19th Century, and, in the Dreyfus affair, victory went to the forces of openness and heterogeneous civil society as the basis for democracy. There have been attempts to revoke the victory, notably by World War II era collaborationists and the contemporary radical right, under the leadership of nationalists like Jean-Marie Le Pen. But in Central and Eastern Europe there have been few such signal victories, and as Adam Michnik has suggested, the issue is a very current one: "In both France and Poland the question was whether the nation was to be open and the state tolerant and multicultural, or whether the state was to be based on authoritarian principles and nationalistic doctrine. And I think this has been the central question ever since. Whenever the shadow of anti-Semitism arose in Polish public life, it was an unmistakable signal that people with antidemocratic, intolerant views were on the political offensive."[30]

It would be good, but not enough, to say that tolerance should reign within states. Even multinational, multicultural states require more than simply tolerance among subsidiary peoples. They require public discourse. Citizens from different nationalities, as from different regions, religions or occupations, need to be able able and willing to engage each other in discourse about the social arrangements which hold them together and order their lives—in brief, about the common good. Moreover, the same is crucial within nationalities. There is no reason to accept monolithic conformity within any one nation or people. Not only may states be multinational or multicultural, nations themselves must admit and encourage internal diversity whether they are coterminous with states or exist as subsidiary identities within states. It is necessary, in other words, that the nation be open to democracy and diversity whether or not the close link between nation and state is severed. In power, extreme nationalists do not just repress other peoples, they repress the diversity and creativity of people within the very nation they cherish.

Without diversity, democracy is hardly distinct from a dictatorship of the mass. Indeed, it is hard to imagine how such a monolithic mass could be sustained beyond an ephemeral uprising except by means of centralized totalitarian power. Nationalism is only benign when it does not tend towards this pseudo-democracy of sameness. And this is where civil society comes in. Civil society is the locus of diverse groups and individuals and more importantly of their contact with each other. Division of labor and other sources of difference may arise within civil society or be brought into it from the family or other less public realms. But in civil society, the exchange not only of goods but of ideas can take place. Advocates of democracy in the late 20th century are called upon to discover whether the virtues of diversity, sociability and tolerance associated with the ideal of the cosmopolis can be combined with the self-governing political community of the polis. Can political arguments be considered on their merits, at least partially autonomous from the identities of the arguers?[31]

But this cannot happen simply through direct interpersonal relationships in cities. It must happen also through television and newspapers. It must happen on the scale of millions of people in powerful states. Political parties with their patronage, bureaucracies and public relations staffs will mediate the relations between groups as much as cafes with their intellectual arguments. These parties must remain open to diversity for they are crucial means of achieving not consensus so much as reasonable compromises where consensus is impossible. If democracy is to flourish, nationalism must not become the enemy of difference.

The events of 1989 showed the power of mass media to further an internationalization of culture and politics. I was in Beijing that spring, and watched with amazement. Chinese students deliberately echoed Poland's Solidarity movement, and within days protesting students in Eastern Europe marched with headbands and placards proclaiming their sympathy with the Chinese. And today Chinese democrats—and nationalists—look to Eastern Europe for inspiration. The nationalism which figured centrally in these movements is an international phenomenon—as nationalism was in 1848. Not only is it shared through mass communication, it is driven by global processes which value and privilege nations as categories of identity between the immediately interpersonal and the local. It is often repeated that the twin tendencies of the present era are towards globalization and localization. This has an element of truth, but it is an overused mantra. Simply to repeat this leaves the door open to a globalization which is simply a further centralization of power —particularly economic power. And it suggests that the division of the world into ever smaller units of putative internal sameness is the only way to achieve happiness in our immediate lifeworlds. It is as though someone decided that Durkheim's mechanical solidarity is the only kind that works. Nationalism encourages the identification of individuals not with locality *per se,* not with the webs of their specific interpersonal relationships, but with an abstract category. This category of nation may be a helpful mediation between the local and the global, but not when it is used to override other identities, both within and across national boundaries.

And what of democracy? Is it possible to build states and even confederations of states in which cohesion and self-rule are established through public discourse across lines of difference? Can we conceive the growth of a cultural unity within such states or confederations which does not devalue or demand the obliteration of other sources of personal and political identity? Or must we fall back on nationalism alone as our shelter in a world grown too frightening, or as the one immediately satisfying identity with which to confront the globalization of capital? When it is one of many intermediate identities between the world as a whole and our individual existence, nationality can be important and benign. When touted as the essential basis of identity, it is the enemy of both democracy and sociable civil society.

Notes

1. In January 1990, the editor of the *Annual Review of Sociology* asked me to write an article on "agency and structure." As more abstract discussion of this dualism did not excite me, I declined, but offered to write an article on nationalism. The editor wrote back that the *Review's* board thought this subject was passé and encouraged me to reconsider. When I insisted on the importance of nationalism, the editor did commission the essay, but with the stipulation that I deal with "ethnicity" as well.

   The view of the editorial board presumably stemmed from a general lack of sociological attention to nationalism (as well as a relatively slow movement of public issues into the professional discourse of sociologists). Nationalism figures only at the margins of the founding work of Marx, Weber and Durkheim; Marcel Mauss (in an unfinished book; see *Oeuvres*, vol. 3; Paris: Editions de Minuit, 1985) was the only 'classical' social theorist to explore it in detail. And though important analyses of nationalism have been written more recently, they have consumed much less paper than, say, methodological discussions of the role of path analysis in the study of status attainment. See review in Calhoun, "Nationalism and Ethnicity," *Annual Review of Sociology,* (1943): 211–239.

2. See Charles Taylor, "Modes of Civil Society," *Public Culture,* vol. 374 (1991): 95–118; Jeffrey Weintraub, "The Theory and Politics of the Public/Private Distinction," in J. Weintraub and K. Kumar, eds., *Public and Private in Thought and Practice.* (Chicago: University of Chicago Press, forthcoming). Jean Cohen and Andrew Arrato, *The Political Theory of Civil Society* (Cambridge, MA: MIT Press, 1992). The last is by far the most substantial and theoretically developed modern treatment. Readers should note, however, its strong Hegelian roots and relative neglect of Anglo-Saxon and French thought, including such key figures as Ferguson, Montesquieu and Tocqueville. This affects in particular their discussion of the concrete social organiza-

tional bases for the democratic political culture they describe, including the important themes of intermediate associations and mediating institutions.

3. See Georg Lukacs, *History and Class Consciousness* (Cambridge, MA: MIT Press, 1922); Calhoun, "The Infrastructure of Modernity," pp. 205–36 in N.J. Smelser and H. Haferkamp, *Social Change and Modernity* (Berkeley: University of California Press, 1991).

4. See Habermas, *The Structural Transformation of the Public Sphere* (Cambridge, MA: MIT Press, 1989) and the various qualifications, extensions and refinements suggested by the essays in Calhoun, *Habermas and the Public Sphere* (Cambridge, MA: MIT Press, 1992).

5. Even if one could point to completely self-contained island cultures somewhere in the South Pacific (and my reading of the anthropological evidence is that one cannot), these would not be nations in anything like the modern sense of the term, for that implies the definition of one by contraposition to others.

6. "What is a Nation," trans. by M. Thom, pp. 8–22 in H.K. Bhabha, ed.: *Nation and Narration* (London: Routledge, 1990), quotation from p. 11).

7. *Imagined Communities* (New York: Verso, 1983).

8. National identity, thus, in its main Western ideological form, is precisely the opposite of the reckoning of identity and loyalty outward from the family. Where the segmentary lineage system suggests "I against my brothers, I and my brothers against my cousins, I, my brothers and my cousins against the world," nationalism suggests that membership in the category of the whole nation is prior to, more basic than any such web of relationships. This suggests also a different notion of moral commitment from previous modes of understanding existence.

9. Hans Kohn: *The Idea of Nationalism* (New York: Macmillan, 1944); Andrzej Walicki: *Philosophy and Romantic Nationalism: The Case of Poland* (Oxford: Oxford University Press, 1982); Joan S. Skurnowisc: *Romantic Nationalism and Liberalism: Joachim Lelewel and the Polish National Idea* (New York: Columbia University Press, 1981); Friedrich Meinecke. *Cosmopolitanism and the National State* (Princeton: Princeton University Press, trans. R.B. Kilmer, 1970.

10. (Fichte, quoted in Meinecke, *Cosmopolitanism and the National State*, 89).

11. William Bloom: *Personal identity, national identity and international relations* (Cambridge: Cambridge University Press, 1990).

12. Nils Kjoer to Ibsen on the celebration of his 70th birthday (1898), quoted p. 7 of Margrethe Aaby, ed. "Henryk Ibsen—Our contemporary," Oslo. The 1991 Ibsen Stage Festival in Norway, 1991.

13. E. Weber: *Peasants into Frenchmen* (Stanford University Press, 1976).

14. Susan Cott Watkins: *From Provinces into Nations: Demographic Integration in Western Europe, 1870–1960.* (Princeton: Princeton University Press, 1991)

15. See C. Calhoun, "Imagined Communities and Indirect Relationships," in P. Bourdieu and J. Coleman, eds.: *Social Theory for a Changing Society* (Boulder, CO: Westview Press, 1991).

16. "The Theory and Politics of the Public/Private Distinction," p. 16.

17. *Nations and Nationalism* (Oxford: Blackwell, 1983), p. 6.

18. As Hobsbawm writes, "we cannot assume that for most people national identification—when it exists—excludes or is always or ever superior to, the remainder of the set of identifications which constitute the social being" (*Nations and Nationalism since 1780*, Cambridge: Cambridge University Press, 1990, p. 11). But part of nationalist ideology is precisely the notion that national identity does "trump" other identities.

19. This point is made with some force by Eric Hobsbawm in *Nations and Nationalism since 1780* (Cambridge: Cambridge University Press, 1990) and Ernest Gellner in *Nations and Nationalism* (Oxford: Blackwell, 1983). Both authors stress that this is not accidental, for "a world of nations cannot exist, only a world where some potentially national groups, in claiming this status, exclude others from making similar claims, which, as it happens, not many of them do" (Hobsbawm, p. 78).

20. Though Anderson's notion of "modular" nationalism may overstate the case to the point of denying creativity and indigenous roots to later nationalist discourses. See Partha Chatterjee: *Nationalist Thought and the Colonial World: A Derivative Discourse?* (London: Zed Press, 1986).

21. Resentments seem especially central to some nationalisms of Central and Eastern Europe. Some domestic religious traditions, like Russian and other "Eastern" Orthodoxies, seem to encourage xenophobia beyonnd any influence of historical wrongs or current international threats. See Liah Greenfield, "The Formation of the Russian National Identity: The Role of Status Insecurity and *Ressentiment*," in *Comparative Studies in Society and History* 32:3 (1990): 549–91.

22. Albert Nenarokov and Alexander Proskurin: *How the Soviet Union Solved the Nationalities Question* (Moscow: Novosti Press Agency Publishing House, 1983).

23. Katherine Verdery: *National Ideology Under Socialism: Identity and Cultural Politics in Ceausescu's Romania* (Berkeley: University of California Press, 1991).

24. Communism has always been linked to nationalism in China, though the label "nationalism" was appropriated by its competitor the Guomindang. In general, a kind of modernizing nationalism has often been part of communism's appeal, and it is no accident that communism has flourished especially in settings where people have felt cheated of their due stature by the capitalist world system (not in the advanced centers of capitalism as Marx predicted). As the case of largely ethnically homogenous China illustrates, nationalist aspirations are not limited to the constitution of states or the alteration of their boundaries, but include pursuit of a range of goals including regeneration, liberation, modernization, and power.

25. Ivo Banac: *The National Question in Yugoslavia: Origin, History, Politics* (Ithaca: Cornell University Press, 1984); Walker Connor: *The National Question in Marxist-Leninist Theory and Strategy* (Princeton: Princeton University Press, 1984).

26. It was, of course, this same nationalism and this same weakness of other cultural and movement forms which rendered the Transcaucasus unable to sustain its federation in after 1917, and unable to mount significant resistance to the Red Army's imposition of Soviet rule.

27. Similarly, it is analytically untenable to try to treat "nationalism" and "patriotism" (or other labels amounting to "good" and "bad" nationalism) as though they were fundamentally different ideological species. Artistic inspiration, needed identity, will to power and politics of repression can be and often are bound inseparably together. The differences among nationalisms come as much from the nature of international contexts as from differences in internal form or content.

28. See Charles Taylor, *Philosophy and the Human Sciences* (Cambridge: Cambridge University Press, 1985); Calhoun, "Culture, History and the Problem of Specificity in Social Theory," pp. 244–88 in S. Seidman and D. Wagner, eds.: *Postmodernism and General Social Theory* (New York: Blackwell, 1991).

29. Charles Taylor has argued that identity and moral commitment are intimately intertwined, so that it is almost redundant to say "identities or values." See *Sources of the Self* (Cambridge, MA: Harvard University Press, 1989).

30. "Poland and the Jews," *New York Review of Books,* May 30, 1991, pp. 11–12, quote from p. 11.

31. This is, of course, a core theme to Habermas's work from *The Structural Transformation of the Public Sphere* to the present. One may accept the centrality of the question without accepting quite the extreme of abstraction from issues of personal identity which is characteristic of Habermas's work.

The Geopolitics of Ethnic Mobilization: Some Theoretical Projections for the Old Soviet Bloc

Randall Collins and David V. Waller
University of California, Riverside

In the aftermath of the Soviet breakup, one of the most obvious legacies is ethnic nationalism and conflict. Can we theorize this phenomenon? Was it foreseeable on general principles, and can its future be predicted by anything more solid than ad hoc extrapolations of short-run trends? Our answer to these questions is yes. Our line of argument is that, in its overall patterns, *ethnicity follows geopolitics*. This is not the conventional way in which ethnicity has been studied; but it has its antecedents, especially in Max Weber's mode of analyzing nationalism. Generally speaking, theory of ethnicity has been a weak spot in the social sciences: not from lack of attention, but from a fragmentation among contradictory approaches, the tendency to put description in the place of comparison, and often the ideologically heated nature of these discussions. Ethnicity has not been sufficiently treated in a broad enough context, particularly in terms of large-scale configurations of states and inter-state power.

We will attempt to show by means of some historical comparisons that a geopolitical theory can do the job. We begin by briefly considering the analyses of ethnicity which are conventionally used, and suggest that they are quite indeterminate unless their processes are placed within the larger context of geopolitical dynamics. We go on then to review some basic geopolitical principles which explain the expansion and contraction of state power and accordingly the internal prestige and legitimacy of national identification with the state. As we shall see, the media of cultural identification, including education and language, do not have a fixed effect on ethnic identification, but vary in the direction of the state's power prestige. Polar cases may be labeled the "Americanization model," in which ethnic amalgamation has high prestige in a geopolitically expanding state; and the "Balkanization model," in which medium-sized ethnic units are mobilized as centers of opposition to a geopolitically disintegrating state. Finally, we apply these principles to the successor states of the USSR, and derive some long-term extrapolations of the trajectories of ethnic nationalism in each region.

Generalizing About Ethnicity: Primordialists and Assimilationists

In recent years it has been popular to emphasize the enduringness of ethnicity. This often has a celebratory tone: "ethnicity forever!" The theme is connected to the mobilization of ethnic protest and rebellion in the U.S. since the 1960s, and obviously in the recent waves of enthusiasm for ethnic rebellion in the demise of the USSR. One might say it has become "politically correct" to be pro-ethnic nationalism. Now very much out of fashion is the emphasis on ethnic assimilation which was prominent in the 1950s and earlier. Critique of the older assimilation models made several useful points: that assimilation is not ethnically neutral, but is typically the cultural domination of one group over others; that a trend towards larger and more universalistic group identifications is not always the case; that modern social processes can reinforce ethnic identification and segregation rather than undermine them. More often than not, this critique became polemic, and the opportunity for a more balanced analysis was lost. Assimilation theory, although containing its own ideological elements, was not made up out of thin air; it attempted to explain certain real processes which took place in some countries at certain points in history—and for that matter, continue to go on in particular places. (For instance, assimilation of many groups of Asian-Americans into Anglo-American society in the late 20th century and the beginning of the next is indicated by many trends; the pan-Europeanist movement suggests another possibility of massive inter-ethnic assimilation.)

A theory of ethnicity useful for explaining these different patterns will have to be a theory of dynamics and variations. Ethnicity is a variable in at least two dimensions: (1) How large are the ethnic boundaries? That is to say, which people are identified with which cultural label and with the structures of group association that go along with it? (2) Given a particular ethnic boundary, how intensely do people identify with it, and how strongly do they mobilize for group action on either side of that boundary? Most analyses in recent years have focused on the second question. We suggest this is short-sighted because it tends to take for granted the answer to the question of boundaries. Thus, most theories of ethnic mobilization and conflict tend to be primordialist; to assume that ethnic identities have always existed, or at least they were formed some-where back and out of the purview of the explanatory theory. In contrast, we argue that the boundary question is the crucial one; that if ethnic boundaries could be changed in the past they can be changed in the pres-ent; and that explaining this pattern of change will give us strategic lever-age for answering other questions about the intensity of ethnic action.

When are Ethnic Boundaries Expanding, Stable, or Contracting?

A theory of assimilation is an explanation of how ethnic boundaries widen. Typically assimilation theories assumed that the target boundary was that of the national state, but this is just one stopping point in the possible range. There are also assimilation processes which take place on a much smaller scale; for instance "Italian-Americans" are the result of assimilation among Sicilians, Calabrian, Neapolitans, Genoans, and so on; and those regional ethnicities themselves were the product of upwards assimilation among previously fragmented villages or clans. The same is true of "Chicanos," the result of assimilation among Indios, Mestizos, Spaniards, et al.; the category-in-formation "Hispanics" is further along the boundary continuum yet.

Assimilation theories are those which concentrate on dynamics of change along the boundary continuum in one direction only, the growing size and inclusiveness of ethnic boundaries. In contrast, there are theo-ries of ethnic fragmentation. In principle, these ought to be theories of how boundaries are drawn more narrowly than at a previous time. Such analysis has not usually been very sharply focused, however; it has tended to be confounded with an explanation of ethnic stability at the size of rela-tively smaller boundaries than some larger "target" or "standard;" i.e., what we have here usually are anti-assimilation theories, which are con-tent to show where ethnic boundaries do not expand towards greater inclusiveness. Analytically, we need explanations for three types of movement along the continuum: bigger boundaries (assimilation), no change in boundaries in a situation of ethnic multiplicity (ethnic stasis), and increasing numbers of divisions (fragmentation).

What is not well recognized is that a theory of ethnic fragmentation comes up against strong limits. Fragmentation cannot proceed very far down the continuum. Certainly it is impossible to reach the level of "one person, one ethnic group," if only because ethnicity involves a shared cul-ture, and group structure large enough to sustain a marriage pool. Moreover, the very process of ethnic fragmentation tends to involve some mobilization and assimilation; at least if it is a process of conflict (and not a process of pure migration into essentially virgin territories, such as happened at one time in New Guinea or Oceania), conflict along some boundaries brings pressure to mobilize overriding other lines of distinction within. Thus Calabrians and Sicilians acquired a united front as Italian-Americans because of conflict with Anglo-American society; in the same way, *some* of the potential lines of ethnic division, say within Croatia or within the Ukraine, will be overridden by conflict with Serbians or with Russians. Raising this point of course is not the same thing as providing a theory of which lines of ethnic division will override which, or how far down the continuum of fragmentation the situation will go in particular instances. We defer the issue to later in this paper, but can anticipate this much: the degree of fragmentation is part of the more general question of what causes movement along the boundary continuum in either direction; and that is a matter of geopolitical conditions at that particular location.

Processes of Ethnic Stasis: The Reproduction of Ethnicity and the Intensification of Ethnic Conflict

Most contemporary theories focus on the processes by which stable boundaries are maintained; some varieties of these theories go on to provide a dynamic within a limited range: that is, they explain how pre-existing identities become more salient and give rise to vociferous ethnic movements and overt inter-ethnic conflict. The American tradition of research of prejudice and discrimination is of this sort; so is historically oriented research on the mobilization of ethnic movements. We overview this material cursorily, with an eye towards showing how it fits into the larger geopolitical dynamics. Our main these is that these meso-dynamics of ethnic reproduction and conflict are relatively short-run and of variable strength; they are reinforced by particular geopolitical configurations, overridden by others.

One structural basis of ethnic distinctiveness is geographical regionalization. This was the main determinant of proto-ethnicity in pre-state and agrarian-coercive (feudal/extractive) societies.[1]

The development of a market economy, division of labor, urbanization, and bureaucratic administration can break down these regionally-based distinctions and set in motion a process of assimilation to some larger-sized group. However, as the experience of agrarian conquest states shows, it is possible for these structures to develop while leaving narrower ethnic boundaries in place, or at least producing no more than small-scale movements along the continuum of assimilation into larger groups. The Parsees in India, the "King's Jews" in medieval Europe, the Hanseatic Germans in the Baltic, are only a few examples out of many of ethnic enclaves situated precisely in the centers of trade and administration.

The generalization here is that even in a complex division of labor and exchange, stratification can reinforce ethnic distinctiveness. Ethnic groups can find enclaves as specialties within the division of labor, a tendency of which the Indian caste system is only the most extreme example. Although at one time sociological theorists assumed that such ethnic division of labor was characteristic only of pre-industrial and pre-bureaucratic societies, there is ample evidence from contemporary societies that it can continue to exist in every form of economy yet known. (The split labor market of high and low wage sectors; the protection of particular markets by unionization, by ethnically based credit associations, by monopolization through privileged ethnic groups, by "racial" discrimination, are some of the structures through which this operates.[2]

The point of our sociological theorizing should not be merely to draw up a scorecard of how much ethnic segregation happens to be structured into a particular case of the division of labor, but to explain the extent to which such patterns exist. Any existing historical situation is the result of a balance between opposing tendencies of differing strengths. The division of labor and other administrative centralization can operate in opposite directions upon the continuum of ethnic boundaries. In one direction, any kind of contract and co-participation among distinct ethnic groups has the potential for producing assimilation across their boundary; as long as people come together, there is always the prospect of forming a common culture, a new language or *patois*, making friendships and intermarriages, forming a united front in conflict against more remote parties. Whether this potential for assimilation is realized, or whether, on the contrary, contact merely heightens a sense of boundaries, depends upon whether motivation to assimilate across the boundary are stronger than motivation to quarrel. This motivation, we will show in the sequel, is determined by whether there is a strong enough prestige of participating in a common culture legitimated by the state.

Similarly with the effects of stratification. In general, we are most familiar with the processes by which stratification reinforces ethnic segregation. Differences in class cultures add onto (and sometimes also create) differences in ethnic cultures, and vice versa. We are familiar with many such self-reinforcing loops: in the contemporary U.S., the material condition of the suburbs vis-a-vis the inner city flows through family, educational, and attitudinal patterns which reinforce the distinctiveness between black "street" culture and middle-class white culture, with the circle closed by occupational stratification and the perpetuation of material inequality. The pathos of such self-perpetuating models has become virtually the sociologists' stock in trade.

Nevertheless, from an analytical vantage point, stratification does not necessarily result in static ethnic boundaries. Stratification can also set up tendencies towards assimilation. Stratification gives prestige to the culture of the dominant class. Such culture has often spread to middle and subordinate classes, by the processes of imitation or trickle down. If class stratification is correlated with ethnic stratification, such processes bring about assimilation of ethnic cultures. In addition, stratification fosters motivation for upward mobility; insofar as subordinated ethnic groups move up in the class structure, and especially move into the centralized organizations of the economy and state, they tend to bring about full-scale ethnic assimilation by structural amalgamation of group boundaries.[3] The issue, then, is the relative strength of the tendency of stratification to reinforce ethnic boundaries, versus the strength of the opposite tendency to motivate assimilation. This again, we suggest, depends on the geopolitically-given power-prestige of the state and hence of the ethnic culture of its rulers.

There is an additional loop between economic interests and ethnic antagonism which has received much attention. The mobilization of ethnic antagonism has often been attributed to underlying economic conflicts. Insofar as ethnic groups form enclaves in the division of labor and the lineup of classes, any change in the economic standing of these groups mobilized class conflict, which surfaces most easily in the form of ethnic antagonism. For example, anti-Semitism, rare in Christian Europe before the 11th century, was replaced by violent attacks on Jews, initially in the Rhineland and subsequently in Eastern Europe, from 1100 A.D. onwards. This has been attributed to the spread of mercantile economy, of which Jews were the spearheads, often in alliance with centralized rulers, making anti-semitism a convenient rallying point for traditionalist classes, the peasantry and nobility.[4] Similar structures help account for antagonism to Armenians in the old Soviet sphere. We should bear in mind, however, that such analyses assume the pre-existence of ethnic boundaries. Ethnic antagonisms based on enclaves within the division of labor are not uniformly mobilized throughout the world history; there are many instances in which they are not mobilized at all. Again we suggest that such tendencies to ethnic conflict are just on of several causal forces, which can be overridden by stronger conditions elsewhere. The most central of such conditions, we have suggested, is the geopolitically-based power-prestige of the state's rulers. Let us now turn to consider its dynamics.

Geopolitics and Ethnic Prestige

Max Weber, in discussing the phenomenon of nationalism, noted that the boundaries of a state do not necessarily coincide with linguistic, religious, or ethnic divisions.[5] What makes a difference for national identity, he argues, is what is constructed through the political experience of people with their state. Nationalism is not primordial; it waxes and wanes. The most important of these common experiences, in Weber's view, is an all-out military mobilization. French nationalism was forged above all in the *lev'ee en masse* of the Napoleonic wars; German nationalism, overcoming the regionalism of the *kleinstaaterei*, was above all created in the war of liberation against Napoleonic conquest (which not incidentally destroyed many of the minor states and left Prussia, the leader of the liberation war, as the center of national identity). Similar arguments can be made about such multi-ethnic cases as Switzerland or (to a considerable extent postdating Weber) the U.S..[6]

Weber's argument is about nationalism, but it can be extended to ethnicity in general. Put another way: nationalism is the form which ethnicity takes when the gradient of movement is towards expanding ethnic boundaries so that they coincide with the state. The classic statements of "assimilation" come from the period of nationalism, and implicitly assumed that the target boundary was that of the state. Weber's argument takes us into the terrain of geopolitics. Ultimately the core of the state is its capacity to wield military power to control a territory. In fact, neither the boundaries of states nor their power vis-a-vis each other are static; geopolitics gives the principles which determine the increases and decreases in external state power.

We may add an important corollary: the power prestige of the state in the external arena heavily affects the legitimacy of its rulers in the internal arena. There are of course other, domestic sources of legitimacy, but we assert that in a dynamic analysis, the most important factor affecting legitimacy is external power prestige.[7] The most extreme evidence for this connection is revolution: revolution depends almost always on delegitimatization of rulers and on splits within the elite, and these in turn have reached the necessary extreme proportions typically as the result of geopolitical defeat or accumulated effects of geopolitical strain.[8] Conversely, the prestige of state rulers rises with military success; even in the absence of war, the ability of a strong state to dominate other states in diplomacy reinforces the legitimacy of its rulers. In short: external geopolitics affects internal legitimacy.

Let us extend this argument from the legitimacy or rulers to the legitimacy of dominant ethnic groups. Now we have the corollaries: when a state is geopolitically strong, the prestige of its dominant ethnic group is also high. Conversely, a geopolitically weak state lowers its ethnic prestige. The principle affects inter-ethnic relations both within the state, and across its borders. As an instance of the former, consider the prestige of the English vis-a-vis Welsh and Scots during the time of the expanding British empire, and the motivation for assimilation into English culture and the English elite; or the prestige of France (really the region of Isle-de-France) over Brittany, Occitanie, and other ethnic identifications during the height of French military power; and conversely the growth of ethnic separatism in the French provinces after the loss of the French world empire post-WWII. In the external arena, let us contrast two opposing forms of nationalism in the 19th century: Panslavism, and "Balkanization." Panslavism is a movement towards large-scale assimilation into the largest possible ethnic boundary; it is a phenomenon based on the accelerating power-prestige of the Russian Empire during the 19th century. On the other hand, the 19th century is a period of geopolitical weakness and dissolution of both the Austro-Hungarian and Turkish empires; and it is in their zone of geopolitical loss, the Balkans, where nationalistic particularities and movements for ethnic independence are strongest.

"Americanization" vs. "Balkanization"

We have argued that the subsidiary, meso-level processes within the division of labor, ethno-class stratification, and cultural mobilization in themselves have indeterminate effects: they can promote either ethnic distinctiveness and conflict, or foster motivations towards assimilation. Which of these happens depends upon contextual conditions, above all the geopolitical trajectory of the state. We may label two polar types. The "Americanization model" is the case in which the state has an expanding geopolitical position. Accordingly the prestige of the dominant ethnic group is high, and the prevailing motivation is towards assimilation. In the "Balkanization model" on the other had, the geopolitical trajectory is downhill; the state is crumbling; the prestige of the dominant ethnic group is low; ethnic separatism rather than assimilation is the direction of mobilization. To be more precise, in the "Balkanization" model the dominant ethnic group is not merely lacking in attraction; it becomes a *negative* referent point, so that anti-Austrian and anti-Turkish sentiments are major mobilizing points for political and social action. In the same way, Russian ethnic identity at the time when their Russian-controlled Soviet empire comes apart becomes a negative reference point for non-Russians.

We have perhaps loaded the dice with the "Americanization" model. The U.S. was not only a geopolitically expanding power since the early 1800s, reaching a standing of major world power by the time of World War I;[9] it was also a territory of great economic resources, and perhaps it was this land of wealth rather than its power prestige which attracted large numbers of immigrants. We may be tempted to modify the theoretical principles to add: not only geopolitical prestige but also economic opportunities increases the legitimacy and prestige of ruling elites and ethic groups; conversely not only geopolitical weakness but economic decline reduces ruling ethnic prestige. (This modified principle would have application to predicting post-Soviet-breakup conditions.) However, there are grounds for giving geopolitics primacy in affecting ethnic prestige. The prestige of Anglo-assimilation in the U.S. has been high from the early 1800s until the 1950s; if it has been challenged since that time, the correlation is not with economic decline but with geopolitical setbacks: above all the Vietnam War, but more generally the Korean stalemate, the Iranian/Islamic challenge, and the emergence of a polycentric world. This underscores the point that geopolitical prestige is a matter of trajectory, rather than absolute standing; "what have you done lately" seems to be more important than one's absolute level of geopolitical resources.

The history of the U.S. is not the only example of the "Americanization" model of ethnic assimilation processes. Another example is the prestige of "Germanization" from the early 1800s on into the 30s, linked to the geopolitical rise, first of Prussia and subsequently of the Empire. In our own times, the most important case is the trend of Europeanization, which may be expected to accelerate with the growing geopolitical prestige of the European Community.

Geopolitical Prestige and Struggle
Over the Means of Cultural Production

In our discussion of meso-level conditions which affect ethnic boundaries we omitted the cultural media, such as education and language. These have important middle-range effects upon both ethnic assimilation and ethnic struggle. As with all such meso conditions, the question is: which effect happens when? Thus in one (assimilation-oriented) model, mass education produces a common culture; the mass media spread a common language; expanding access to these media eventually eliminates ethnic enclaves except for a few residual traditionalists. In the other (assimilation-resistance or ethnic fragmentation) model, the opposite occurs. The spread of literacy, newspapers, television and the like become the basis for mobilization of cultural separatists; "modernization" does not promote universalism but provides the instruments for reinforced particularities. In this vein, education operates in a "damned-if-you-do, damned-if-you-don't" fashion. If the state attempts to impose cultural uniformity through the education system, the result is resentment by aggrieved ethnic groups; here we have Lithuanian, Ukrainian, or Armenian nationalists keeping their culture alive under Russian educational imposition, ready to burst out when the opportunity arrives. On the other hand, if the state allows cultural pluralization (as Soviet reformers did increasingly in the 1980s), it hands the weapons of group mobilization to its opponents.

The key to which scenario takes place is not the structure of the education system (or the mass media) but the geopolitical conditions which set the overarching gradient of ethnic prestige. A culturally unified educational system and an imposed linguistic monopoly on the means of dissemination will fail if the prestige of the dominant ethnic group is low; at least this will be the case over the time period (apparently several generations under modern conditions) during which state weakness eventually leads to a crumbling of central controls. But we should not dwell too strongly on the image of a strong, vibrant current of cultural separatism, meeting in basements and waiting for the time when it can come into the open air; rebellious ethnic nationalisms are to a large extent constructed, and fairly sudden shifts in the political wind can bring about enthusiasm for an ethnic culture of separatism that was carried for a long time by only a few die-hards. The "Balkanization" process can be long and slow, with state control visibly crumbling for decades or centuries; in the case (the 19th and early 20th century Balkans) overt cultural resistance and mobilization is continuous. Or "Balkanization" can emerge rather rapidly, as in the weakening of central control in the USSR from the mid-1980s onwards; in this case whatever twist occurs in the rulers' cultural line all feeds the same direction of resistance.

On the other hand, the "Americanization" model of cultural hegemony can operate without much more than market processes. Although there were some efforts by Anglos to impose their culture upon immigrants in the public schools of the late 19th and early 20th century, the prestige of Anglo culture seems to have been the dominant factor in bringing about linguistic and educational assimilation. There was never any national control over education, and a good deal of local initiative existed. Variant forms of education were tried: a huge Catholic school system, staffed mainly by non-Anglos; a huge multiplicity of religious colleges; a number of foreign language schools were tried (out of which only the Hebrew academies have had any staying power). The variant forms of education soon lost their distinctiveness, as all emulated the high-prestige model: the sequence leading up to the traditional Anglo-Protestant college.[10] Not that multi-ethnic competition within the U.S. had no effects upon the educational marketplace; but its effects were to heighten competition over a common currency of educational credentials, resulting in the most massive expansion of schooling at all levels of any society in world history.[11] The result was inflation of the educational currency, not fragmentation into separate ethnic enclaves.[12] In the same way, separate ethnic-language newspapers and other cultural media have not flourished in the U.S. in competition with the Anglo-American mass-culture. No state restrictions were significant in bringing about his result; the prestige of the Anglo culture merely out-competed that of the ethnic separatists.

Principles of Geopolitics

What then are the key determinants of the geopolitical trajectory of the state? The following set of principles provides the backbone.

(1) *Size and resource advantage*. The society with the bigger population and larger economic resources tends to win wars over smaller and

poorer societies. This advantage/disadvantage is cumulative; over time the strong get stronger, the weak get progressively weaker.

(2) *Marchland advantage.* The society with fewer rivals geographically adjacent tends to win wars in the long run and to increase their realm of power; a society with enemies on many fronts tends to lose and contract. Again there are cumulative results: marchland states (those on the borders of populated territories) tend to expand; middle states are subject to balance of power processes which even out over time. In the long run, marchland states grow at the expense of middle states, which tend to fragment and eventually are swallowed up.

(2a) *Showdown wars.* Principles (1) and (2) accumulate time and reinforce each other. The pure tendency is for a geopolitical area eventually to simplify into two rival marchland states which have swallowed up the intervening territory, fighting a ferocious showdown war for "world" dominion. The result of such showdowns has usually been the mutual exhaustion of the resources of the rivals and eventually a power vacuum filled by a third force.

(3) *Overextension and disintegration.* The further from its home resource base a state attempts to project military power, the more difficult it becomes to defeat enemies, and the more likely it is to suffer major defeat. Defeat in a posture of overextension tends to bring disintegration which is much more rapid than the process of expansion. Overextension is due to two processes: the fact that logistics eats up an increasing proportion of military resources with greater distance; and the tendency for ethnic/cultural difference to increase with distance, resulting in a more deep-seated basis for mobilization of resistance.

(4) *Internal political legitimacy follows geopolitical success.* A state's rulers derive much of their domestic prestige from their external geopolitical position, especially its dynamic trajectory; the process of victory generates emotional solidarity on behalf of ruler, whereas defeat or prolonged frustration of ambitions tends to delegitimize. A basic principle of revolution follows as a corollary: defeat in foreign war (especially through coercive resource depletion via overextension) tends to produce a collapse in domestic power.[13]

Are geopolitical principles specific to a particular historical epoch or do they apply to all social formations? We argue for the latter. Principles one through four were formulated largely by analyses of the agrarian conquest states, including the long-term history of China.[14] Additionally, resource advantage remains a key in industrial/capitalist military power; Kennedy[15] depicts overextension dynamics from the 15th to the 20th century; Collins'[16] projection of the decline of the Russian empire used all four principles in the argument[17] that modern transportation technology eliminates geographical limits (in effect eliminating principle three and reducing world dynamics to the cumulative effects of principle one, making a single world empire inevitable) is countered by the fact that costs of logistics and military equipment have risen about as rapidly as extensions in range.[18]

The Geopolitical Trajectories of the Successor-States of the USSR

Our line of argument has been that the direction of ethnic boundaries towards assimilation or towards fragmentation, is determined mainly by the rising or falling geopolitical power of the state vis-a-vis its neighbors; geopolitical power, in turn, is predictable from the set of principles just given. Consider briefly the way such analysis helps to explain the differing ethnic lineups of several regions of the world: The U.S. from 1800 to 1960, our prime example of the assimilation ("Americanization") dynamic of expanding ethnic boundaries, expanded into the territory of North America against minimal local opposition; by the the late 1800s, the size and economic resource advantage of the U.S. was formidable on the world scale; in the 20th century the U.S. was in the position to pick up the pieces of the costly showdown wars among the major European powers. After 1960, mild geopolitical decline took place, due to a costly arms race (a "cold showdown war") vs. the USSR, the marchland state on the other side of the old European battle zone; further strains resulted from logistical overextension against populous enemies in Korea and Vietnam. This explains the high ethnic prestige of Anglo-American culture as a target for assimilation, with some falling of in this prestige after 1960.

The example we have given of ethnic "Balkanization" is the region of the breakup of the Austro-Hungarian and Turkish empires. Here we have states confronting potential enemies on multiple fronts; these states also were at size and resource *dis*advantage against most of their neighbors. The accumulation of disadvantages led to repeated episodes of division and redivision of the middle zones, resulting in the fragmentation and localistic ethnic mobilization of the Balkans. On the scale of world history, the region at an agrarian level of development which has had the most prolonged geopolitical fragmentation has been India, and it is also the region in which ethnic fragmentation has been most deeply institutionalized, in the form of the caste system.[19]

This set of geopolitical principles has also proven effective for predicting future developments; Collins[20] used them to predict the reversal of five centuries of Russian expansion and the breakup of the Russian empire. Given the array of successor states as of 1991, what do these principles imply for their medium to long-run futures?

Russia

Russia was of course the core of the Soviet Union, and its empire was an extension of the expanding geopolitical trajectory of the Russian Empire. Russian geopolitical advantages turned negative in the 20th century, however, and Gorbachev's efforts to reduce logistical overextension by currying military commitments resulted in the rapid delegitimization of the ruling group.[21] It would appear, however, that whoever the successor group to Gorbachev's geopolitico-strategic reforms may be, they will benefit from a more modest and improved geopolitical position. Russia's size and economic resources are considerably depleted; but so are those of its immediate neighbors. It is now playing in a different geopolitical ballpark; instead of the U.S., NATO, and Iran, its most immediate rivals are now the Ukraine (52 million), Kazakhstan (17 million), Belarus (10 million), the Baltic states (8 million), against its own 148 millions and more than proportionate economic resources.

Russia is in a good medium-to-long run position to exercise dominant power-prestige over its neighbors. This does not mean that Russia necessarily will expand against its neighbors, or fight with them. Geopolitical power-prestige is exercised in peacetime as well as in war; it exists as well in the diplomatic leverage which its relative resources gives it vis-a-vis its neighbors, manifested in a combination of implied threat and attractiveness as an ally. In addition, as we shall detail shortly, most of Russia's neighbors are states with geopolitically disadvantageous middle positions among rival states; whereas Russia returns to something more like its favored marchland position of Petrine days.

Russias main geopolitical weakness is in the Far East. Its resource-rich eastern Siberian region is geopolitically accessible to two very large states: Japan and China. Furthermore, China during both the Ming (circa 1415) and the Manchu (Ch'ing) dynasties (circa 1760) held portions of current Russian territory along the Amur.[22] With continuing weakness (including internal economic decline and political strife), it is within the realm of geopolitical possibility that China or Japan would acquire this territory in the next few decades; the Japanese in particular have already been involved in economic development in this region. There is, however, one geopolitical feature which favors Russian power in the Far East: the fact that there are two potential rivals for it, not one. Japan and China would likely stalemate each other's moves into this area; in addition Korea, a sizable economic resource bloc, which historically has always been the first line of Japanese expansion, would no doubt ally against Japan. Yet a further strategic consideration is the U.S.. Since the demise of the Cold War, Japanese-U.S. relations have worsened noticably; this is not surprising in that their common enemy was what held them together. Given further weakness in Russia with concomitant threats to its Far Eastern territory, it is not at all unlikely that the U.S. would make alliance with Russia, propping it up as a counterbalance against Japan. This too has historical precedent; in the geopolitical lineup of the 1800s when the U.S. was in tension with the British Empire (especially over the Canadian frontier), the U.S. and Russia were allies. Their accommodation in the northern Pacific was the cause of the transfer of Alaska to the U.S..

On the whole, then, the truncated Russian state appears to have a relatively favorable middle-to-long run geopolitical future. The result should be that the power-prestige of Russian ethnicity will be high, in relation to its ethnic rivals. There are two consequences, one internal to the Russian Federation, one external. The internal consequence is that we should not expect much if any further ethnic fragmentation *inside* Russia. There are of course numerous ethnic minorities within the Russian Federation; many of them have an already existing administrative structure in the form of Autonomous Republics and Autonomous Regions. Nevertheless, few if any of them appear to be viable as independent states.

These ethnic districts are found primarily (1) in the Caucasus region; (2) in the Urals; (3) in the Altai mountains along the Chinese border; (4) in Siberia. Some of the Siberian autonomous republics and regions are quite large on the map, but their populations are miniscule; the largest of them, Komi, Khanti-Mansi and Uakut-Sakha each have populations of 1.1–1.2 million, but all have Russian ethnic majorities (of 58%, 66%, and 50% respectively, against multi-fragmented minorities); and the other such regions in Siberia have populations down to the range of 40,000–80,000. Whatever their legal status, these regions locked within

Russian territory are bound to be Russian satellites. The same is true for the Urals ethnic districts; here the most trouble should come from Tatarstan (3.6 million, 43% Russians against 48% Tatars), and indeed it had riots affirming independence in October 1990; but its geographic position effectively neutralizes its sphere of independent action.

Overall, the regions which have the biggest potential for geopolitical autonomy are those with relatively large populations, an indigenous non-Russian majority, and a position on the edge of Russian territory. Three regions fit that description: Chechen-Ingushetia (1.2 million, Chechens 53%, Russians 29%), located on the Georgian border in the Caucasus; North Ossetia (Population 620,000, Ossetians 53%, Russians 30%), located on the Georgian border; and Tuva (population 300,00, Tuvinians 64%, Russians 32%), located on the border of Mongolia. Not surprisingly, all three of these regions have already had ethnic conflicts. Chechen-Ingushetia (the only one of these big enough to be a real state) had a pro-Muslim coup in October 1991 and forced the withdrawal of Russian troops in November. In Tuva, with its substantial local ethnic majority, Russians were fleeing ethnic violence in 1990. North Ossetia, on the other hand, has been most concerned to make ethnic solidarity with South Ossetians, who are struggling for autonomy from Georgia; appealing to Russian power-prestige, they want South Ossetia to become part of the Russian Federation.[23]

One may predict, then, that with minor exceptions in non-Russian dominated border-regions, Russia itself will undergo few further ethnic secessions. There is of course the possibility of further fragmentation of Russian territory, but this would take place not under the auspices of ethnic independence, but as struggles of regional warlords or other units, struggles among the Russians themselves. In general, the power-prestige of Russians as an ethnic group should be high throughout its own territory; and since Russia should do better geopolitically than most of its neighbors, we can expect that it will anchor a continuing high ethnic prestige for Russians in those regions as well. This bodes well for the Russians within Russia; for other ex-Soviet states with sizable Russian populations, it portends trouble for local ethnic majorities bent on de-Russification.

The Baltic States

These are rather small states (the largest, Lithuania has 3.7 million population) but with fairly substantial local ethnic majorities (Latvia is least homogeneous, with 34% Russians). In geopolitical resources they are weak. To avoid Russian domination they would be expected to attach themselves strongly to Western allies; and indeed the Baltic states are prime candidates for joining the European Community. Given that the power-prestige of the European Community is the major growth trajectory in world geopolitics, the ethnic prestige in this region should be towards pan-Europism. Hence we may expect that the revolutionary upsurge of ethnic nationalism in Estonia, Latvia, and Lithuania will be short-lived, a phenomenon of transition; the center of ethnic gravity should be the neutral pan-Europism of the European Community.

The Ukraine

With a population of 52 million and considerable economic resources, the Ukraine is the one true challenger to Russian power-prestige among the successor-states of the USSR. With 73% Ukrainians and 22% Russians, it will be able to maintain internal Ukrainian ethnic dominance in the short run. But geopolitical conditions suggest long-run problems with Ukrainian power-prestige. The Ukraine has a position as an interior state, with fairly strong neighbors on most borders. The strongest is Russia, triple its size; the post-Soviet breakup jockeying for power and for dividing up the military and other resources (likely including territory) will probably start down the path of mobilizing ethnic hostilities on both sides. The presence of sizable ethnic minorities on each other's side of the Russian/Ukrainian borders is likely to provide structural grounds for outrage in both camps; control of Russian-populated Crimea to is likely to be one such focus. One would expect Russia/Ukraine ethnic conflict to be one of the worst.

Ukraine also has borders with some sizable East European states (Poland, Czechoslovakia), and some weak ones (Romania); this is the direction in which the Ukraine would be able to exercise greater power, but also risks complexities of balance-of-power politics. The Ukraine looks like a long-range trouble center. It should be noted that Ukrainian ethnic identity has never been highly prestigious, due to its long history of conquest by its neighbors; the upsurge of nationalism that has come with the breakaway from the Russian empire has the nature of filling an ethnic prestige vacuum, rather than the more strongly based prestige of military success or having led a successful revolution. Future geopolitical projections imply the Ukraine may be expected to have a rather embattled ethnic identity, a weak attractor for ethnic prestige and assimilation within its own borders.

The Caucasus and Central Asian States

The Caucasus states, with their mountainous terrain, ports on the the Black and Caspian Seas, and borders with Turkey and Iran, are geopolitically open to alliance and influences in numerous directions. This has been their situation throughout history, and the ethnic fragmentation of the region goes back to the patchwork of small states across here as early as the ancient Persian empire. It is not surprising that when the Soviet empire began to weaken, conflicts started here the earliest. The Caucasus will likely continue to be a region of ethnic conflicts; none of its states is likely to be strong enough to provide assimilation-attraction to anyone else; while the balance of power is too complicated to allow any of the states to destroy most of its rivals.

The central Asian states fall into two categories: the big ones, Kazakhstan (17 million), and Uzbekistan (20 million); and the three small ones, Tadzikistan, Turkmenia, Kirgizia, (between 3.6 and 5.3 million each). The overriding geopolitical reality is that all of these states are small compared to the closed big powers, Russia, Iran, and China. The geopolitical history of this region has been that Turkmenia, Uzbekistan, and parts of Kazakhstan (the region southeast of the Aral sea) were usually parts of an empire based in Iran. The predominance of Islam in this region is a heritage of the fact that its connection was historically more with the Middle East than with the Russian north.

In the late 20th century, once again we find Iran as the biggest and richest state in the Middle East (population 59 million; GNP $80 billion). Given the balance of geopolitical resources, a reasonable long-term prediction is that Iranian or other powers from the south (including Afghanistan) will at some time again absorb some of this region. In Azerbaijan as well, the power-prestige of Iran has already led to opening of contacts. Especially as the war against Armenia and its ethnic enclaves in Azerbaijan goes on, we may expect Azerbaijan to become more of an Iranian satellite. Armenia, in turn, has already made overtures to the Turks (despite memories of atrocities early in the 20th century). Medieval patterns of conflict between Turks and Iranians are likely to play themselves out over this region again. The Turkic entho-linguistic heritage of many of the central Asians (Turkmen, some Kazaks) also suggests another pattern of diplomatic alliance. Turkey (population 59 million, GNP $178 billion) and Iran are the two big players in the region; between the two of them, one may expect long-term geopolitical instability in Causasia and south central Asia. Ethnic power-prestige should anchor Turkic and Iranian ethnic identities, likely reinforced by the corresponding religious divisions (Sunni and Shi'ite).

The one central Asian state likely to go its own way is Kazakhstan. Geopolitically, Kazakhstan is furthest from the major Islamic challenging states; it has a buffer of two states between itself Iran, and Turkey is even more remote. It has a border with China as well as with Russia; and since Uyghur tribal peoples overlap the Kazakhstan/China border, troubles on the other side of the border could easily spill over into Chinese claims in Kazakhstan territory. This region, furthermore, was at times incorporated into the farthest western extent of Chinese empires (which sometimes reached as far as Samarkand, in today's Uzbekistan). All these factors, we suggest, should motivate Kazakhstan to maintain an alliance with Russia. The Chinese border is likely to be a source of trouble, but not an indefensible one; on the Chinese side of the border is the thinly populated frontier region of Sinkiang. The Kazakhstan region traditionally constituted overextension for Chinese military power, and the unraveling of empires frequently started with the exhaustion of military ventures in this region (e.g., the disintegration of the T'ang dynasty began in 751 with a defeat by troops of the Arab Caliphate northwest of Alma Ata). Internally, Kazakhstan is ethnically divided; Kazaks are a minority, at 38%, Russians a slightly bigger minority, at 40%. Given that we expect the long-term power prestige of the Russians to be the highest of any of the ex-Soviet states, Russian ethnic identity in Kazakh will be appealing. By the early or middle decades of the 21st century, when Iranian/Islamic inroads have been made into the nearer states of Central Asia, Kazakhstan may well experience severe internal ethnic conflict, between the two externally-anchored centers of ethnic prestige: Muslim and Russian.

Short-Run Considerations

We have argued that geopolitical principles will determine the degree to which ethnicity will become a focus of solidarity in successor states and in neighboring countries. The sudden and rapid breakup of the Soviet Union has left in its wake a number of successor nation-states that have formed along the boundaries of the former union republics. The medium and long-run ability of these new nation-states to manage their territorial integrity and to successfully resist challengers' claims will be influenced by a number of factors. Given the underlying global distribution of power-prestige and wealth in the present international system, we regard the distribution and control of military capabilities in the region to be an important short-run factor that will influence the viability of the newly created national-states. The principal other short-run factor is the success of the current economic experiments being developed within the Russian Federation.

Which successor states gain what level of control over which military resources of the former Soviet Union will have an impact on their international power-prestige and their capacity to manage anti-state challenges by mobilized internal (ethnic) opposition. States which inherit war-making capabilities from the former Soviet Union will have a greater chance of success than states that fund and organize standing armies anew. The sooner emergent national-states gain control over coercive resources, the greater will be their chance of success, all else being equal. Generally speaking, militarily viable states will be more capable of resisting challenges from exterior powers and hence their prestige will likely increase vis-a-vis those powers (i.e., Russia and other regional contenders). Likewise, the more concentrated is a state's control over military resources, the greater are its advantages over contentious subordinates in the event that armed struggle brakes out. Moreover, militarily strong states will be more likely than weak ones to become centers of ethnic solidarity. States which undergo prolonged upheaval and internal struggle over the short-run will be less likely to emerge as centers of ethnic solidarity.

The present is a unique and important historical period. The remnants of the Soviet Union are just now being divided among successor states or being withdrawn to the USSR's internationally recognized heir, the Russian Federation. There are two primary components of military resources which are the focus of negotiations among the former union republics: nuclear and strategic capabilities, and conventional forces. Although no small question, the vast bulk of the nuclear and strategic forces appear to be safely heading toward the Russian Federation. Kazakhston, Belarus, and the Ukraine may in the end balk at this arrangement, although the Ukraine is more likely to than either Kazakhston or Belarus. Conventional forces may suffer a different fate. Currently there is pressure to maintain a unified army under the auspices of the Commonwealth of Independent States. As of January 1992, Ukraine, Azerbaijan, Belarus, and Moldova have stated their intention to establish their own national armies. The likelihood of others making similar claims may grow if internal or regional instability increases. Control over conventional military forces, whether collective or individual will be essential for the short run security of the new national-states vis-a-vis one another in terms of minority challenges from within.

The other short-run factor most likely to influence the success of the new nation-states is the outcome of Russia's current experiments with market reform. On more than one occasion Yeltsin has tied his own political future to the success of these programs. Yeltsin, per se, is not as crucial as the "success" of his reforms. It is important to note that many of the most well organized factions in Russia have the greatest stake to lose if liberalization experiments succeed. If they fail on a large scale then it could bring on a conservative backlash. A wide range of scenarios is possible. The floor of such a backlash could be confined to the present territorial claims of the Russian Federation. Its ceiling could involve territorial claims of the Russian Federation or Eastern Europe, although this scenario becomes increasingly less likely over time. Some middle ground is equally probable, say an attempt to re-establish some semblance of the territorial boundaries of the now defunct USSR. In any event, a conservative backlash in the short-run could directly challenge the efforts to divide up the military capabilities of the former Soviet Union. Generally speaking, the possibility of a conservative backlash in the short-run is the greatest source of uncertainty concerning the future of the new national-states. The short-run outcome of economic reform in the Russian Federation is a source of uncertainty in the entire region. The global implications are equally profound. If a conservative backlash is successful, the principal threat will probably be to regional security. However, if economic collapse can be avoided in the Russian Federation, then centrifugal pressures working to breakup the Soviet military may succeed as well. The economic condition of the Russian Federation and the dismantling of the former Soviet military are the two most important short-run factors affecting the success of the new successor states.

So far we have linked the short-run successes of centrifugal processes governing the geographical redistribution of military capabilities in the region to the economic viability of the Russian Federation. Moreover, we have suggested that a minimal level of success of the current economic program and regime may be necessary for the transfer of control over military capabilities in the region. We offer one qualification for these remarks: the longer the current regime in Russia remains in power, the greater is the likelihood that the decentralization of military power will be carried through. Finally, we have suggested that the transfer of the means of coercion and the legitimate control over their use from the Soviet military to the emergent national-states will have an impact on the future of ethnic mobilization within and between these states.

The geopolitical disintegration of the Soviet Union which greatly intensified in the last few years involved in part the mobilization of medium-sized ethnic units in opposition to the central government. The declining international power-prestige of the Soviet Union in recent years virtually ensured that the central government would be a provocation for ethnically organized anti-state opposition and violence. Following the breakup of the Soviet Union, successor states enjoy a relatively high level of prestige despite their relative weakness vis-a-vis adjacent states and contentious minorities within their borders. But such prestige may be short lived if the leaders of the new national-states fail to build strong national economies from the remains of the collapsing and ailing production and distribution networks that were once part of the Soviet economy. Moreover, the prestige they now enjoy is of the kind that battle champions enjoy in the first moments of victory. It is not the kind of prestige enjoyed by strong resource-rich states. Only economic prosperity or military success gives the state the cultural and material capital around which ethnic groups mobilize and coalesce. Consequently, the new nation-states will be particularly vulnerable to the contentious acts of ethnic minorities who until recently had been mobilized against the central state of the Soviet Union. Access to the coercive resources of the Soviet military may give successor states the means to effectively manage external challenges, and it compounds the advantageous position of the ethnic group controlling the apparatus of the state. Despite a fair number of minor border disputes, many of the successor states presently enjoy more or less mutually exclusive territorial claims and more or less exclusive sovereign authority. Its leaders enjoy a tremendous resource advantages over their contenders which they are able to reproduce and to extend by manipulating the organizational and cultural resources of the state.

The middle-to-long run outlook for the successor states to develop into centers of ethnic solidarity is only partially influenced by Russia's economic trajectory and by degree of decentralized control over the former Soviet Red Army. Despite their current successes, these states face the long-run challenges of state building and economic prosperity. The situation of most of the smaller states is complicated by their geographical proximity to large, economically and militarily strong states. Issues such as which states remain viable sources of ethnic solidarity and which gain international prestige cannot be settled in the short run. However, as they become resolved, we are likely to see the continuation of historical patterns which demonstrate the applicability of the theoretical principles of geopolitics that we have elaborated above.

Endnotes

1. "Proto-ethnicity" in the sense of cultural characteristics, group associations, and marriage pool producing somatic patterns; terminologically, one might want to reserve "ethnicity" for patterns of identification when there is consciousness of a boundary with alien groups, which would not exist if these groups are totally isolated.

2. For example: Bonacich, Edna, "A Theory of Ethnic Antagonism: the Split Labor Market," *American Sociological Review*, 37: 547–559, 1974. Hechter, Michael, "The Political Economy of Ethnic Change," *American Journal of Sociology*, 79: 1151–78, 1974. Light, Ivan, *Ethnic Enterprise in America*, University of California Press, Berkeley, CA, 1972.

3. Late 20th century social science, with its bias towards the enduringness of ethnic difference, has generally lost track of the time frame in which such processes operate; we have no very careful measurements but under conditions when geopolitical factors favor assimilation, this seems to take several generations. Consider for example the history of British society in the centuries after the Norman conquest, when a French-speaking upper class ruled Celtic and German groups; and again the patterns of English/Scottish and English/Irish assimilation and conflict since the unification (by dynastic marriage and by conquest, respectively) of those peoples in the 1600s. All such analyses must be careful to consider the interaction of several conditions: geopolitics, common division of labor, and ethnic stratification.

4. Murray, Alexander, *Reason and Society in the Middle Ages*, Clarendon Press, Oxford, UK, pp. 69–90, 1978.

5. Weber, Max, *Economy and Society*, Bedminster Press, New York, NY, pp. 901–40, 1922/1968.

6. Nationalism has often been connected with the rise of universal military conscription and with free/compulsory mass public education. These are not separate phenomena; the first states to produce the one tended to develop the other. The extent to which these nation-building institutions are popular, or merely a source of grievances, depends on an additional factor, the geopolitical success of the state.

7. For elaboration, see Collins, Randall, *Weberian Sociological Theory*, Cambridge University Press, Cambridge and New York, pp. 145–66, 1986.

8. Skocpol, Theda, *States and Social Revolutions*, Cambridge University Press, New York, NY, 1979.

9. Kennedy, Paul, *The Rise and Fall of the Great Powers; Economic Change and Military Conflict from 1500 to 2000*, Random House, New York, NY, 1987.

10. As demonstrated by Jencks, Christopher, *The Academic Revolution*, Doubleday, New York, NY, 1968.

11. Collins, Randall, *The Credential Society: An Historical Sociology of Education and Stratification*, Academic Press, New York, NY, 1979.

12. Hence, even today, with the late-20th century mobilization of non-white ethnic minorities into demanding separate pieces of the educational pie, the

pieces demanded are for credentials within the unified schooling sequence, rather than for ethnically distinct school systems.

13. Most of these principles have been stated in the previous literature. Size and resource advantage is indicated in military analyses such as Liddel-Hart, B.H., *History of the Second World War*, Putnam, New York, NY, 1970; march-land advantage is repeatedly pointed out by McNeill, William H., *The Rise of the West; A History of the Human Community*, University of Chicago Press, Chicago, IL, 1963. Overextension was formulated by Stinchcombe, Arthur L., *Constructing Social Theories*, Harcourt, New York, NY, pp. 218–30, 1968; as a principle of logistics costs, and is the theme of Kennedy, 1987 (op. cit., note 9), historical analysis. Weber, 1922/68 (pp. 901–04, op. cit., note 5) enuciated the principle that domestic legitimacy follows the power-prestige of the state; the military cost/breakdown model of revolution is in Skocpol, 1979 (op. cit., note 8) and elborated by Goldstone, Jack A., *Revolution and Rebellion in the Early Modern World*, University of California Press, Berkeley, CA, 1991. Here we state these principles in a form in which we can see their cumulative nature as long-term processes and their effects upon domestic power.

14. Collins, Randall, "Long-term Social Change and the Territorial Power of States," *Research in Social Movements Conflicts, and Change*, Louis Kriesberg, ed., Vol. 1, JAI Press, Greenwich, CT, 1978.

15. Kennedy, 1987 (op. cit., note 9).

16. Collins, Randall, "The Future Decline of the Russian Empire: An Application of Geopolitical Theory," Colloquium at Yale University, Columbia University, March/April 1980. Published in Collins, 1986 (op. cit., note 7).

17. Boulding, Kenneth, *Conflict and Defense*, Harper and Row, New York, NY, 1962.

18. As discussed in Collins, 1986 (op. cit., note 7), pp. 167–85. A main criticism of geopolitical arguments (e.g. Mann, Michael, "Comments on Paul Kennedy's The Rise and Fall of the Great Powers," *British Journal of Sociology*, 40: pp. 331–35, 1989) is that they ignore diplomacy and ideology which can offset specific geopolitical disadvantages and form interstate rivalries according to non-military criteria. We argue, on the contrary, that ideology tends to follow geopolitics (as we can see, for example, in the initial conditions for the rise and spread of Isalm: Collins, 1978 (op. cit., note 14)); this is apparent again in the late 20th century, as the geopolitically-based collapse of the Russian empire has had a strong delegitimating effect upon socialist ideology, while the success of the Iranian revolution and the opportunities for geopolitical rearrangement in the Middle East and Central Asia give impetus to Islamic fundamentalism. The argument for countervailing effects of diplomacy is not historically documented; one could demonstrate the contrary analysis that diplomacy is a device for geopolitical expansion by states whose position on principles (1–3) is favorable; the balance-of-power diplomacy favoired in early modern Europe holds mainly in stalemated situations of multiple rivals within a middle zone.

19. The Maurya empire approached a universal state during 300–180 BC; the next fairly large state, the Afghan-based Islamic conquest state of the Moghuls, held the north and briefly other parts of India during the 1600s. The British colonial moved into the power vacuum of the Moghul disintegration; it exercised a mixture of direct and indirect rule lasting from about 1860 to 1947. Although British ethnic prestige was high for a while, it fell of in the

20th century as Britain became increasingly strained by European wars; and it was during these times of geopolitical strain that Indian national separatist movements mobilized. The ethnic conflicts of India in the late 20th century are based in this long-term geopolitical heritage, heightened by the growing prestige of Islamic nationalism in the states to the west: the anti-Western Islamic revolution in Iran, and the successful Afghani war against Soviet military domination. It is predictable that further successful Islamic movements in ex-Soviet Central Asia will increase the power-prestige of Islamic ethnic identification, and anchor still more ethnic conflict within India.

20. Collins, 1980/86 (op. cit., note 16).

21. Ibid.

22. The 1905 Russo-Japanese War took place in the adjacent territory of south Manchuria, which was subsequently held by the Japanese until 1945; the southern part of Sakhalin Island (across from the Amur) was also taken at this time. The Kuriles were annexed in 1875, the first act of modern Japanese imperialism. Current Russian/Japanese tensions thus are rooted in their previous conflicts.

23. Los Angeles Times, November 22, 1991, p. A5.

Protection of the Rights of Minorities —
Back to the League of Nations?

Ambassador Petrus Buwalda
The Netherlands

Introduction

One of the most urgent problems to emerge after the collapse of Marxism in Central and Eastern Europe is undoubtedly that of the protection of the rights of minorities. Marxism-Leninism claimed to have solved the problems of the minorities which had caused so many conflicts and wars in Eastern Europe and Russia. In the spirit of "Internationalism" all peoples were supposed to live happily together and to enjoy the march towards true Communism. We in the West have always had our doubts about that—and saw those doubts confirmed—but quite a few leaders in the former Soviet Union seem to have believed their own slogans and to have been genuinely surprised by the nationalistic outbursts which ensued almost as soon as Glasnost made them possible. And even while nationals in the various republics of the Union obtained autonomy and later independence, minority groups inside those Republics demanded equally to be heard and to be given their autonomy or even independence. What happened in this respect in another former communist country, Yugoslavia, hardly needs to be emphasized here.

The intention of this essay is to trace the history of the protection of the rights of minorities and the lessons it teaches us for the present. Thereafter I shall discuss whether some new system could usefully serve to defuse the tensions and conflicts ensuing from the power vacuum after the fall of the Marxist regimes and the rush of nationalistic feelings within the numerous minority groups in Central and Eastern Europe that followed.

During the nineteenth century the most important example of a minorities-clause was contained in the documents emanating form the Congress of Berlin in 1878. Certain states which used to belong to the

Ottoman Empire became independent and their independence was recognized by the Big Powers on the condition that all parts of the population would have equal rights as far as their religion was concerned. This clause remained largely a declaration of principle, because no mechanism was created for its supervision, although the "Big Powers" of that era did keep an eye on the situation.

It was only during the First World War that comprehensive studies were made concerning minorities and their protection. Three elements were identified which could lead groups to consider themselves a minority: race, language, and religion.

Protection of the Rights of Minorities in the Peace Treaties of 1918–1919

The first systematic attempt to create a system to protect the rights of minorities was undertaken during the peace negociations after the First World War. Once again new states were born in Eastern Europe and once again recognition was made dependent on the acceptance of protection of minorities in those states. But this time a supervision mechanism was added to the treaties with those newly independent states. The relevant clause which was inserted in each treaty reads as follows:

> In as far as the stipulations of the aforegoing articles affect persons belonging to minorities of race, religion or language, those stipulations constitute obligations of international interest and will be placed under the guarantee of the League of Nations.

It is interesting to note that the protection of minorities was provided for in the individual treaties concluded with the states in question and not in the Convenant of the League. President Wilson, who had included the protection of minorities in his famous speech of January 22, 1917, proposed two "additional articles" to the Convenant which would have provided for equal treatment and security of all racial and national minorities within a member state, and a promise by all member-states not to issue laws which hinder the free exercise of religion by their nationals. Neither article made it into the final text and even one of Wilson's advisers, D. H. Miller, concluded that it was impossible to treat the question of minorities in a general sense.

To a considerable extent, it was due to the constant pressure exercised by Jewish lobbying-groups around the peace conference that a system for the protection of minorities was finally devised and inserted in each of the individual treaties which concluded with the states with large minority populations on their territory. These Jewish groups never demanded an extension of this system to all member states, realizing that limitation to the states of Eastern Europe was the only realistic position at the time. Not even Italy, which received a large German speaking minority in South Tirol, or Germany were included. Several of the other states involved at first protested against what they saw as an infringement on their national sovereignty. In the end, however, those states were forced to accept the new system.

The System for the Protection of the Rights of Minorities of the League of Nations

The system created as a result of the peace-treaties consisted of the above mentioned guarantee by the League of Nations. It had to be—and was—formally accepted by the Council of the League which alone was empowered to approve changes in it.

Next to this guarantee it was agreed that each member of the Council was entitled to bring to the attention of the Council violations, or the danger of violations, of any of the provisions regarding the protection of minorities.

Finally, the treaties stipulated that differences of opinion pertaining to legal or actual questions regarding the protection of minorities between member-states had an international character and could therefore be submitted to the International Court of Justice, but only at the request of a member of the Council. Thus is was made clear that the supervision of the stipulations regarding the protection of minorities had been put in the hands of the members of the Council of the League alone.

Nevertheless, for the first time in history an international organization, the League of Nations, would be supervising the protection of minorities in Eastern Europe.

But how would the League exercise this function? It was the Secretariat of the League that devised a practical and eventually successful procedure. Members of the Council, it was quickly realized, would not easily avail themselves of their right to bring a violation of the treaties by a specific state before the Council. Such a question was highly political and a public discussion of a violation might—and probably would—pitch the accusing state against the accused and lead to a battle of prestige, thereby increasing tensions rather than facilitating solutions. Therefore, it was considered of the greatest importance that questions regarding the minorities be dealt with as much as possible in an informal atmosphere and through quiet discussion with the governments involved, before—and preferably instead of—a public discussion in the Council.

In the beginning of its existence, the Council of the League approved several resolutions establishing the procedure which was followed thereafter. Often these resolutions were drafted by the Norwegian Director of the Minorities-section of the Secretariat, Erik Colban. They stipulated that not only member states, but also representatives of the minorities themselves could send petitions regarding violations of the treaty clauses concerning the protection of minorities to the Secretariat. The Secretariat would send any petition which did not originate with a member state to the Government of the "accused" state. That state would then have three weeks in which to inform the Secretariat whether or not it wanted to submit a commentary on the petition, and another two months to formulate such a commentary. Thereafter, the petition and the eventual commentary would be distributed to all member states of the League. The Council President would then form a committee of three, consisting of himself and two other members which would ascertain whether the petition was well-founded. After that it was up to any member of the Council to decide whether or not to bring the question before the Council.

During the deliberations of a committee of three, an important role was played by the Minorities Section of the Secretariat. It would prepare the sessions and submit written comments regarding the facts or the legal questions raised in the petition. Often the committee would request additional information. This might require contacts with the government involved. The Head of the Section therefore traveled regularly to the countries in Eastern Europe where large minorities existed. He, and sometimes his assistants, made themselves available for petitioners and talked to the officials in charge— at first only to those in the Foreign Offices, but gradually more and more to those who were actually dealing with the minorities. Thus they provided an outlet for the complaints and frustration of the minorities themselves. Last, but not least, the Minorities-section was sometimes charged by a committee to keep specific cases under review, and thus could exercise a certain measure of restraint, if not control, over the authorities directly involved.

It should be realized, of course, that the committees of three—let alone the Minorities Section—had no power to enforce any decisions. They could only threaten to submit the question to the Council with all the ensuing publicity, which was generally not welcome to governments in question. But even the Council could do no more than rebuke the sinning state—and that was rare in an era that considered national sovereignty an overriding consideration in the conduct of international affairs.

The governments of the States involved often tried to have petitions declared non-receivable, on the pretext that the petitioners did not belong to a minority. The question of the definition of what constitutes a minority has been discussed endlessly in international fora, and has never been resolved. The Permanent Court of International Justice in The Hague did give a definition in 1923, however, which proved effective within the system at the time. It stated that an ethnic minority consisted of persons who differed from the majority qua race, language, or religion, independent of citizenship. The court added in 1933 that such a minority characterized itself also by the will to cultivate its ethnic traditions and the wish to raise its children in those traditions.[1]

The treatment of the minorities in the States bound by the treaties of 1919–1920 was certainly not always exemplary and the rule of national sovereignty was predominant. Very few cases reached the League Council, and even then no strong measures were taken. The application was limited, of course, to Eastern Europe and was never meant to be extended to other parts of the world. Although now and again the establishment of a permanent committee on minorities or the formation of a special committee to draft a Convention on Minorities was proposed, such proposals were never accepted.[2]

Nevertheless, up till 1934, the minorities covered by the relevant treaties had an outlet for their complaints and a certain measure of control was exercised in the name of the "committees of three" of the League Council by the Minorities Section of the League Secretariat. The system depended to a great extent on the active interest of the main powers in the Council and on the cooperation of the states with large minorities in Eastern Europe. Both began to wane after 1934, when Germany left the League and Poland declared that it would no longer cooperate with the League in questions regarding minorities, and the system lost is effectiveness. By 1939, it had no longer any influence on the protection of minorities.[3] However, "it is unjust to view the failure of the minority system of the League of Nations independently of the general international conditions of its time. Inevitably the minorities system depended on the general state of international order and relations, and inevitably the system collapsed with it..."[4]

Protection of the Rights of Minorities
After the Second World War

After World War II the system for the protection of Minority rights of the League of Nations was not revived in the United Nations Organization. Why did the international community no longer see the need for separate protection of minorities as a group?

The Dutch researcher Joost Herman believes that every minority was regarded as a potential "fifth column," in view of the misuse of Hitler of the German minorities in Czechoslovakia and Poland just before the outbreak of World War Two. For that reason, according to him, ethnic minorities no longer merited a separate position and had to look for help within the general context of the protection of individual human rights.[5] I do not deny that such sentiments may have played a role, but would not give them too much prominence.

A French expert, Mme. Josepha Laroche, blames the countries of the "New World," according to her only interested in assimilation, for the lack of interest shown by the United Nations in the protection of minority group rights. As proof, she quotes the decision not to include a proposed article on the rights of national, linguistic, and religious minorities in the Declaration of Human Rights.[6]

However, in this context one should not overlook the optimism created by the foundation of the United Nations and the special protection of human rights contained in its Charter. It was believed the "respect for human rights and fundamental freedoms for all, without distinction as to race, sex, language, or religion," would also provide for the protection of the rights of minorities. In that way the principle of non-discrimination, one of the traditional aspects of any international system for the protection of minorities, was included among the basic principles of the Charter. However, this principle was now put in the context of the protection of human beings, individuals, and no longer in that of measures especially designed for the protection of minorities, i.e., groups, and still less for the protection of certain groups only, as had been the case under the League system. A study prepared by the Secretary-General of the U.N. in 1950 makes this very clear:

> If the problem is regarded as a whole, there can be no doubt that the whole minorities protection regime was in 1919 an integral part of a system established to regulate the outcome of the First World War and create an international organization, the League of Nations. One principle of that system was that certain States and certain States only

(chiefly States that had been newly reconstituted or considerably enlarged) should be subject to obligations and international control in the matter of minorities.

But the whole system was overthrown by the Second World War. All the international decisions reached since 1944 have been inspired by a different philosophy. The idea of a general and universal protection of human rights and fundamental freedoms is emerging. It is therefore no longer only the minorities in certain countries which receive protection, but all human beings in all countries which receive a certain measure of international protection. Within this system special provisions in favor of certain minorities are still conceivable, but the point of view from which the problem is approached is essentially different from that of 1919.[7]

It was symptomatic that a separate committee on minorities questions was never set up within the U.N.. The Commission on Human Rights, created by the Economic and Social Council on February 16, 1946, was directed to work on five subjects of which "protection of minorities" was only one. That last subject was relegated to a sub-committee which was to discuss not only minorities questions, but also the "prevention of discrimination."

The U.N. Convenant on Civil and Political Rights

The 1950 the General Assembly asked the Commission on Human Rights and its sub-committee "to make a thorough study of the problems of minorities, in order that the United Nations may be able to take effective measures for the protection of racial, national, religious, or linguistic minorities." This study resulted in 1962 in the adoption by the third committee of the General Assembly of an article on minorities to be inserted in the "Covenant on Civil and Political Rights" which was then being drafted. This Covenant was finally adopted by the Assembly on December 16, 1966. The article on minorities became *art. 27* in the final text and reads as follows:

In those States in which ethnic, religious, or linguistic minorities exist, persons belonging to such minorities shall not be denied the right, in community with the other members of their group, to enjoy their own culture, to profess and practice their own religion or to use their own language.

In this way the United Nations created a basis for its own handling of the problems of minorities and the system of the League officially ceased to exist. It should be noted, however, that the emphasis was once again on "persons belonging to minorities" and not on minorities as a group.

Moreover, no control mechanism was set up which could have taken over the tasks that had been carried out by the Minorities-section of the League Secretariat.

It is true that under *art.8* of the "International Convention on the Elimination of all Forms of Racial Discrimination" a "Committee on the Elimination of Racial Discrimination" was established which is entitled to receive and consider communication from individuals within its jurisdiction claiming to be victims of a violation of any of the rights set forth in the Convention. But the Committee can only do so provided the "accused" State has declared beforehand that it recognizes the competence of the Committee. It is also restricted to individuals and to racial discrimination.

The Human Rights Committee, set up under the "International Convenant on Civil and Political rights," studies only reports submitted to it by States parties to the Convenant. Under an "Optional Protocol" States parties to this Protocol recognize the competence of the Committee to receive and consider communications from individuals subject to its jurisdiction who claim to be victims of a violation. But once again, this competence is limited to States having accepted the Protocol beforehand and to individual cases of human rights violations and does not enclose the rights of minorities as a group.

Capotorti notes that the Subcommittee on discrimination and minorities for a long period (1954–1971) concentrated its work on questions of discrimination and that only the decision to request a special report by a rapporteur (Capotorti himself) brought the minorities question back to the focus of its attention.

I should add that the relative neglect of the minorities question during the initial decades of the existence of the U.N. was almost certainly influenced by a political factor at the back of the minds of the diplomats: practically all the minorities involved in the system of the League of Nations during the interbellum were now under communist rule. The climate of the Cold War would undoubtedly have prevented the constitution of a new specific system for the protection of those minorities, even one as weak as that under the League Council had been.

All endeavors to draft a definition of the concept of a minority have failed. Both the Commission on Human Rights and its Sub-Commission recognized already in 1954 that it was difficult, if not impossible, to group together under a generally satisfactory definition every minority group in need of special measures of protection. Capotorti concluded in 1977 that:

"At the present stage, it would be illusory to suppose that a definition likely to command general approval could be achieved."

Recently the Committee on Human Rights and its Sub-Commission on Prevention of Discrimination and Protection of Minorities have again intensified their attention to the problems of the protection of the rights of (persons belonging to) minorities. The Committee approved on February 21, 1992, a declaration on the rights of people belonging to national, ethnic, religious, and linguistic minorities[8] on which an informal open-ended working group had been working since 1978. At the same time it decided to discuss the item again at its next session with a view to considering measures to give effect to this declaration when adopted by the Economic and Social Council. However, as its title states, the declaration once again concerns the rights of individuals rather than groups.

More interesting from the point of view of this paper is a new approach by the Sub-Commission which was initiated in 1989. After another attempt to find a generally accepted definition of minorities had failed in 1985,[9] it decided to embark upon an examination of possible ways and means to facilitate the peaceful and constructive resolution of situations involving racial,[10] national, religious, and linguistic minorities. The emphasis would be on "the handling of minority situations in real life." The mandate therefore required "an examination of national experiences so as to construct models for peaceful and constructive solutions of minority situations." This examination clearly would include the rights of minorities as a group.[11] Mr. Asbjörn Eide of Norway was named rapporteur and he has already submitted two interesting progress reports. In the introduction of the first one he states inter alia:

> Minority situations frequently give rise to conflicts. It will often be impossible or undesirable to seek to "solve" the conflicts in the sense of making them disappear altogether. If that is sought they tend to reappear and often in more destructive forms. The task will rather be to find peaceful and constructive ways to manage the conflicts in cooperation with members of the minority and representatives of the State.

He then suggests that *art.* 27 of the Convenant on Civil and Political Rights constitutes a minimum which should be respected.[12]

This approach, it seems to me, is a promising one and could in time lead to ways and means to peacefully manage conflicts involving minorities. At the same time it must be conceded that this is a long-term approach and that a generally approved method of protecting the rights of minorities as a group is still far off.

No Protection of the Rights of Minorities as a Group

Thus there is presently no instance which could intervene in behalf of the rights of minorities as a group or in cases other than those of individual racial discrimination or violation of individual human rights.

In can be argued—and I would agree—that such an instance, e.g. a special U.N. committee on the protection of the rights of minorities, would not be able to function on a global scale, if only for the lack of a generally accepted definition of the concept of a "minority." I do not believe the situation in that respect has changed since the statement of the U.N. Subcommittee quoted above.

I believe therefore, that a possibility to create a better protection of the rights of minorities as a group exists only if the problem is approached on a regional scale. The problems of minorities vary too much from one region to the next to lend themselves to prescriptions of universal application. The only way out is to devise special measures for limited regions, perhaps even for separate groups.

Protection of the Rights of Minorities in Europe

While practically every region in the world has its own minority problems, the recent developments in Central and Eastern Europe have undoubtedly given them a special urgency for the old continent. Both the Council of Europe and the Conference on Security and Cooperation in Europe have given special attention to minorities during the last few years.

The Council of Europe

The council had already paid attention to minorities in the past. In its "European Convention for the Protection of Human Rights and Fundamental Freedoms" of November 4, 1950, *art. 14* states: "The enjoyment of the rights and freedoms set forth in this convention shall be secured without discrimination on any ground as...national or social origin, association with a national minority." This provision operates, of course, only within the context of the individual enjoyment of human rights.

Of more recent date is the work of the "European Commission for Democracy through Law" set up by resolution of the Committee of Ministers of the Council of Europe on May 10, 1990. The Commission believes that the drawing up of a binding European legal instrument would offer in the long run the best solution to the problem of minorities. It has drawn up a "set of principles" which could be incorporated in such a legal instrument.[13] It is an excellent document which, as far as I can see, covers practically all the rights a minority could desire. But this very fact makes it unlikely that a binding legal instrument on that basis will be accepted by all the countries involved in the near future. It should be noted that the members of the Commission acted in private capacity and emphasized themselves that their solution was for the long run.

The C.S.C.E.—The Second meeting of the Conference on the Human Dimension in Copenhagen

The organization which is in my opinion best suited to take more immediate action as regards to minority problems in Europe is the Conference on Security and Cooperation in Europe (CSCE). This conference has originally, like the U.N., treated minority questions under the heading of the protection of individual human rights. The first CSCE document accepted by the consensus of all participating States, the "Helsinki Final Act" of August 1, 1975, mentions national minorities in the "Declaration of Principles." However, the reference is to "persons belonging to minorities" rather than to minorities as a group.

The turning point came at the second meeting of the Conference on the Human Dimension of the CSCE, held in Copenhagen in June 1990. For the first time specific attention was paid to the protection of the rights of minorities as a group. The Dutch human rights expert Arie Bloed concludes that "the closing document of this meeting contains a number of agreements which are an important step forward on the difficult road to *communis opinio* about the status of national minorities in international law and relations."[14] At the same time he has to recognize that the language used is still full of escape clauses, as had been the custom in so many previous CSCE documents.

The beginning of paragraph 32 of the closing document sounds positive enough:

> The participating States will protect the ethnic, cultural, linguistic and religious identity of national minorities on their territory and create conditions for the protection of that identity. They will take the necessary measures to that effect after due consultations, including contacts with organizations or associations of such minorities...

Thus for the first time after the Second World War the protection of the identity of minorities as a group is mentioned in an agreed document, and not just that of people belonging to minorities. Moreover, there is recognition of the role of their own organizations which thereby obtain a status as the proper and accepted representatives of the group.

But then the escape clauses begin. The consultations with the organizations of the minorities have to be "in accordance with the decision-making procedures of each State." This is a very murky phrase, but at worst it could mean that the left hand takes back what the right hand has just given; if the "decision-making procedures" of the State in question do not include consultations with organizations of the minorities, such consultations might not have to be held. The paragraph continues with another caveat:

> Any such measure will be in conformity with the principle of equality and non-discrimination with respect to the other citizens of the participating State concerned.

That sounds fair enough, but it touches one of the most difficult problems with regard to the protection of the rights of minorities. The Secretary-General of the United Nations stated already in 1949 that: "Minorities...may desire positive support from the State in the preservation of their distinctive characteristics or partial of full autonomy..."[15] In other words,it may not be enough to grant a treatment to a minority equal to that of the majority. It may be necessary to give them, on a temporary or permanent basis, extra support to maintain their ethnic, linguistic or religious identity. This possibility seems to have been denied in the paragraph just quoted.

The Copenhagen meeting has also tried to address the difficult problem of the definition of a minority. It has not attempted a clear-cut definition, but approached the problem from a different angle by stating in paragraph 32 of the closing document:

> To belong to a national minority is a matter of a person's individual choice.

This is an important innovation and addition to international practice.

The Copenhagen meeting further recommended that a special meeting of experts be called to study in depth the problem of the protection of the rights of national minorities. That was done by the Summit meeting held in Paris in November 1990, which decided that a special "Meeting of Experts on National Minorities" would be held in Geneva in July 1991.

The Experts Meeting in Geneva 1991

The experts meeting discovered once again that a minority means something quite different from one state to the next, even within Europe. Greece, for instance, did not consider its Turkish speaking Muslim minority in Thrace a "National Minority" in the sense in which they understand that term,[16] fearing such recognition could lead to territorial claims. The U.S. continued to regard the problem of minorities mainly from the point of view of non-discrimination and assimilation—the melting pot. France continued its opposition to the notion of minorities as such. Since the French Revolution it believes the legal equality of all its citizens within the administrative unity of the State to be a "higher principle of law."[17]

No wonder that, while much was said about the rights of individuals belonging to minorities, little could be agreed upon with regards to improved protection of the rights of minorities as a group. Yet the following clause was accepted (as always in the CSCE, by consensus) in the final report of the meeting:

> Issues concerning national minorities, as well as compliance with international obligations and commitments concerning the rights of persons belonging to them, are matters of legitimate international concern and consequently do not constitute exclusively and internal affair of the respective State.[18]

The experts also followed the example of Mr. Eide and included in their final document an enumeration of measures already taken by various Participating States to protect the identity of national minorities and which could be helpful in improving the situation of national minorities on their territories. For the rest, the meeting limited itself to strengthening the commitments already undertaken in Copenhagen.

A New Netherlands Proposal in CSCE

The already mentioned CSCE-Summit in Paris also created several permanent structures for the CSCE which had up till then only been meeting regularly in various capitals. A permanent Secretariat was established in Prague, a Crisis Prevention Centre in Vienna and a Office for Elections in Warsaw. The latter was renamed Office for Democratic Institutions and Human Rights by the Ministerial Council held in Prague in January, 1992.

In that same Council the Minister of Foreign Affairs of the Netherlands, Mr. Hans van den Broek, made a new proposal regarding the protection of the rights of minorities as a group. He suggested that a CSCE High Commissioner for Minorities be appointed who could bring the plight of minorities to the attention of the Committee of Senior Officials of the CSCE and thus to that of the entire community. Mr. Van den Broek emphasized that such a Commissioner would *not* involve himself in a detailed examination of individual cases. He would be supported by the Office for Democratic institutions and Human Rights in Warsaw.

This is an interesting proposition. A CSCE High Commissioner could, it seems to me, fulfill some of the tasks which under the League system fell to the Head of the Minorities-Section of the League Secretariat. As we have seen, this section was assisting the members of the "Committees of Three" of the League Council who, in theory, were only charged with determining whether petitions were addressed to the Council could be received, but in fact could and did quietly discuss problems of minority rights with the governments involved, as well as with the representatives of the minorities themselves. In their name the Head of the Minorities-Section and his assistants could exercise a certain restraint over the governments through frequent visits and discussions.

The Netherlands proposal for a CSCE High Commissioner for Minorities (HCM) has been further developed and will be introduced at the CSCE Follow-up meeting held on March 24, 1992, in Helsinki. It is placed in the context of a search for ways for the CSCE to deal with ethnic tensions, such as "early warning" and "good offices."

Conclusion

The need to improve the protection of the rights of minorities in Europe is urgent. This is so not only because the human rights of millions of persons belonging to minorities are being or may be violated, but also because minority problems are one of the most serious causes of conflict, in particular in Central and Eastern Europe as the wars in former Yugoslavia have made all too clear.

Protection of only individual rights of persons in not sufficient for the great majority of the members of a minority. They consider themselves as a distinct group and want to maintain the identity of that group, all the more so if that identity is the same as that of the population of a neighboring country. That especially makes minority conflicts such an explosive issue. I very much agree with U.N. Rapporteur Eide when he says that it will often be impossible or undesirable to seek to "solve" those conflicts in the sense of making them disappear altogether. We should rather, as he states, try to find peaceful and constructive ways to manage them in cooperation with representatives of both the majority and the State involved, while of course keeping in mind the sovereign equality and the inviolability of the national unity and territorial integrity of States, as provided for in the U.N. Charter.

It is to be welcomed that the United Nations in the mandate given to Mr. Eide recently seems to have accepted at least the possibility of discussing measures to deal with minorities as a group, rather than with individuals only. The same can be said for the Council of Europe. However, in both cases not only a more or less binding text, but also the formation of any institutional body which could mediate in conflicts—or at least help to manage them—seems far off.

I believe that only the CSCE may be in a position to offer a quicker, if perhaps only a partial, solution by accepting the Netherlands proposal for a High Commissioner for Minorities. The return to the concept of an independent official who could quietly, but with a high international standing and the clout of threatening publicity behind him, try to resolve problems of the minorities in, especially, the newly emerging democracies in Central and Eastern Europe (and perhaps in the former Soviet Republics in Central Asia as well) is attractive. Such an official could contribute to a solution for one of the most dangerous legacies of the collapse of Marxism.[19]

Endnotes

1. Herman, Joost, "The Protection of Minorities in the League of Nations: Again Applicable?", in *Transaktie*, No.1, 1991, p.33.
2. Gütermann, Dr. Christoph, *Das Minderheitenschutzverfahren des Volkerbunds*, Duncker und Humblot, Berlin, 1979, p. 145.
3. Ibid., p. 148.
4. Bagley, T. H., *General Principles and Problems in the Protection of Minorities*, Imprimeries Populaires, Geneva, 1950, p. 126.
5. Herman, J., (op. cit., note 1).
6. Laroche, Josepha, *Les Minorités et Leurs Droits depuis 1789*, Paris, 1989. She adds: "L'individu est affirmé seul sujet de droit, comme si les garanties de 1789 suffisaient toujours et le génocide des juifs n'était qu'une parenthèse dans l'histoire."
7. *Study of the Legal Validity of the Undertakings Concerning Minorities* (E/CN.4/367 and Add.1), chapter 14.
8. U.N. Document, (E/CN.4/1992/L.11), p. 31.
9. Proposal by Mr. Jules Deschênes in U.N. Document (E/CN.4/Sub.2/1985/31).
10. Since shortly after World War II, the world "racial" to describe a minority had been dropped in favor of "ethnic" or "national." It reappears here for the first time.
11. Resolution of the Sub-Commission 1989/44.
12. U.N. Document (E/CN.4/Sub.2/1990/46).
13. See Annex III of U.N. Document (E/CN.4/Sub.2/1990/46) p. 20.
14. Bloed, A., *Netherlands Quarterly of Human Rights*, Vol. 8, 1990. p. 249.

15. Memorandum by the Secretary-General, Dec.27, 1949, p. 15.
16. Greece and several other countries maintain that "ethnic, linguistic or religious" minorities do not necessarily constitute "national" minorities and thereby limit the scope of the latter term. This interpretation was reluctantly accepted by the other participating States in order to obtain consensus on the final report. See: "Report of the CSCE Meeting of Experts on National Minorities," Geneva, 1991, paragraph II.
17. Daniel Luchack in *Les Minorités et Leurs Droits depuis 1789*, states flatly that the notion of a minority as a group is ignored in French law. The French Permanent Representative to the U.N. on September 16, 1976, wrote to the Director of the Division of Human Rights to the effect that the French people recongnized no distiction based on ethnic characteristics and thus ruled out any concept of minority.
18. Report of the CSCE-Meeting of Experts on National Minorities, Geneva, 1991, paragraph II.
19. Since this article was written, the proposal has been accepted and the first High Commissioner, the former Dutch Foreign Minister Max van der Stoel, appointed.

Asymmetrical Reciprocity in Market Exchange: Implications for Economies in Transition*

James M Buchanan
George Mason University

I. Introduction

Western visitors to those parts of the world that before 1991 were politically organized as the Soviet Union have been impressed by the attitudes of persons toward behavior in ordinary exchanges, attitudes that seem to be so different from those in Western economies. The essential elements of an "exchange culture" seem to be missing, and this absence, in itself, may be central to the effective functioning of market economies.[32] Individual participants in ordinary exchange relationships in Western economies act as if they understand the simplest of all economic principles, namely, that there are mutual gains from trade, that the benefits are reciprocal, that exchange is a positive-sum game. This "as if" understanding, which remains perhaps below our level of consciousness in the West, is largely missing from the public attitudes of citizens of the former Soviet Union, who behave as if the gains from trade do not exist, or at least are one-sided rather than mutual.

There is a familiar story that illustrates the thesis: "In the Soviet Union, both parties to an exchange lose; one party loses the goods; the other party loses the money." This statement may offer a concise, if exaggerated, summary of the general attitude toward exchange that seems to describe the behavior of many (of course, not all) persons in the republics that were formerly parts of the Soviet Union.

In this paper, I propose to build upon, to extend and, in part, to modify these arguments. I propose to offer an *economic* explanation for some of the differences in behavioral attitudes that we observe, as between Western economies and those of the Eurasian republics. In the West, with developed market systems, economists concentrate initial attention on the mutuality of trading gains and on the *reciprocity* in any exchange relationship. And a recognition of this reciprocity seems to inform public participation in markets. What is often overlooked is the asymmetry in the reciprocal relationship between buyer and seller in developed money economies. The buyer of goods and/or services who offers, or "sells," money in exchange possesses a bargaining advantage that is often overlooked. The central command economy reverses the direction of advantage, even when exchange dealings are permitted. The differences in the incentives that confront participants in the two organizational settings generate predictable differences in observed behavior and in behavioral attitudes.

I should stress at the outset that my focus is exclusively on the economic as opposed to the ideological sources of explanation of observed behavior in the exchange process. The ideological denigration of market exchange, as a general system of organizing economic relationships, may have exerted influences on individual behavior over and beyond those analyzed here. And, of course, at some higher system level where organizational-institutional decisions on structure were made, ideological motivation may explain why persons were confronted with the circumstances that contain divergent economic incentives.

In Section II, I shall introduce the formal analysis by reference to the workings of an idealized model of a barter economy in the absence of transactions costs. This model is introduced solely for the purpose of comparison with the workings of a money economy, still idealized, but as made minimally necessary by the presence of transactions costs. This second model is examined in Section III. In Section IV, I shall identify the asymmetry in the reciprocal exchange relationship, even in the idealized money economy, and I indicate observable features of Western economies that do not falsify the hypothesis that such an asymmetry exists. Section V takes the obvious next step and extends the analysis to the command economy that does not allow full scope for the operation of the institutions of market exchange. The results suggest that the behavioral roles of participants in such economies may become quite different from those in market cultures. In Section VI, I discuss some of the implications of the analysis for problems of transition from a command to a market structure.

II. Idealized Exchange – A Pure Barter Economy

Consider a setting in which the exchange process operates ideally in the analytical-conceptual sense and beyond any feasibility limits imposed by the limits to human capacities. Persons enter into exchange dealings, one with another, in the full knowledge of all potential trading opportunities. Further, the exchange network, the economy, is sufficiently large such that, for each and every buyer or seller in the market for each and every good or service, input or output, there exist large numbers of sellers or buyers, among whom any single buyer or seller may choose. Finally, there are no costs incurred by any buyer or seller in shifting custom from one alternative to another.

Note that, in such an idealized, zero-transactions-cost setting, no person, whether buyer or seller, in any exchange relationship secures any differential gain from exchanging with the single seller or buyer with whom a particular exchange is effectuated. Neither party's action, in making the particular cross market transfer, generates benefits for the other, for the simple reason that alternative buyers or sellers are available at no cost to whom trade may be shifted. The gain emerges, of course, as between any person, whether buyer or seller, and "the market," inclusively considered.

For my purpose, the noteworthy feature of this idealized model is the implied behavioral indifference that each participant in the exchange network will exhibit toward those with whom exchanges are made. In such a setting, nothing that might be called an "exchange culture" would have meaning. Each participant may, if he or she chooses, behave as if he or she exists in total independence of others, despite the complete interdependence among all persons who participate in the inclusive network. No buyer need invest any effort in persuading, cajoling, or convincing any seller to offer goods and services, and no seller, similarly, will find it rational to try to persuade any buyer to take his wares off the shelf. The reason is straightforward: there exists a sufficiently large number of alternative sellers or buyers to insure that, if one person does not trade, a replacement immediately appears to whom trade can be shifted and at no differential cost.

III. Idealized Exchange with Money

I now propose to modify the idealized exchange model described in Section II in only one respect. Assume, as before, that there are no costs of making exchanges, and that all participants have full knowledge about the qualities of goods. Further, assume, again as before, that the economy is large, and that there are many sellers and many buyers in the market for each good and service. Assume now, however, that there are limits to the knowledge that any participant has about the location of those persons in the economy who seek to purchase precisely the same good he or she seeks to sell, and *vice versa*. That is to say, direct barter is costly in the sense that each participant in a potential trade must undergo some search effort in locating the desired matching trading partner.

Recognition of the costs of search that make direct barter inefficient provides an economic explanation for the emergence of money, either in the form of some good that comes to be widely accepted as a medium of general exchange through some process of cultural evolution, or in the form of some good or some symbolic representation, the value of which is guaranteed by the collective body that protects private property, that is, by the state. The existence of money allows sellers to eliminate costly searches for other persons who are themselves sellers of goods that are desired in exchange. Similarly, money allows buyers to purchase goods that they desire without the necessity of searching for persons who seek to buy precisely that which they offer in exchange as sellers. The familiar metaphor that refers to money as the lubricant of the exchange system is helpfully explanatory.

Under the severely restrictive conditions assumed to exist, however, the behaviorally relevant conclusions reached above with reference to the idealized exchange economy seem to continue to hold. Since there are many buyers and many sellers in the markets for any good or service, any input or output, the individual participant need not be at all concerned about the person with whom an exchange is effectuated. The seller of red shoes need not invest in efforts to convince potential buyers to purchase his stocks since, by definition, there exist alternative buyers who will purchase the stocks and with no cost to the seller. Similarly, the buyer of red apples need not invest in attempts to persuade any single apple seller to offer his wares, since, again by definition, there exist many alternative apple sellers to whom the apple buyer may turn and without cost. There is no economic basis for the emergence of any attitude other than behavioral indifference toward specifically identified cross-exchange partners.

IV. Asymmetrical Reciprocity

The summary analysis of the preceding paragraph is, I submit, incorrect at worst and misleading at best. The introduction of money, even under idealized settings for the operation of an exchange economy, modifies the presumed anonymity, and consequent symmetry, in the pairwise buyer-seller relationship; and this modification has important behavioral implications.

Consider, again, the working properties of an idealized money economy. Figure 1 reproduces the familiar "wheel of income" diagram from introductory textbooks in economics. The individual at A, whom we may call A, who either possesses or produces a good or service (perhaps an input into some process) that is not desired for his own or internal use, enters one market as a seller of that good or service, which we may call X. If we ignore sequencing here, we can say that this individual simultaneously enters another market as a buyer of that good or service (or bundle of goods and services) that is desired for final end use; say this good or service is Y. The individual in question is a supplier of X and a demander of Y, in the two separated markets.

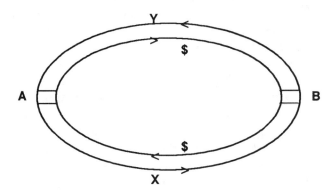

Figure 1

A person cannot, however, enter unilaterally in any market. The reciprocity relationship requires that each participant in an exchange enter simultaneously as buyer and seller. The individual identified above as the seller-supplier of X and the buyer-demander of Y enters the market for X and the market for Y in the necessary reciprocal positions as a buyer-demander of money (\$) in the X market, and a seller-supplier of money in the Y market. The generalized or fully fungible good, money, becomes the intermediate instrument of value that allows the individual entry into the two markets of his or her ultimate interest.

The asymmetry enters when we recognize that the money side of any exchange has an inherent "transactions costs" advantage, which in turn improves the "bargaining" power of the person who takes such a role. Consider, once again, a pure barter economy without money, but with some limits on knowledge. Clearly, the person who possesses or produces a good that is, relatively, more generally desired than others will find it less costly to effectuate exchanges for whatever good is ultimately desired. Money becomes the limiting case of a good that is generally desired by all participants in the exchange network, even if not intrinsically but instrumentally. The trader who accepts money for units of any nonmoney good or service secures a nonspecific medium of value that facilitates reentry into any market. The ideal fungibility of money gives the supplier-seller of money an asymmetrical claim to the gains from exchange. By the very definition of what money is, the possessor, and hence potential supplier, of money faces lower transactions costs in completing any exchange than the possessor, and potential supplier, of any nonmoney good or service. The fungibility of money provides the possessor with enhanced power to "walk away" from any exchange for goods and services, a power that the possessor of any nonmoney good or service simply does not have.

The basic asymmetry in the money-goods exchange is obscured by the proclivity of economic theorists to "define away" the features of the exchange process that are sometimes of most interest. As noted, if transactions costs are, literally, defined away, there would be no need for money at all; the pure barter economy would operate with ideal efficiency. When the rigorous assumptions required for the working of a pure barter economy are modified, however, and money is recognized to be an efficiency-enhancing institution, attempts are made to idealize the operations of the money economy by postulating that each and every buyer and seller, whether of goods or money, faces a sufficiently large number of cross-exchange options to guarantee that no person has market or exchange power, in the differential sense instanced above. Once transactions costs are introduced at all, however, there seems to be no plausibly acceptable logic for refusing to acknowledge differentials in "bargaining" advantages as between those persons who enter markets as suppliers-sellers of money and those who enter as demanders-buyers. To put the same proposition conversely, it is the demanders-buyers of goods and services that have an asymmetrical advantage over the suppliers-sellers, and in all markets.

As we move away from the abstracted models for the working of a production-exchange economy and toward a more descriptively satisfying appreciation of the economy as it actually seems to function, the basic asymmetry identified here may become painfully obvious, and my whole discussion may be taken to represent trituration. I suggest, however, that the money-goods asymmetry assists in an understanding of much of the behavior that we observe in developed economies, both historically and currently. The institutions of market exchange, as we know them, incorporate a recognition of this asymmetry, even to the extent that their familiarity breeds analytical oversight.

In markets as we know them, sellers of goods and services peddle their wares, advertise, create attractive displays, adopt attitudes of deferential demeanor toward potential buyers and behave, generally, as if their customers' interests are their own. "We aim to please" – this slogan describes the attitudes of those traders on the goods-and-services side of the goods-money exchanges, rather than *vice versa*. And we should find ourselves surprised if this behavior were absent. We do not observe buyers of goods and services setting up their own market stalls with signs that read "we buy apples," except in unusual circumstances. In product markets, we see some, but not much, buyer advertising. Potential buyers of goods and services apparently feel under no compulsion to act as if the interests of a seller are of relevance. Such buyers remain behaviorally indifferent toward the interests of any identified seller.[33]

The distinction between the two sides of the money-goods exchange stressed here does not depend on the pricing institutions that are in place. In developed economies, sellers tend to offer their wares to potential buyers at quasi-fixed prices, and the latter remain free to purchase varying quantities. In many developing economies, by contrast, sellers do not fix prices in advance, save as some preliminary move in what becomes a complex bargaining game with buyers. In both sets of pricing arrangements, however, we observe sellers-suppliers in the active roles of seekers for potential buyers and investors in efforts at persuasion, rather than the opposite.

The asymmetry stressed here is, of course, implicitly recognized in the usage of the term "consumers' sovereignty" to describe the exchange economy. This term, which might be better replaced by "buyers' sovereignty," suggests that sellers of goods and services, or suppliers, are, and must be, responsive to the interests of buyers, and, hence, that the latter are the ultimate sources of evaluation. Conventional discussion of the consumers' – sovereignty feature of market economies does not, however, take much note of the relevant behavioral implications.

An alternative way of discussing the asymmetry in the money-goods exchange relationship is to introduce the differential specificity of valued assets, as held by each party prior to exchange. Whether we analyze a pure exchange economy, in which persons commence with determinate endowments of goods, or a production-exchange economy, in which persons commence with endowments of talents that may be organized to produce goods, the potential supplier in any exchange for money is, by definition, locked in, relatively, by the specificity of the valued asset in possession, preexchange, and, for this reason, is more vulnerable to terms-of-trade manipulation than the potential cross-exchange demander, whose preexchange valued asset takes the form of money.[34]

V. Asymmetry Inversion in Command Economies

How would it be possible to remove or even to reverse the asymmetry in the basic exchange relationship in an economy? Reversion to a system of barter through some prohibition of a generalized money medium could remove the asymmetry here, but only at the expense of gross inefficiencies occasioned by the costs of search. In such an economy (one without money but with transactions costs) each market participant is both a buyer and a seller of goods (services), and there is no generalized advantage to either side of an exchange. As noted earlier, there would be particularized advantage to either the buyer or seller of the goods that are in relatively wider usage in the economy.

Let us consider, now, an economy in which money has been introduced, but where money is not, in itself, a sufficient medium to insure the effectuation of an exchange. Such an economy would be described by money prices for goods, but accompanied by some set of complementary nonmonetary "prices," or arrangements, that would be required to complete a transaction. The nominal money prices for goods and services would be politically established and at a level below those prices that would clear markets, that would equate demand and supply. Straightforward public-choice analysis of the incentives of persons in bureaucratic authority to set money prices suggests that such prices will remain always below market-clearing levels.[35] Bureaucrats lose any rationing authority if prices are set at market-clearing levels, and such authority is desired both for its own sake and as a source for the extraction of favors (rents). There will tend to exist excess demands for the supplies of goods brought forth in all markets. Each seller will tend to face more demanders for his or her product than can possibly be satisfied.

In such a setting, any reason that a seller-supplier might have for acting as if he or she is motivated by the interests of buyers is absent. Sellers will be behaviorally indifferent toward each and all potential buyers; they will have no incentive to please particular buyers, not even to the extent of providing quality merchandise, since there will always be buyers ready and willing to purchase whatever is made available to them.

Consider, by contrast, the behavioral stance of the participant who enters the exchange relationship as a potential buyer, who possesses a stock of money in the hope of securing goods and services. Each person in such a role will face the frustration experienced in an inability to get the goods in the quantities desired, and of the quality standards wanted. Buyers, with money, become the residual claimants to the gains from exchange, a role that is directly contrary to that which buyers occupy in the well-functioning money economy, as analyzed earlier. "Buyers' sovereignty," which was mentioned earlier as a shorthand description of the central feature of the exchange economy, is replaced by "sellers' sovereignty," provided we are careful to include within the "sellers" category those persons who hold bureaucratic authority to establish arrangements for nonprice rationing among demanders of goods and services.

In the command economy, as sketched out in capsule here, buyers of goods and services become the supplicants, who must curry favor with the sellers and their agents, who must, somehow, "aim to please," over and beyond some mere offer of generalized purchasing power in the form of money. Sellers remain indifferent to the pleas of buyers, and not only because of the excess number of demanders. Sellers also realize that if they exchange goods for money, they, too, must return to other markets as buyers, who must, in turn, expect to encounter the frustrations of buyers throughout the system.

The chronic "shortage" of goods that describe the workings of the command economy stems directly from the imposed politicization of money prices, as does the generalized supplication of buyers toward sellers-suppliers, including the relevant members of the bureaucratic apparatus. The institution of money, as such, is not allowed to serve its standard efficiency-enhancing function. The nonprice rationing arrangements, which emerge as supplementary to money prices, become analogous, in their economic effects, to the search costs that barter involves in the absence of money.

The command economy, with politicized money prices, along with supplementary rationing arrangements, will be characterized by a "money overhang," that is, by a supply of money that is in excess of that which is needed in exchange transactions, at the politically set money prices. Indeed, without such "money overhang" the authority that is exercised by the whole central price-setting regime loses its "bite." Unless potential consumers-buyers are provided with more money (through wage payments) than they can spend on products, at the controlled prices, the authority of bureaucrats to ration scarce supplies becomes unnecessary. This excess money supply, in its turn, sets up additional incentives for the emergence of exchange transactions that are outside the boundaries of legitimacy in some formal sense. Black, shadow or underground markets will emerge more readily when persons are unable to satisfy their demands for goods through standard exchange channels and when they have available, at the same time, unused and unusable stocks of money. As this shadow sector increases in size over time, as measured either by the volume of transactions or by the number of participants, the behavioral norms that describe the operation of the whole legal order must be undermined.

The fact that money is not allowed fully to perform its efficiency-enhancing role in the economy must also set in motion evolutionary pressures toward the emergence of some good that will secure general acceptability as "real money," quite distinct from the money issued by the state monopoly. In Russia, and in other former socialist economies, the currency of developed nations (dollars, marks, Swiss francs) has emerged to fill this role, at least in part. And, in the shadow exchanges between these monies and goods, the asymmetry observed in Western economies is partially restored. Sellers of goods do, indeed, seek out and court potential buyers who are thought to possess hard currencies.

This transitional stage aside, however, the point to be emphasized is that, in the command economy, as it traditionally functions, the whole economic culture is dramatically different from that which we observe in Western market economies. The near-total absence of seller-supplier efforts to attract custom and to please potential buyers shocks Western observers who visit the territories of the former Soviet Union. The paucity of billboards in the Moscow of 1990 was not primarily attributable to regulatory prohibition. This result emerged directly from the fact that no seller-supplier of any good or service felt any economic pressure to respond to customer interests or to expand the demands for product. The sales clerk at the kiosk, as a selling agent, behaved very differently from her Western counterpart, but not because of ethnic origins; she behaved differently because in the Russian mindset that permeates the citizenry generally, the seller-purveyor of goods need not be concerned about customers.

The Russian visitor to the United States is equally surprised when the behavior of sellers-suppliers is observed, both directly and indirectly. Such a visitor is overwhelmed by the neon blazes, by multicolored billboards, slick magazine pages and the TV commercials, as well as behaviorally by the stance of those persons who act as agents for suppliers of almost all goods and services. Coming out of an economic culture where buyers are the universal supplicants, the Russian visitor stands aghast at the supplication of sellers and their agents. Neither this Russian visitor nor his American counterpart in Moscow understands that the dramatic differences in the two cultures can be explained, at least in large part, by variations in the incentive structures. The American setting allows the asymmetry in the money-goods exchange relationship to be played out fully in the development and operation of its market institutions. The Soviet Union, by contrast, attempted, throughout its existence, to counter this asymmetry by the politicization of money prices, with an acknowledged major increase in the costs of making transactions, but also with the unrecognized impetus given to the emergence and operation of an economic culture that must be subversive in any effort to move toward the market structure.

VI. Implications for the Transition from a Command to a Market Economy

This paper is not presented as a contribution to the explanation of the operation of either an exchange (market) economy, or a command (socialized) economy. My emphasis is on and my interest is in the behavioral differences that the separate systems tend to motivate and to accentuate, differences that are readily observable, and on the implications of these differences for the problems of transition from a command to a market economy, the transition that the countries of Central and Eastern Europe now face.

In my earlier paper (see footnote 1), I concentrated attention on the apparent failure of participants in the socialist economy to recognize the reciprocal nature of the exchange relationship and the presence of mutuality of gain to all parties. I did not, of course, suggest that participants in the developed market economies of the West explicitly understand even this most elementary principle of economics and that a comparable understanding was missing in the command economies. I did suggest, however, that the basic principle of reciprocal exchange had come to inform the consciousness of many persons in Western economies, even if there seems to be little or no articulation of such a principle within the range of ordinary competence.

In that paper, which was advanced only in an exploratory fashion, as is this one, I attributed the absence of such an "exchange mentality" or mindset to the conjectural history that persons accept as descriptive of their social development. I suggested that in Western societies, and especially in the United States, the central notion of gains-from-trade emerges naturally from a historical imagination that traces economic and social development from family independence and self-sufficiency (the frontier homestead) through stages of increasing interdependence as specialization proceeds, always accompanied by increasing standards of living. In this imagined history, however, the exit option, the potential for withdrawal into independence, remains at the back edge of understanding and interpretation, thereby insuring that the expansion of trade and exchange must enhance well-being for all members of the society.

I suggested that participants in the former Soviet economy carried with them no such historical imagination of economic development, and that there was no comparable conjectural history of self-sufficient independence from which the economy emerged. Instead, cooperation was always imagined, not as achievement of mutual gains through exchange, but as taking place within a collective-community enterprise. Individual cooperative behavior, even as idealized, was modeled exclusively as the fulfilling of tasks assigned in a collective endeavor, assigned by some command authority. When I sketched the elements of my analysis to a Russian intellectual, he aptly described, and accepted, the thesis as, "the Russians are natural slaves; the Yankees are natural traders."

I see no reason to back off from or to withdraw the arguments made in my earlier paper; I remain convinced that the analysis contributes to an understanding of some of the difficulties in making the transition from a command to a market economy. I now think, however, that the arguments advanced in this paper supplement and extend those of the earlier paper usefully, and allow me to offer an economic explanation of some of the apparent differences in mindsets that need not be so critically dependent on a presumed divergence in historical imaginations. The importance of historical imagination may have been exerted at a more fundamental level than that discussed in the earlier paper. An imagination that is grounded on the liberty and independence of individual families might have proved a formidable barrier against collectivization of the economy. A "socialized United States" may never have been within the realm of the possible. History, and the historical imagination that it shapes, matters. And different national experiences may affect the feasibility of adaptation to different organizational structures. In the view of many observers, Poland's role in the revolution against the Communist regime was due, in part, to the historical position of the Catholic Church.

The possible oversight of the earlier treatment lay in my failure to appreciate that the "exchange mentality" that I took to be descriptive of Western attitudes toward markets generally, is manifested largely, even if not exclusively, in the observed activities of those who find themselves in roles as sellers-suppliers (or their agents) of goods and services, and that their behavior finds its origins, at least in part, in the asymmetry of the goods-money exchange. Conversely, I generalized the behavioral indifference of sellers or selling agents in the former Soviet Union to the whole culture, without noting that the structure within which exchanges takes place removes incentives for sellers to behave in ways comparable to their Western counterparts.

Entrepreneurial or leadership roles in implementing exchanges-transfers of valued goods among persons and units in the command-control economics have been taken by those persons who possess differential access to nonmoney means of influencing choices, through personalized relationships, through extra-market barter arrangements, through sublegal bribes, payoffs, kickbacks. In other words, the entrepreneurial talents that have been rewarded in the command economy, as it operated, were those of the "fixers" rather than those which might have represented some differential ability to recognize latent demand in nonexisting goods and to design and organize the production of such goods in response to such demand. In other words, there was little or no supply-side entrepreneurship, as such, in dramatic contrast with Western-style capitalist economies, where, at least in principle, such entrepreneurship should remain a dominant feature.

The entrepreneurship manifested in the activities of the "fixers" is not, of course, absent from Western economies, especially as these economies have developed to include large and rapidly growing socialized or public sectors. As governments have grown, in all dimensions, over the course of the century, there has been the developing recognition that private profits may be located in the exploitation of public as well as private opportunities.[36] Entrepreneurs who seek to capture the rents created by the artificially contrived scarcities stemming from politicized economic regulation, sometimes called "rent-seekers," are behaviorally similar to those that emerge in the more pervasive regulatory structure of command economies. We need only point to the thousands of lawyer-lobbyists whose activity consists exclusively in exploiting loopholes in the complexities of tax law and in seeking the creation of still further loopholes through new legislative changes.

The unanswered empirical question is whether or not the scarce set of entrepreneurial talents is generalizable over the two quite distinct roles. And the answer here will be critical for the problems of transition. Is a successful rent-seeker, who has demonstrated an adeptness at implementing value transfers in a regulated-politicized setting, likely to be equally successful when, as and if the incentive structure shifts and success requires that attention be paid to organizing production to meet demands of consumers? Or do the distinct entrepreneurial roles require quite divergent talents? These questions stand as a challenge to my economist peers who place their primary reliance on direct empirical results.

My own intuition-interpretation suggests that the experience of the command economy, in which there has been little or no differential reward offered for supply-side creativity, will exert relatively long-lasting effects, and that the transition to a market economy will be made more difficult because of this absence of an entrepreneurial tradition. Those persons who have been skillful in responding to the disequilibria of the command structure may find the switch to the new role beyond their limits.

Entrepreneurs are, of course, emerging in the transition economies. Both those who were and might have been the "fixers" and those who held positions of bureaucratic authority are moving to take advantage of the opportunities opened up by institutional changes. The question is not so much whether entrepreneurship will emerge as whether that which does emerge will prove sufficiently creative to stimulate the impoverished and sluggish economies in ways that may prove necessary to insure that the revolution's ultimate result will be positive.

A useful distinction may be made at this point between the Kirznerian and the Schumpeterian definitions of entrepreneurship, a distinction that has been the source of longstanding debates within the subdiscipline of Austrian economics. Israel Kirzner, who has long stressed the importance of the entrepreneurial function in an economy, models the entrepreneur as responding to disequilibria, essentially as an arbitrageur, who locates and exploits disparities in potential exchange values as among separate locations, persons and production opportunities.[37] In this conceptualization of the entrepreneurial role, there should be relatively little difficulty encountered in transforming the "fixer" of the command economy into the equilibrating supply-side organizer of production and distribution in the operative market economy. By contrast, Joseph Schumpeter models the entrepreneur as a disequilibrating force, as a creator of destruction to established ways of doing things, as a disrupter of existing and predicted channels of exchange.[38] In this conceptualization, the supply-side entrepreneur acts quite differently from the arbitrageur, even if the latter is defined in the broadest possible terms. The entrepreneur creates that which does not exist independently of his or her action. To the extent that the ongoing market or capitalist economy is understood to be progressively created by Schumpeterian entrepreneurs, there can be no easy transition from the command system, quite independently from the institutional reforms that may be put in place.

Both types of entrepreneur can coexist as highly productive contributors to the successful transition toward market economies and to the growth of such economies, once established. In my own view, the supply-side or Schumpeterian entrepreneur is unlikely to become dominant in the economies that are now in transition. And, indeed, such entrepreneurs may have almost disappeared in Western economies. In this perspective, while successful transition to a market economy is possible for the former command systems, there will be no *Wirtschaftswunder* (economic miracle) in the near term, East or West.

Endnotes

*I am indebted to my colleague, Roger Congleton, for helpful discussions.

A modified version of this paper was published under the same title in *Social Philosophy & Policy* 10(No. 2, June 1993): 51–64 which was also published in *Liberalism and the Economic Order*, ed. Ellen Frankel Paul, Fred D. Miller, Jr. and Jeffrey Paul (Cambridge: Cambridge University Press, 1993), 51–64.

1. James M. Buchanan, "Tacit Presuppositions of Political Economy: Implications for Societies in Transition," (George Mason University, Fairfax, VA: Center for Study of Public Choice, 1991), mimeograph. The present essay builds on, extends and modifies the argumens of this earlier paper.

2. Labor markets may seem to offer an exception to the generalizations suggested here. The absence of homogeneity among separate units demanded may offset, or even reverse, the direction of effect emphasized here generally.

3. The relationship between differential asset specificity as between parties to contract, and the vulnerability to opportunistic behavior, has been discussed by Armen Alchian and Susan Woodward, "Reflections on the Theory of the Firm," *Journal of Institutional Theoretical Economics (Z. Ges. Staatswiss.)*, vol. 143, no. 1 (1987), pp. 110–37. More generally, economists have analyzed the effects of asymmetric information in the operation of exchange. The pioneer in these efforts was George Akerlof, "The Market for 'Lemons': Quality Uncertainty and the Market Mechanism," *The Quarterly Journal of Economics*, vol. 84, (August 1970), pp. 488–500.

4. David Levy, "The Bias in Centrally Planned Prices," *Public Choice*, no. 67, vol. 2 (November 1990), pp. 213–26.

5. For a generalized discussion, see James M. Buchanan, Robert D. Tollison and Tullock, eds., *Toward a Theory of the Rent-Seeking Society* (College Station: Texas A & M University Press, 1980) and especially my introductory paper (1991).

6. Israel Kirzner, *Competition and Entrepreneurship* (Chicago: University of Chicago Press, 1973).

7. Joseph A. Schumpeter, *Theorie der wirtschaftlichen Entwicklung* (Leipzig, 1912); English translation, *Theory of Economic Development* (Cambridge: Harvard University Press, 1934).

Conservative Political Philosophy and the Strategy of Economic Transition[1]

Peter Murrell
Fellow Woodrow Wilson International Center for Scholars
and
University of Maryland

1. Introduction

Social science, especially economics, does not center its efforts on the processes of socioeconomic change. The concern within economics has been traditionally on end points: how to achieve the first-best Pareto efficient outcome, rather than deciding which problem to solve first; the implications of behavior under rational expectations, rather than the study of learning processes. This lack of emphasis on change has become increasingly apparent as scholars apply existing theories to the most momentous economic changes of our times—the Eastern European economic revolutions.

There are a few scholarly traditions that have placed the analysis of change at the center of concern.[2] Important among these is a set of works that might be grouped under the rubric "conservative political philosophy" or, perhaps more appropriately in the present context, "principle of democratic social reconstruction."[3] The leading works in this genre are Burke, Popper, and Oakeshott.[4] In this essay, I examine the lessons of conservative political philosophy for the process of economic change in Eastern Europe.

The following two sections lay out the central assumptions of philosophical conservatism and explore the important distinction, due to Popper, between utopian and piecemeal social engineering. Sections four and five use this distinction to examine policies for the Eastern European economic transition in two important areas: the place of workers' management in the transition and the relative properties of large scale and small scale privatization. The analyses of these two policy areas are provided as examples of the application of the conservative philosophy of reform, which can in principle be brought to bear on all the major policy decisions in the economic transition from socialism.

2. Assumptions

A central concern of conservative political philosophy is the way in which societies use the knowledge that is available to them. This concern arises most notably from two inter-related assumptions. First, there is the view that a large part of socially useful knowledge is acquired in the context of the prevailing set of socioeconomic arrangements and is usable only in a narrow domain of that set. Second, there is the hardly controversial notion that politico-economic systems are vastly complicated constructs, especially when viewed in the light of limits on human intellectual capacities. These concerns run through the discussion that follows and are elaborated in the context of that discussion.

In almost all societies, the socioeconomic framework has been built up in a gradual process of accumulating small changes.[5] As each new institution arises, it is fitted into a larger pre-existing structure. Therefore, the effectiveness of each piece of the socioeconomic structure is deeply dependent on the existence of a network of institutions. The functioning of each institution cannot be understood as an isolated phenomenon, but only in the context of the particular set of working arrangements in which that institution sits. One might be able to understand and predict the effects of small changes or the marginal consequences of the presence or absence of a particular institution. However, one cannot hope to break down the major elements of a society's socioeconomic processes into separate components and then understand how the whole society works (at least at the present stage of the development of social science).

A society's institutional structure is an organic whole—the result, in successful societies, of a long historical process. The human capacity for understanding is small in relation to the complexity of such organisms. Therefore, in political matter, "we can never walk surely but by being sensible for our blindness."[6] Or, according to Popper, "It is not reasonable to assume that a complete reconstruction of our social system would lead at once to a workable system."[7]

Thus, there is at the center of conservatism an extreme skepticism concerning the workability of any blueprint for a new society. Implicit in this view is the assumption that a vast number of rearrangements of society's institutions would produce worse outcomes than those that presently exist, while only a few would result in improvement. Moreover, since the present state of knowledge on socioeconomic processes is so limited, policy-makers have not been able to discriminate between workable and disastrous theoretical blueprints for new social systems. This might be called the "bad bet" argument against radical change. (But not, as we will see, against change.)

The preceding argument requires the assumption that the existing structure of society has been built by a process that selects those arrangements that, at least partially, take into account social welfare. If today's arrangements are randomly chosen—or worse, inimical to welfare—then a bad bet on a new blueprint might still be one that is worth taking. But this is a minimal requirement. This assumption does not imply that the present arrangements are anywhere near first best; the insistence is solely on some attention to human welfare in existing arrangements. For reasons discussed in the following paragraphs, this minimal amount of attention to the functional needs of society is unlikely to be present in a society that results from the implementation of a blueprint.

A distinct, but related, argument for conservative change begins with observations on the nature of a society's stock of knowledge and especially on the association between this knowledge and existing socioeconomic arrangements. Following Oakeshott,[8] one might distinguish between two types of knowledge.[9] The first is a technical knowledge, the set of explicit rules and articulatable procedures that are used in undertaking an activity. This is the type of knowledge that can be conveyed by lecturers and systematized in textbooks. It is the type of knowledge that knows no borders and no boundaries.

In contrast, one has practical, or personal, knowledge, although this term should not be allowed to evoke the mundane. Practical knowledge is that inarticulate knowledge that is required in the effective performance of any activity and that can be acquired only by direct acquaintance with the activity. It is the knowledge of the scientist who has an instinct for the correct experiment to make; it is the knowledge of the experienced businessman who senses opportunities through a cloud of disparate facts. Because personal knowledge is acquired through activity, it is inherently specific to particular contexts. It can only be communicated between individuals by joint sharing of experience and activity, as, for example, in apprenticeship.

All activities—whether science, art, politics, or economic policy-making—use both types of knowledge. To the extent that one type of knowledge is missing or inappropriate, the resulting outcome will be that much poorer. This point is hardly worth stating for the first type of knowledge; we all know, for example, that it would be inadvisable to have judges and lawyers who have not studied the legal code. But the value of the second type of knowledge is often overlooked. It is frequently suggested, for example, that legal codes can be transferred between countries, replacing existing codes and practices wholesale. What this suggestion fails to recognize is the practical knowledge that is essential to the interpretation and use of a legal code. Without this practical knowledge, which only exists in the working arrangement of a set of lawyers and judges, there is no reason to suppose that the transplanted legal code will have positive value.

Practical knowledge—of an economy, of legal arrangements, of a political system—is always acquired in a particular institutional context. Hence, the knowledge possessed by a society is most fully applicable within that society's present context. Practical knowledge loses much of its value when applied far from the framework of activity in which it was acquired. It is hardly likely to be productive in deliberating on the consequences of implementing some radial blueprint for a new society.[10]

Recognition of the existence of personal knowledge suggests that the productivity of small changes will be much greater than that of large changes. The ability of policy-makers to identify good policies decreases rapidly as those policies move society further from its existing position. Moreover, the nature of personal knowledge suggests that societies cannot quickly acquire the knowledge required to implement a blueprint. Many years of practice and, in the meantime, poor and very costly decisions are required to acquire the practical knowledge that is needed if the blueprint is to be implemented.[11] Thus we have reached a second argument for conservative change—this might be called the "use of knowledge" argument.

3. Utopian and Piecemeal Policies

In order to draw out the implications of the forgoing, it is useful to employ a distinction drawn by Popper between Utopian and Piecemeal social engineering.[12] Although the distinction is somewhat strained, it is apposite for expositional purposes in the present context. As with many artificial dichotomies that are useful for expository purposes, the contrast is really between the two extremes of a continuum, rather than between the only two possibilities.

Utopian social engineering begins most often with a radical critique of the existing arrangements of society, a denial that there is anything worth preserving in these arrangements, and a picture of what a better world would be like. The driving force of utopian policies is a blueprint of the end state of society, which usually has little in common with present arrangements. Policy measures en route are always framed in terms of this destination, rather than as departures from the initial situation, which contains nothing of worth. Since the existing institutions of society are so different from, so incompatible with, those that are in the target blueprint, and since these existing institutions are presumed to have no value, the initial phases of utopian engineering always center more on destruction than creation.[13]

Of course, there will be some institutional construction that can be done at the beginning of reform. However, the sheer complexity of creating workable social arrangements argues that the whole blueprint cannot be created quickly. Moreover, implementation of the blueprint is in principle impossible due to the inevitable inaccuracy and imprecision of the blueprint that exists for the epistemic reasons outlined above. Hence, those positive measures that occur in the early phases of a utopian project will inevitably involve planting in place one of the pieces of the blueprint jigsaw, even though the remaining pieces are nowhere to be found quite yet.[14]

The emphasis on the final destination and the willingness to throw away existing arrangements both lead to policies that are inevitably irreversible. In the utopian approach, reversible policies are harmful. For those with faith in the blueprint and the ability of a society to implement it, the tenacity of the old, together with its intrinsic worthlessness, mean that irreversible polices have much benefit. Policy-makers must ensure that society can never go back because that isolated island in the storm is simply a temptation not to advance to more fertile shores.

Given the view of knowledge described in the previous section, it is easy to see why a conservative perceives grave dangers in the utopian approach to social change. The "use of knowledge" argument stresses that a radical move destroys much of the valuable knowledge in society. Practical knowledge, dependent as it is on a specific configuration of society's arrangements, is only useful for judging the effects of small changes. Hence, individual policy-makers will have little ability to construct new arrangements that will lead society reliably to the destination laid out in the blueprint.[15] In the process of trying to get to the destination quickly, one destroys the knowledge of how to get there certainly. Then the "bad bet" assumption becomes relevant—unanticipated consequences become a major determinant of the outcome and there is every probability of finishing up in a worse position than at present.

The foregoing critique of the utopian approach can be challenged, of course, by denying its central assumptions. The following seem the most important criticisms:

1. One might argue—and this is heard frequently in the Eastern European context—that existing arrangements really have one utility (presumably compared to those that can be easily established at the beginning of a move to a final blueprint). This is also an argument that was made very strongly by socialist revolutionaries in the early part of this century.

2. It might be claimed that we really do have a good understanding of how societies work and that this understanding is relevant outside the specific historical context in which it was acquired. In the present context, this means that economists really do know how capitalist societies work and that this knowledge is relevant outside developed capitalist countries. Keynesian economists—the majority in the 1960s—of course frequently used this argument against their conservative critics.

3. These understandings can be communicated quickly to the policy-makers who will be implementing the new policies. In the present context, Eastern European banking officials, legislators, politicians, etc., can be relied upon to acquire quickly the skills that are relevant to their new roles in the market economy.

Suppose, however, that one believes that these three claims are incorrect. Utopian social engineering will then be, at best, unproductive and, at worst, thoroughly dangerous. What alternatives are there? Popper advocates piecemeal social engineering.[16] In this approach to "democratic social reconstruction," the emphasis is not on a blueprint for the state, but rather upon identifying the worst problems of the existing set of arrangements. Intellectual efforts are primarily focused on solving these problems in the specific institutional context in which the solutions will be implemented.

Piecemeal social engineering places an emphasis on reversible changes, insofar as these are possible, since one cannot necessarily expect society's limited knowledge of socioeconomic processes to produce even small changes that are necessarily beneficial. Finally, there is a preference for replicating policies that have been used in a similar institutional context or widening the scope of experiments that have worked on a smaller scale within the existing system.[17] The risks in the introduction of the new are then minimized.

The emphasis is on gradual change for a variety of reasons. First, the larger the number of institutional changes that are implemented simultaneously, the harder it is to design a workable set of arrangements. Second, reversibility is enhanced by making changes slowly. Bad policies can be stopped midstream. Third, with gradual change, society can accumulate practical knowledge of the new arrangements as this knowledge is needed. There is a change to experiment on a smaller scale and to provide usable feedback to which policies work and which do not.

The arguments encapsulated above in the distinction between utopian and piecemeal engineering are summarized in Table 1. These arguments for gradual change are offered in the present context not with any sense that they are obviously correct, but rather with the suggestion that they are worth considering in the context of the massive changes in Eastern

Table 1: Characteristics of Utopian Piecemeal Approaches to Policy

Utopian	*Piecemeal*
1. *End Point Driven.* Choice of initial policy determined by the goal for the final outcome of the process.	1. *Focus on Immediate Problem.* Identifies worst problems, trying to solve them largely ignoring the effects of today's decisions on some long run equilibrium.
2. *Clean the Slate.* Emphasizes inter-relatedness of society's problems and therefore the need to make a decisive break with the past, with the necessity of institutional destruction in the first stages.	2. *Use Existing Institutions.* Recognizes that new structures can be created only slowly and accepts that existing institutions are usually better than either none or hastily constructed alternatives.
3. *Large Leaps.* To make a decisive break from the constraints of the past, advocates bold policy steps that involve packages of many new institutions.	3. *Small Steps.* Emphasizes the risks from going too fast and the impossibility of successfully creating a network in inter-related institutions anew.
4. *Faith in the New.* Willingness to trust in theoretical reasoning as the primary input for the design of society's new arrangements.	4. *Skepticism.* Search for existing models and methods to help in the formulation of institutional changes.
5. *Irreversibility.* In the weak form, willingness to accept large irreversible changes. In the strong form, emphasized the need for them.	5. *Reversibility.* Advocates policies that facilitate feedback on their effects and that can be stopped or even reversed.
6. *Design and Theory.* The most important intellectual resource for policy-makers is the knowledge held by theoreticians and technocrats.	6. *Judgment and Practice.* The most important intellectual resource is the practical experience accumulated in the context of a particular set of institutional arrangements.

Europe. They do derive from an important tradition—one that has given insights into the problems caused by massive socioeconomic changes in the past.

Perhaps the best capsule summary of the arguments offered above is provided by Oakeshott. He lists the implications of the conservative temperament for matters of innovation and change:

> First, innovation entails certain loss and possible gain, therefore, the onus of proof, to show that the proposed change may be expected to be on the whole beneficial, rests with the would-be innovator. Secondly, [the man of conservative temperament] believes that the more closely an innovation resembles growth (that is, the more clearly it is intimated in and not merely imposed upon the situation) the less likely it is to result in a preponderance of loss. Thirdly, he thinks that an innovation which is a response to some specific defect, one designed to redress some specific disequilbrium, is more desirable than on which springs from a notion of a generally improved condition of human circumstances, and is far more desirable than one generated by a vision of perfection. Consequently, he prefers small and limited innovations to large and indefinite. Fourthly, he favors a slow rather than a rapid pace, and paused to observe current consequences and make appropriate adjustments. And lastly, he believes the occasion to be important; and, other things being equal, he considers the most favorable occasion for innovation to be when the projected change is most likely to be limited to what is intended and least likely to be corrupted by undesired and unmanageable consequences.[18]

This summary leads us to one final observation, that the term "conservative" is much misused in many parts of the reforming socialist world. This term does not denote those who are against change *per se*, as seems to be assumed in the Soviet Union. Nor does the term denote those who advocate radical measures to implement capitalism overnight, as is the case in Czechoslovakia, for conservatism eschews ideological blueprints. Nor is there any necessary association between conservatism and the various positions that one might take on such matters as the appropriate size of government, or, for example, the role for income redistribution. One can be a 'liberal' in the American sense or a 'liberal' in the European sense and still be a conservative. For conservatism is about how societies should change, not about where they should finish up.

The importance of the above discussion in the context of deliberations on East European economic policy should be obvious. In the remainder of the paper, I give examples of the application of the conservative outlook for present policy debates in Eastern Europe. The two examples focus on the role of workers' management in the transition and the types of privatization schemes that are being implemented.

3. On Piecemeal Privatization Versus Mass Privatization

There seem to be two basic models for the privatization of large state enterprises in Eastern Europe.[19] The first model is one of a variety of piecemeal actions. This involves waiting for groups of interested parties to arise with sufficient funds; seeking out foreign buyers; constructing ad hoc lease-purchase arrangements; and perhaps giving away some enterprises when there is only one potential "buyer" at a zero price. Above all, this approach to privatization is signified by patience, a heavy emphasis on traditional forms of the market mechanism to exchange ownership rights, and the search for traditional types of owners. These three features are of course interrelated. The need to wait arises from the search for a variety of arrangements for privatization, each identifying a buyer willing to risk his or her own resources in undertaking ownership.

The alternative model stresses the need for speed. Speed implies that a large number of privatizations be carried out simultaneously using a single method. Because privatization on such a mass scale has not been accomplished before, this method requires the creation of wholly new procedures and institutions (voucher trading schemes, new mutual funds, etc.) It must be stressed not only that these institutions and procedures are new to the country in question, but also that there are not close models from other countries on which to base their design. Hence, the foundation of the mass privatization method is pure theory. The builders of the huge institutional structure are primarily technocrats, whose stake in this process is necessarily trivial compared to the amount of resources that their schemes affect. In contrast to the usual mechanism of markets or pluralistic democracies, the mass of the population and important economic interests have limited influence on this process.

The critique of the two methods of privatization is transparent once one combines the few details given in the last two paragraphs with the analysis provided in Sections two and three. There is no need here to provide that critique in detail. Rather, it is given in summary by using the structure of Table 1 to contrast the two schemes. The resultant comparison is provided in Table 2.

Table 2: Characteristics of Two Privatization Approaches

Large Scale	Gradual, Ad Hoc
1. *End Point Driven.* Attempt at immediate implementation of ultimate goal of reform—capitalist economy.	1. *Focus on Immediate Problem.* Unclear property rights can be solved without immediate privatization; solution to lack of competition necessarily lies outside the existing enterprise structure (in the creation of an environment where entry of new firms is easy.)
2. *Clean the Slate.* As soon as possible, erase all non-capitalist ownership forms.	2. *Use Existing Institutions.* Validate and strengthen some existing property rights; rely on state control during the lengthy period before all enterprises can be privatized.
3. *Large Leaps.* Many privatizations handled simultaneously.	3. *Small Steps.* Each privatization is an individual decision involving different actors.
4. *Faith in the New.* Theoretical reasoning establishes the nature of the voucher schemes, the new forms of mutual funds, and new managerial incentive schemes.	4. *Skepticism.* Rely on the tried and tested features of market processes.
5. *Irreversibility.* Once the scheme is launched new property rights are issued, the revocation of which would destroy the whole reform.	5. *Reversibility.* Each separate privatization is, of course, not reversible. However, the general policy can be amended and changed easily.
6. *Design and Theory.* Relies on the skills of technocrats and standard intellectual approaches for the design of new institutions.	6. *Judgment and Practice.* Uses decentralized judgments of many participants on the forms and scale of privatization and the post privatization structure of ownership and corporate control.

5. On Worker's Management in the Transition

It is common to find the argument that there cannot be a third way—between capitalism and socialism—in the transition. Most notably this argument is targeted at those who advocate some form of worker's ownership of enterprises during the transition to a market economy. This argument is ultimately end point based. When emanating from Western economists, it is usually driven by two familiar pieces of logic. The first is the theoretical analysis that implies that several perversities result for workers' ownership in a competitive economy. The second element in the argument is the observation that there are few successful economies in which workers' management has been prominent. Given that this ownership form was perfectly legal in most developed economies, its lack of use shows its inefficiency.

I do not take issue with either the theory in the first line of argument or the empirical interpretation in the second. Moreover, I would agree that these arguments, especially the second, imply that it is unlikely that there will be worker's management at the end of a very long transition. But, as one should guess from the previous discussion, this does not mean that these two pieces of logic sustain the conclusion that worker's management cannot begin the transition. This conclusion relies too much on the notion that initial policies should be guided by the target blueprint, the utopian view.

The piecemeal approach would first ask a series of questions about the importance of worker's management in the economy undergoing reform. It would ascertain whether the principle of worker's management, and its organizational embodiment, is a deep part of the country's tradition. If the answer to that question is in the affirmative, then the short-term productivity of society's practical knowledge will be intimately tied to the continuation of workers, management. In such a situation, the knowledge of how to organize enterprises is contingent on the existence of workers' management, as is the intuitive knowledge that policy-makers possess about the economy's responses to exogenous events and to policy changes. A quick move away from workers' management would destroy this practical knowledge, which cannot be replaced by even the instantaneous and complete acquisition of formal knowledge of the new system. Consequently, the productivity of enterprises and the effectiveness of policy-makers would be reduced to some large degree by the destruction of an existing system of workers' management.

In those society's in which workers' management is important, the piecemeal approach would then seek to determine whether workers' management is the principal cause of the society's problems. Such a determination could not rely on theoretical strictures concerning the behavior of a worker-managed economy compared to an idealized system, since that idealized system is exactly the one that reforming economies will not have in the near future. Obviously, then, ascertaining whether workers' management is really one of the crucial problems of the economy is not an easy matter. But that becomes a crucial point, since a conservative approach would require burden of proof to be on the side of the zealous reformer when scrapping large elements of both society's institutional capital and society's stock of knowledge.

The preceding discussion implies that the decision on the role of workers' management in the transition must begin with a series of questions about the nature of the existing system in a specific country. I have some guesses concerning the answers to these questions and know that these answers vary between countries. In most cases, however, the answers would depend upon deep contextual knowledge about the country in question. This is perhaps the most important point to be made. That point makes it obvious that the blanket dismissal of worker's management as an element of transition policy is totally unsustainable, except in an approach that assumes that the institutions of a new economic system can be designed and reliably implemented instantaneously.

In countries such as Yugoslavia, and perhaps Poland, it is plausible that worker's management is deeply embedded in the existing economic fabric. In that case, there seems to be little justification to eradicate it as the beginning of the process of transition. This does not mean that worker's management is expected to survive the transition, not especially that it should be helped to survive the transition. There will surely be rapid growth of the capitalist sector over the next few years. It is clear that fair competition between this sector and the workers-management sector must be a vital element in the transition process. Competition for survival—the most important missing element under socialism—should determine the end state of the reform, not ideas about the ultimate nature of good societies that are applied at the beginning.[20]

6. Conclusions

The above analysis ultimately rests on a distinct vision of the way in which successful socio-economic systems are created and the way in which some of the most costly socio-economic experiments of history were generated. Those living in Central and Eastern Europe, above all, should need no reminding of the huge costs that can befall societies when utopian blueprints are implemented. It is surely no coincidence that Popper's distinction between utopian and piecemeal socio-engineering should have been developed in the 1930s and 1940s. (And indeed no coincidence that Burke's most famous work was written in 1790.)

The vision of socio-economic progress presented above emphasized that successful socio-economic systems have seen their institutions build up slowly in a succession of relatively small changes. Revolutions against an existing system, intending to destroy it, invariably result in excess in another direction and failure in some other way.[21] Of course, in the present context, it is perhaps fruitless to hope that either East European policy-makers or their Western advisers would take the lessons of Burke, Popper, and Oakeshott seriously. Therefore, I do not hope to offer the above analysis as a normative exercise relevant to the development of East European policy. Rather, it is a predictive exercise for the events of the 1990s. In that case, the successes and the failures of Eastern Europe in the economic transition *from* socialism will provide a test of the applicability of a political philosophy that last had a burst of energy in reaction to the transition *to* socialism.

Endnotes

1. I would like to thank the Wilson Center and the Center for Institutional Reform and the Informal Sector (IRIS) at the University of Maryland for support in the writing of this paper. Norbert Hornstein is thanked for his key suggestions that led me into the literature on conservative political philosophy.

2. In economics, there are the sets of what some called evolutionary economics, Schumpeterian economics, and Austrian economics. Murrell (1992) examines the implications of evolutionary economics for the design of policies in the Eastern European transition.

3. Popper, Karl, *The Open Society and Its Enemies*, Princeton University Press, Princeton, NJ, 1971, p. 1.

4. Burke, Edmund, *Reflections on the Revolution in France*, 1790; Popper, 1971 (op. cit., note 3); and Oakeshott, Micheal, *Rationalism in Politics and Other Essays*, Basic Books, New York, 1962. In classifying these three authors together, there is no implication that there are not important differences between them. However, the similarities are obvious when one reads these works in the light of developments in Eastern Europe and particularly in contrast to the current works on the changes in that region.

5. Moreover it is assumed that this gradual process of change has been the case in *all* successful societies, as discussed later in the paper.

6. Burke, Edmund, *Burke's Politics: Selected Writings and Speeches of Edmund Burke on Reform, Revolution, and War*, Ross J. S. Hoffman and Paul Levak, eds., Knopf, New York, 1949, p. viv.

7. Popper, 1971 (op. cit., note 3), pp. 167–68.

8. Oakeshott, 1962 (op. cit., note 4), pp. 7–8.

9. The distinction between the two types of knowledge has been offered by many authors, most notable Polayni, Michael, *Personal Knowledge: Towards a Post-Critical Philosophy*, University of Chicago Press, Chicago, IL, 1962. It is also the basis of much economic theorizing on the nature of organizations; see Nelson, Richard, and Sidney Winter, *An Evolutionary Theory of Economic Change*, Harvard University Press, Cambridge, MA, 1982; and, Williamson, Oliver E., *Markets and Hierarchies, Analysis and Antitrust Implications: A Study of Economies of Internal Organization*, Free Press, New York, 1975.

10. For those preferring a somewhat mundane example of this principle, the variance of forecast error of regressions increases with the distance from the mean of present observations.

11. The use of foreign advisers, who are experienced in the working of a society similar to that envisaged in the blueprint, might seem to be one way to solve this problem of implementing the blueprint. There are reasons why this is not possible, however. First, the number of policy decisions is much too great compared to the number of foreign advisers that would be available. Second, many of the existing institutional arrangements will remain before the blueprint is implemented. The foreign advisers suffer from lack of the practical knowledge of these arrangements in much the same way that the domestics lack the knowledge of the blueprint society. Therefore, foreign technical assistance must be implemented through a meeting of the minds of foreign experts and domestic policy-makers.

12. It is interesting to note here that Popper did not shrink from the use of the phrase "social engineering" when discussing the types of reforms that should be implemented in a democratic society. He does not argue against social engineering *per se*, but rather against specific types of social engineering. In particular, his arguments are addressed against reforms based on a utopian ideal.

13. There is one philosophy in which destruction is all that is needed. This is the philosophy that derives from primitive economics—perfect competition, with a dash of the Coase theorem—emphasizing that the market is simply the freedom to engage in the propensity to truck, barter, and trade. That is why a belief in a crude *laissez-faire* doctrine interacts most unfortunately with the utopian approach.

14. A perfect example of this occurs when reforming countries implement currency convertibility under the assumption that a working private sector will follow quickly from privatization. This assumption shows all signs of being incorrect for two reasons. First, the privatization process is obviously a very slow one. Second, privatized firms will not necessarily behave in the fashion of classical private sectors which have been created in an evolutionary process.

15. The use of knowledge argument also implies that the blueprint itself will inevitably be flawed.

16. Popper, 1971 (op. cit., note 3).

17. Interestingly, this is a characterization of what is arguably the most successful reform that has yet been implemented in countries moving from central planning. The Chinese began, not with a grand plan on the part of the leadership, but rather with the leaders validating and spreading an experiment that had been conducted under the initiative of the leadership of some localities.

18. Oakeshott, 1962 (op. cit., note 4), p. 172.

19. Of course, this is a gross simplification, again for expositional purposes. See Stark, David, "Privatization in Hungary: From Plan to Market or from Plan to Clan?" *East European Politics and Societies*, April, 3, 1990, pp. 351–292; for an excellent discussion of the various dimensions of privatization.

20. Murrell, Peter, "Evolution in Economics and in the Economic Reform of the Centrally Planned Economies," In Christopher C. Clauge and Gordon Rausser, eds., *Emerging Market Economies in Eastern Europe*, forthcoming

1992; argues that the absence of competition for survival among economic units was the most important problem of Eastern European economies.

21. Those tending to disagree with this statement would, I presume, most readily cite the English Revolution of 1688 and the American Revolution of 1775, as counter examples. This in not the place to discuss interpretation of history. But it must be noted that Burke, for example, interpreted both events as situations where a monarch was overstepping the bounds that had been created in a long period of historical development. Therefore, the majority of "revolutionaries" were in fact quite conservative in intent, as later events indeed showed.

The Role of the State in the Transition to Capitalism

Anders Åslund
Stockholm School of Economics

The transition to capitalism in formerly communist countries in East and Central Europe raises new challenging questions on the role of the state. The idea of an all-pervasive state has simply withered away. Broadly, the Western world represents two perceptions of the state – the liberal[1] state only providing truly public goods and the social democratic social welfare state with a wide range of social responsibility. In addition, many countries in the Third World present a fourth type of state – a totally corrupt state whose aim is to satisfy the rent-seeking of the élite.

The purpose of this paper is to establish what role the state ought to play in the period of transition from a command economy to capitalism. In order to do so, I shall discuss: in what way are the tasks required from the state different under the transition to capitalism? How does the capacity of the state compare with an ordinary Western state? What priority should be given to various possible state tasks? What tasks should the state be absolved from and what kind of state is desirable? Thus, the discussion will range from the empirical to the normative. It will draw on the experiences of the formerly communist countries in East and Central Europe, and particular attention will be devoted to the former Soviet Union and Russia where these issues loom large on the political agenda.

1. In what way are the tasks of the state different in the transition?

An almost universally accepted view is that "the state is expected to further the common interests of its citizens,"[2] that is, the state should provide truly public goods. The most obvious categories are:
- external security (defense and foreign policy);
- legal system (legislation, police, magistrates and courts);
- monetary and financial system.

To these indisputable public goods, three large categories that are partially perceived as public goods may be added to a limited extent:

– social security;

– education;

– physical infrastructure.

Much of the Western debate over the role of the state concerns how much of these functions that should be privatized, but even Friedrich Hayek (1960) acknowledged that the state arguably should take some responsibility in these spheres. Two further categories that should not exist in a liberal state but persist to some extent in all Western countries are:

– state enterprises;

– industrial policy.

The transition of a state from a command economy to a market economy comprises several tasks that an ordinary capitalist economy does not have to face. In most cases (Poland, Yugoslavia, the USSR, Bulgaria, Albania and Romania), the communists have left power as their states have approached very high inflation or even hyperinflation. Hence, a central task of the government is macroeconomic stabilization, for which there are well-known cures, but they require swift, radical and single-minded actions, focusing on the basic macroeconomic indicators.[3] This is not only a question of changed policies. All the vehicles of macro-economic policy must be constructed more or less anew, reconstituting the Central Bank and the Ministry of Finance, as well as payment mechanisms and tax collection systems.

Another essential assignment is the establishment of a legal frame-work. A vast body of civil and commercial law must be elaborated and enacted. Moreover, it must be learnt and the legal system be reformed, for instance so that the prosecutor is not superior to the judge as the Soviet practice goes. Since communist society was based not on law but arbitrary and totalitarian power, there was a shortage of law but an abundance of commands. For the transition to the rule of law, the training of a huge number of lawyers is required. This is also true of auditors, who did not exist in the command economy.

A third task of a state in transition is the privatization of state enter-prises. In effect, this frequently amounts to their nationalization from the *Nomenklatura,* who have unlawfully expropriated most public property to their own benefit.[4] To date, successful privatization remains an unsolved problem in all formerly communist countries.

Fourth, communism has left the social security system in a complete mess. Contrary to all myths about the superior social standards of socialism, a democracy can hardly get away with such poor social facilities at a comparable level of economic development. In addition, the old social safety net was to a considerable extent provided by state enterprises, which neither can nor will fulfill many of those functions when exposed to competition on the market. Since no system of private insurance is at hand, it is natural to request that the state provision of health care and training be further extended. Moreover, the transition to a market economy creates new needs, as unemployment is bound to increase, and long delayed restructuring will be unleashed, causing a variety of human disorientation.

The revolutionary changes of both economic mechanisms and relative prices will compel society to massive restructuring. The communist economies are invariably departing with utterly run-down infrastructures, which are traditional objects of public care. Hence, demands for industrial and structural government policies have become frequent.

Thus, apart from its ordinary functions, the state must pursue macroeconomic stabilization, develop a legal system, privatize massively, provide new social services and possibly engage in the construction of infrastructure. Facing these challenges, it may seem obvious that the state should undertake more activities than in a stable market economy, but before accepting this suggestion, we need to scrutinize the ability of the state apparatus to carry out all these tasks.

2. The capacity of the state apparatus in the transition[5]

The capacity of the state is dependent on many factors. First, we must consider how large resources the state can reasonably control. Second, we have to recognize the nature of a command economy. Third, how accurate and voluminous is the information on which the state would have to act? Finally, what is the quality of the state apparatus?

The two most useful comparative measurements of the economic role of the public sector are public expenditure as a ratio to GNP and public employment as a share of total employment. In developed Western economies public expenditures have varied from 67 percent of GNP in Sweden around 1980 to as little as 20 percent previously in several countries, with a current average of 38 percent in the OECD area. Public employment has been much smaller as a share of the total, since a large share of the public expenditures are transfers, and ranges currently from 6.5 percent in Japan to 32 percent in Sweden.[6]

The East European command economies tended to have a higher share of public expenditures as a share of GNP, about 50–60 percent in the 1980s with a more narrow range than Western countries (cf Pryor, 1968), while public employment tended to account for around 95–98 percent of all employment, with the exception of Poland. The interesting fact is that the East European countries were barely able to raise state revenues over 50 percent. Characteristically, Soviet state revenues peaked at 48 percent of GNP in 1985 and then fell (Åslund, 1991a, p. 194). This suggests that the predominance of the public sector in terms of employment and production must not be confused with the ability of the central state apparatus to control the economy. In fact, Sweden has probably maintained higher public revenues – as distinct from public enterprise revenues – than any socialist state. This also points to the dubious status of "public" property. As Jan Winiecki (1991) has convincingly argued, there is no real public ownership, as its main beneficiaries are apparatchiks and bureaucrats, casting doubts on the socialistic underpinnings of the benefits of public enterprise. For our current discourse, the important fact is that public ownership or public employment cannot be equated with state power or control, which is limited by the state revenues.

As Ronald McKinnon (1990) has pointed out, state revenues inevitably fall during decentralizing economic reform. Traditionally, the three main sources of state revenues in command economies have been enterprise taxes, turnover taxes and foreign trade taxes. Enterprise taxes have been very high – almost 60 percent of total profits, since the remaining profits at the end of a year have been expropriated by the state. With the transition to a market economy, it becomes necessary to cut profit taxes to about 30 percent of profits which is a Western standard. Foreign trade taxes have been pretty high because of excessive protectionism. With the introduction of free trade, state revenues from foreign trade are likely to fall. Turnover taxes were originally very high. However, frequently wholesale prices have risen faster than retail prices, and the turnover tax, which was the residue between them, has fallen or even turned negative, equating subsidies. New turnover taxes may initially rise, but as a multitude of small private trading enterprises emerge, any kind of tax on sales is likely to become ever more difficult to collect. The underexploited tax object is the employee, as income taxes have been very low. However, with little habit of paying income taxes, the public will show little tolerance to them. Moreover, there is barely any revenues service that can collect them, and accountancy is poorly developed. Any attempt to tax individuals in the transition is likely to generate little state revenue (Åslund, 1991a, pp. 193–5), while it may have very harmful effects on respect for law and private supplies.

An additional tax that is almost equally accessible before and after transition is a payroll tax, which is typically geared to social benefits. These conditions call for the wide application of lump sum taxes for small private enterprises. On the one hand, lump sum taxes provide the state with some revenues where little would otherwise be collected. On the other hand, they guarantee small entrepreneurs certain legal and economic security and excellent incentives to increase their supply. Since the dysfunction of the system does not allow for any rational distribution of taxes in any case, such considerations may be neglected during the first years of transition. Various forms of discrimination are inevitable, and the central decision-makers must make sure that it is not directed against private entrepreneurs to whom the future obviously belongs. It is vital to stimulate new private supplies.

As a consequence of these changes of the tax system, caused by the liberalization of the economy, it appears inevitable that the share of state revenues in the GNP falls from almost 50 percent to some 40 percent. Moreover, such a high level would imply very energetic efforts to chase both new indirect taxes, for instance on energy, and substantial new direct taxes. Both kinds of taxes are likely to have a highly detrimental supply effect, as private entrepreneurs will tend to be more cautious if they are subject to a arbitrary tax system, which will be pretty arbitrary as legal standards are missing. Therefore, it would be natural to call for a further reduction of state revenues to some 30 percent of GNP, which would be more appropriate to the level of economic development of Eastern Europe.[7]

From a social point of view, it is easier to defend budget cuts in formerly communist countries and particularly in the former USSR than in the West. A characteristic feature of the Soviet budget has been that social transfers have been minute and total social expenditures have only accounted for some 11 percent of GNP, while more than one tenth recently went to subsidies, and huge amounts to the military sector and investment. Therefore, it is obviously socially beneficial to reduce the budget as a share of the GNP.

A second limitation of the capacity of the state is the very malfunctioning of the old economic system. Most analysis of the Soviet economic system has been devoted to its malfunctioning. It is a strictly hierarchical system based on secrecy, monopoly and protectionism. As Yegor Gaidar (1990, p. 4) has pointed out, "a hierarchical organization can only function efficiently in the presence of social forces and mechanisms which provide effective control over its activity." The very nature of the communist command economy actually excludes its efficient functioning, as has been pointed out time and again since Ludwig von Mises did so in 1920.

Interestingly, the current top economic politician in Russia, Yegor Gaidar, published a book in 1990 called *Economic Reforms and Hierarchical Structures,* which adapted Oliver Williamson's (1975) reasoning on markets and hierarchies to the Soviet Union. The focal point of Gaidar's study is how extremely poorly the hierarchies function in the USSR. Pursuing Williamson's reasoning on the choice between markets and hierarchies, transaction costs turn out to be exorbitantly high *within* the hierarchies. If hierarchies are not competitive in terms of transaction costs, the only reasonable choice is to transfer as many transactions as possible to the market. Ideally, no transactions that can occur on the market should be left to the state.

A third constraint is the shortage of relevant information. The communist state was secretive and gave little information away. When statistics are not subject to public scrutiny but to political desires, their quality swiftly deteriorates, and gradually less and less essential statistics were even collected. Ideological dogmas prohibited the elaboration of many vital statistics. The isolation of statisticians from the outside world rendered them parochial. As the Soviet Union parted with this world, its statistics were left in shambles.[8] The sad presumption is that statistics will grow worse rather than improve. A well-functioning statistical system requires a substantial computer system which is both costly and takes time to develop. The necessary funds are not likely to be allocated in the nearest future of severe economic crisis in the formerly communist countries. The traditional communist statistical systems have focused almost entirely on the state sector, which is set to dwindle. Instead the private sector will expand rapidly, but little of its activities will be registered by the statisticians, who are unprepared and lack motivation, while the new private entrepreneurs are anxious to avoid any kind of registration in order to escape from unnecessary taxation. To this comes the demoralization of civil servants discussed below. The conclusion is that statistics are so poor that there is barely sufficient grounds for macroeconomic decisions (Åslund, 1991b). To suggest a large range of state interventions would be to argue for decision-making based on little or no information.

The dearth of information is aggravated by the poor functioning of the market. In the nascent market economies, the market naturally functions rather badly: monopoly effects distort prices; the price spread is great; certain shortages persist and quality is often poor, as private traders initially skim the market; relative prices swing fast; frequently, established market prices do not yet exist. Therefore, it is more than usually difficult for the state to assess and control the costs of its commitments, which is of course a strong argument for the state doing less. Thus, the dysfunction of the market ironically turns out to be an argument for the state doing less, not more.

A fourth restriction on the capacity of the state is the eventual quality of its apparatus. Virtually everything is wrong with the old state administration. Its very structure with huge industrial wings is designed for a command economy. Its staff has the wrong training, being predominantly engineers rather than lawyers and social scientists. Because of poor language skills, the ability to absorb knowledge from abroad is highly limited. Far-reaching demoralization prevails, because many of the former officials were communists and stick to their old convictions, which makes them both alienated from the new rule and despised by the population. In a time of rapid inflation, it is difficult to maintain reasonably high salaries for civil servants, and relative salaries fall sharply.

Worst however is the extraordinary corruption. It has long been a severe problem in the USSR (Zemtsov, 1976; Simis, 1982). To judge from anecdotal evidence, corruption is worse the greater the general mess in society. Thus, it seems least in Czechoslovakia followed by Hungary and worse in Poland and far worse in the Balkans and in the former Soviet Union. In Russia, a common view is that only a few dozen of the top officials of the Russian government form a mass of still uncorrupted people.

It is not only the numbers and range of corrupt people that are disturbing. The degree of irresponsibility the Russian corruption involves is almost incredible. Money is the ultimate decision-maker.[9] The ultimate form of rent-seeking prevails (Buchanan et al, 1980; Winiecki, 1991). The pervasive corruption is a natural consequence over time of the dysfunction of a command economy. It implies a much greater limitation on the capacity of the state than the financial or information constraints. To argue that the state should do anything that can be done by anybody else under such conditions would be to favor corruption. In many ways, the current post-Soviet society is reminiscent of Europe in the 1840s. The late communist society is rather similar to the feudal society with its all-embracing hierarchy and the delegation of partial property rights to local lords by a sovereign. In particular, neither the feudal society nor the communist society had a rule of law, as that would limit the powers of the ruler. The natural response in the 1840s was the demand for a very far-reaching liberalization, since the malfunctioning state could be entrusted with little (Mill, 1859). The similarity in the situations is reflected in similar demands now being raised in Eastern Europe. Typically, the radical liberal economists in East Europe (Kornai, 1990; Winiecki, 1991) are rather more moderate in their demands than the neoliberals now emerging in Russia (Piyasheva, 1991; L'vin, 1992).

L'vin's (1992) line of argument is particularly interesting. Its essence is that a very far-reaching revolution has occured which has devastated the whole former state apparatus in depth and on such a wide scale that it will take a long period for it to recover in a new form. The old hierarchy has been liquidated; the old state ethics that determines the relationship between civil servants and citizens has disappeared, and no new state norms or rules have yet emerged. As a result, the state must be deprived of as many functions as possible, and L'vin argues for a society resembling that of Hayek (1960), but on the basis of his observations of how the post-Soviet society actually works rather than with reference to liberal theory.

The conclusion that arises is that the capacity of the state in the transition to capitalism is extremely limited, far more so than is generally perceived. To require that the state should do anything means to ask the uninformed and corrupt for assistance. The simple fact is that apart from a limited number of directly applicable decisions from the very top of the state apparatus, the state apparatus in incapable of making informed and publicly-responsible decisions. Therefore, the only defensible recommendation is that the role of the state be limited to a bare minimum in the period of transition to capitalism. This stand should not be dependent on perception of what the state should do under more normal circumstances in a developed democracy, because states in transition face extreme conditions. Then radical solutions are rational.

It might appear commonsensical that if a country has a big public sector, it would be natural to maintain a bigger public sector than others. Indeed, in the Western world the size of the public sector even in the rather long term seems more closely related to its prior size in that particular country than to the tasks the society is facing. However, that is under ordinary circumstances when a wide range of options are open, and the issue is degree of efficiency rather than failure or success of society as such. In Eastern Europe, the question is exactly that: whether the transition to a free and stable market economy will succeed or not. Therefore a stark and rational choice need to be made. The suggestion that follows from this argument is that the formerly communist countries need to shift to extremely liberal economies in a radical deregulation reminiscent of the liberalization in the United Kingdom in 1846. It was hardly by chance that *laisser faire* followed upon feudalism. From a simple analysis of transaction costs, it follows that the state hierarchies, that were rudimentary, had not capacity for accurate decision-making, in particular as markets were poorly developed and could not present market prices in many cases. Therefore, the rational response of the time was to defer as many decisions as possible to the market. *Laisser faire* was not a mistake but a rational response to the prevailing situation.

It might be appropriate to differentiate for various formerly communist countries with regard to their preconditions. The more orderly the state administration and society in general, the wider is the choice for what role to give the state. Hungary may get away with a much more interventionist policy than Russia would be able to do. It is characteristic that Hungary has settled for a greater role for the state than Poland or Russia, though even so the Polish state might be more intrusive than the country can actually afford. In Czechoslovakia the top politicians, notably Minister of Finance Vaclav Klaus, have simply chosen a highly liberal policy.

3. What tasks should the state focus on?

The two first sections of this paper have brought out a stark contradiction between demands on the state and the very limited capacity of the state. In fact, much of this apparent contradiction can be resolved, since many of the tasks that the state is called to perform may be undertaken by the private sector with more or less stimulation by the state. When asking what the state actually should do, we are both asking what is most urgent and what can only be done by the state. Our focus on the state provides new insights into how the transition should be undertaken.

In general terms, the limited capacity of the state means that little precision is possible in the design of the transition to a free market economy. It is striking how proponents of a gradual and well-planned transition to a market economy, for instance Galbraith (1990), seem completely unaware of the limited capacity of the state, which seriously undermines his argument. Corrupt, incompetent and irresponsible bureaucrats cannot be expected to further the well-being of society contrary to their own pecuniary interests.

There are a number of basic functions that can hardly be performed by any other body than the state, at least not fast enough. The state obligations with regard to foreign policy and defense remain, but we shall focus on economic tasks. First, for the functioning of the market, a stable and preferably convertible currency can be established. Therefore, swift macroeconomic stabilization is so important. Under the frequent conditions of very high inflation after the collapse of communism, this implies a rapid elimination of any budget deficit, strict monetary policies and possibly an incomes policy. The very requirements of a swift macroeconomic stabilization preclude a gradual approach (Blanchard et al, 1991; Dornbusch, 1991; Lipton and Sachs, 1990a).

Second, a well-functioning market economy requires a rule of law. A rudimentary legislation for a market economy needs to be adopted as fast as possible, since many basic economic legal acts were missing under communism. If anything, legislation is the imperative of the state. An unfortunate mistake in Poland and Czechoslovakia has been not to adopt a constitution fast enough, leaving the whole legal framework in suspense. The adoption of a good constitution is easier in the first year of transition, because the actual knowledge required is little, and as time passes by, a variety of vested interests wake up and complicate the adoption of a fair and balanced constitution (Dahrendorf, 1990).

Third, law without sanctions is of little value. The next major task in terms of priority is to develop a legal system with police, magistrates and independent courts, but a precondition is the cleaning up of corruption. It will require a lot of time and effort. The major method must be far-reaching deregulation, which by definition renders bribery impossible. The old state apparatus must be cut to a minimum and be made as transparent and legally controlled as convenient. Regardless of what society we ultimately aspire to, a new state apparatus must be constructed. At the heart of each country, a central state administration of some size is needed which will ultimately be motivated by moral incentives, such as professional pride, ambition, appreciation and an *ésprit de corps*. Therefore, young highly educated citizens should be given elite training and decent economic conditions, so that their professional pride and economic sufficiency will help them out of the corruption of the state apparatus.

Fourth, considering that the state will fail in most of its tasks, it is vital that the state does its utmost to allow others to succeed where it fails itself. In effect that means to provide primarily private enterprises with as liberal conditions as just possible. No licensing can be accepted, though simple registration of enterprises may be justified in order to identify them as legal subjects. Naturally, domestic trade and other contracts between individuals and enterprises of any kind should be completely free. Similarly, foreign trade should be as liberal as possible, though foreign trade is admittedly a suitable object for taxation. Still, the main aim of foreign trade policy in the short term should be to vitalize enterprise, stimulating trade and competition, so that the functioning of the market can improve rapidly.[10] If sufficient taxes initially can be extracted from state enterprises (given that a small budget is desired), is it at all necessary to tax private enterprises? The arguments for taxation would then be equality and income redistribution, which are weak as no precision is possible under the prevailing conditions.

My suspicion is that a major shortcoming of government policies in the countries under transition so far has been the coyness in deregulation of private enterprise. It is not enough to declare certain liberties. It is necessary to ensure that no old regulations persist and that local and regional authorities are not introducing new regulations, legally or not, on their own. In Poland, domestic as well as foreign businessmen complain bitterly about red tape and corruption being worse than ever. There are usually more complaints about local and regional authorities than about the central authorities, whose quality tends to be better.

Enterprise hybrids without actual owners, so-called public enterprises, cannot function well. The very idea of privatization is to get rid of them. Then, the state should discriminate heavily against them, as long as it does not disturb the functioning of the market as such. In the interim, unemployment is likely to grow and the state provision of social benefits and services will function badly. Private enterprise should be stimulated to fill the void quickly, providing its new employees with both employment and income, while contributing to the saturation of the market. Moreover, it is inevitable that new private enterprises will pay little or no tax initially, at the same time as massive restructuring is required. Under such circumstances, the state would be well-advised to leave the nascent private enterprises alone, so that they can develop and the market stabilize. Later on, the state can turn its attention to them and apply ordinary ideas of non-discriminatory taxation. Formally, this could be arranged as a period of grace of a couple of years for all private enterprises, possible below a certain size.

Fifth, privatization is of vital importance. No normal market economy has more than one third of its employment in the public sector. This must be considered an emergency task. Before two thirds of employment has passed to the private sector, little economic or political stability can be expected, given the problems with the soft budget constraint of public enterprises. It remains an unresolved issue what form of privatization that is to prefer, but the importance of speed is undisputable (Grosfeld, 1990; Lipton and Sachs, 1990b).

Sixth, the state must provide a social safety net and education. Here many different perspectives need to be considered, and it is not obvious what kind of compromise between them should be reached. Previously hardly any private system of social services and education has existed. Although private alternatives develop fast in some spheres, notably management training, basic private services are likely to develop slowly. The public sector will remain necessary to fill the void. The public health and education services have been so limited in the formerly communist states that what is needs to be maintained in order to have a reasonable amount in relation to their level of economic development. In addition, rising unemployment and restructuring pose new challenges to the public services, at the same time as state revenues are being reduced. My suggestion would be that as much as possible of the eventual state revenues are devoted to these social purposes, but this is based on the idea that the state has a considerable responsibility for the health and education of its citizens. If the private sector has not developed far enough to take care of them, these responsibilities rest with the state.[11] It would be reasonable if education and social expenditures account for a larger share of public expenditures than in an average Western country.

Seventh, whether it likes it or not, the state can hardly avoid a certain responsibility for the development of the physical infrastructure for the simple reason that no private entrepreneur would dare to undertake the large-scale investments frequently required without having an idea of the intentions of the government. Still, a reasonable state policy would be to provide private investors – foreign or domestic – with such legal guarantees that they dare to go ahead with necessary big investments in infrastructure. Considering that the state has small resources for such investments, it would be harmful if the state insisted on any kind of public monopoly, since the outcome would be that infrastructure becomes a permanent bottle-neck as is the case in many state-dominated economies in the Third World.

Finally, as Mancur Olson (1982) has shown, a national crisis offers a great opportunity to set institutions right, as the ordinary play of vested interests is overtaken by the necessity to put things right. Although the current slogan throughout the postcommunist world is "no experiments!", it would be foolhardy not to exploit the actually received wisdom, and it points in a highly liberal direction.

As a summary, the state should focus on vital issues to society that requires relatively little management capacity, but preferably at a high level, which is particularly important for the swift transition to a market economy. The first leaders brought in with democratization are not likely to be corrupt, and the important decisions should rest with them, before they have become corrupted. The degraded and possibly corrupt apparatus should preferably be abolished, especially at local and regional levels. This should be the main task of the first postcommunist administration.

It follows from our line of argument that it would be unsuitable for the state to run and own enterprises. Unfortunately that is already the case. Before its speedy privatization of these enterprises, the state leadership can try to isolate itself from their running through a swift transformation of the enterprises to corporations and their commercialization. The government should not manage enterprises. Regulation of the economy is basically not acceptable, apart from the necessary elements of domestic liberalization, macroeconomic policy, tax policy and foreign trade liberalization.

Industrial or structural policy might appear more justified. Massive structural changes are in the offing. A decline in registered industrial production of some 35 percent during the two first years of systemic change appears standard. The restructuring will cause the displacement of a large part of the labor force, which will be exposed to considerable stress. The structural changes are complicated by whole industries and regions losing their economic justification. Should not the state intervene? No. Our knowledge of what structural changes that are likely is very limited. At the outset of the systemic changes in Poland in 1990, there was a general expectation that light and food industry would do well, while heavy industry would decline fast. The opposite occured. It turned out that the enterprises in light and food industry were highly inefficient or even produced a negative value added (for instance, turning nice fresh vegetables into inedible conserves), while heavy industry could survive for a while because of remaining cheap raw materials and cheap labor. Machine-building enterprises are frequently dependent on their ability to attract a foreign partner, and in most specific industries, the number of potential foreign partners is limited to a handful or even less. In many cases, an enterprise is an inorganic composition, while several parts of the enterprise can become viable independent enterprises. To this comes poor statistics, poor accounting and swiftly changing relative prices, which are not likely to stabilize very fast. The necessary information for any structural policy is not at hand. Nor do state officials possess the necessary skills, and they are neither motivated, responsible nor honest. Any structural policy would be costly, but the scarce funds available should either be invested in viable private enterprises or infrastructure or given to suffering citizens. Under such conditions, a great belief in the competence of the state is necessary for any advocacy of industrial policy.

Conclusions

The role of the state in the transition from a command economy to capitalism is in several important regards different from the role of the state in an ordinary Western society. On the one hand, there are many tasks that are peculiar to the transition, such as macroeconomic stabilization, the creation of a legal framework and privatization, at the same time as the social demands on the state are mounting. On the other hand, the capacity of the state apparatus is far more limited than generally perceived. State revenues decline with reform and a fall to 30 percent of GNP seems preferable; the command economy is not an efficient system and all its flaws are preserved in the state administration; little information on anything worthwhile is available; the state apparatus has been geared to completely different tasks, and in its demoralization its corruption becomes almost total in the countries most degraded by communism. Thus, the state cannot intervene in an informed manner in other than a few major issues, and more interventions are essentially providing corrupt rent-seekers with additional gains.

Central issues of such significance that the state even so needs to take responsibility for them are: macroeconomic stabilization, the establishment of rule of law (fundamental legislation and a legal system), the evolution of a small noncorrupt civil service, consistent liberalization of the economy (preferably with positive discrimination of private enterprise), privatization, the provision of a social safety net and education, and the development of physical infrastructure. The state should avoid anything but strategic tasks as far as possible, but also activities that are likely to involve rent-seeking, such as industrial policy.

This paper entirely focusses upon the formerly communist countries in transition to capitalism, and without going into any discussion about ordinary Western societies, it is apparent that it is much more difficult to defend extensive state intervention in the period of transition. The ultimate argument is the degree of corruption, but there are many auxiliary arguments, such as the damage to supply caused by excessive taxes, the sheer incompetence of the old civil servants, and the shortage of accurate information.

Notes

1. Throughout this paper, "liberal" is used in its classical European sense, implying a minimum of state intervention.
2. Olson, 1965, pp. 6–7.
3. Bruno et al, 1988.
4. Voslensky, 1980.
5. I have discussed this theme in less detail in Åslund (1991b).
6. OECD statistics. I leave differences of definition aside as only the broad picture is of interest here.
7. Russia has settled for an almost balanced budget of 35 percent of GNP in 1992 *(Nezavisimava gazeta,* March 7, 1992, p. 1; Memorandum, 1992).
8. I have discussed the miserable shape of Soviet economic statistics in Åslund (1991c).
9. Health inspectors of restaurants and food are literally disinterested in anything but their bribes. A local health inspector even tried to close the luxury hotel of Lufthansa in Moscow, when he was refused a bribe. When a British plane with meat was refused permission to unload in Moscow, the general understanding was that the inspector was either refused a bribe or wanted to keep the meat out in order to assure that the free meat price did not fall. Realizing that health inspection is not related to sanitary standards of restaurants or food but only to bribery, the liberal Russian government has felt forced to prohibit much health inspection.
10. Foreign trade regulations seem poorly suited for any kind of industrial policy at the initial stage of transition, which McKinnon (1991, pp. 162–186) has advocated. As the market functions so poorly, all means must be applied to vitalize it. Domestic monopolies need to be checked through foreign competition; domestic producers should be exposed to higher international quality standards; domestic producers should not be hampered by unnecessary supply bottlenecks. Initially restructuring, bankruptcies and unemployment

have been slow to appear, so that there is little empirical evidence of the danger of excessive social disruption in the early stage of transition.

11. Needless to say, no luxury can be afforded, and no distortion of incentives can be tolerated. Even so, the state should provide a minimum of social welfare and as much education as it can.

References

Åslund, Anders (1991a) *Gorbachev's Struggle for Economic Reform*, 2nd ed., Pinter, London.

_____ (1991b) "Four Key Reforms: the East European Experiment Phase II", *The American Enterprise*, 2, no. 4, pp. 48–55 (July–August).

_____ (1991c) "How Small Is the Soviet National Income?" in Rowen, Henry S., and Charles Wolf, Jr., eds., *The Impoverished Superpower*, ICS Press, San Fransisco.

Blanchard, Olivier, Rudiger Dornbusch, Paul Krugman, Richard Layard and Lawrence Summers (1991) *Reform in Eastern Europe*, MIT Press, London.

Bruno, Michael, Guido di Tella, Rudiger Dornbusch and Stanley Fischer, eds. (1988) *Inflation Stabilization*, MIT Press, Cambridge, Ma.

Buchanan, James M., Robert Tollison and Gordon Tullock, eds. (1980) *Toward a Theory of the Rent-Seeking Society*, Texas A & M University Press, College Station.

Dahrendorf, Ralf (1990) *Reflections on the Revolution in Europe*, Chatto, London.

Dornbusch, Rudiger (1991) "Priorities of Economic Reform in Eastern Europe and the Soviet Union", CEPR Occasional Paper no. 5.

Gaidar, Yegor T. (1990) *Ekonomicheskie reformy i ierarkhicheskie struktury*, Nauka, Moscow.

Galbraith, John Kenneth (1990) "The Rush to Capitalism", *The New York Review of Books*, October 25, pp. 51–2.

Grosfeld, Irena (1990) 'Prospects for Privatization in Poland', *European Economy*, No. 43, pp. 139–150 (March).

Hayek, Friedrich A. (1960) *The Constitution of Liberty*, Routledge & Kegan Paul, London.

Kornai, Janos (1990) *The Road to a Free Economy*, Norton, New York.

Lipton, David, and Jeffrey Sachs (1990a) "Creating a Market in Eastern Europe: The Case of Poland", Brookings Papers on Economic Activity, no. 1, pp. 75–147.

_____ (1990b) 'Privatization in Eastern Europe: The Case of Poland', Brookings Papers on Economic Activity, no. 2, pp. 293–341.

L'vin, Boris, "Kak delat' revolyutsiyu. Neskol'ko sovetov pravitel'stvu Rossii", *Nezavisimaya gazeta*, March 10, 1992, p. 5.

McKinnon, Ronald I. (1990) "Stabilising the Ruble", *Communist Economies*, 2, no. 2, pp. 131–42.

_____ (1991) *The Order of Economic Liberalization*, John Hopkins University Press, Baltimore, Md.

"Memorandum Pravitel'stva Rossii", *Nezavisimaya gazeta,* March 3, 1992, pp. 1, 5.

Mill, John Stuart [1859] (1975) *On Liberty,* Norton, New York.

von Mises, Ludwig (1920) "Economic Calculation in the Socialist Common-wealth", Nove, Alec, and D.M. Nuti (eds.), *Socialist Economics,* Penguin, Harmondsworth, 1972.

North, Douglass C. (1981) *Structure and Change in Economic History,* Norton, New York.

Olson, Mancur (1965) *The Logic of Collective Action,* Harvard University Press, Cambridge, Ma.

_____ (1982) *The Rise and Decline of Nations,* Yale UP, London.

Piyasheva, Larisa I. (1991) *Mozhno li byt' nemnozhko beremennoi?* Polifakt, Minsk.

Pryor, Frederic L. (1968) *Public Expenditures in Communist and Capitalist Nations,* Allen & Unwin, London.

Simis, Konstantin (1982) *USSR: Secrets of a Corrupt Society,* Dent, London.

Voslensky, Michael S. (1980) *Nomenklatura. Die herrschende Klasse der Sowjetu-nion,* Moewig, Vienna.

Williamson, Oliver E. (1975) *Markets and Hierarchies,* Free Press, New York.

Winiecki, Jan (1991) *Resistance to Change in the Soviet Economic System. A Property Rights Approach,* Routledge, London.

Zemtsov, Ilja (1976) *La corruption en Union sovitiéque,* Hachette, Paris.

Liberty or Prelude to New Disasters? The Prospects for Post–Revolutionary Central and Eastern Europe

Daniel Chirot
University of Washington, Seattle

Two years after the Revolutions of 1989 in Central and Eastern Europe the mood has soured. The economic transitions to capitalism have not been smooth, and throughout the area, even in eastern Germany, they remain unfinished. High unemployment, declining production and standards of living, the collapse of entire industrial sectors, particularly those that specialized in trading with the defunct CMEA,[1] and fear about the uncertainties of the future have eliminated the optimism so evident in early 1990. The overthrow of police states was welcome, but it has been accompanied by sharp increases in visible crimes. The end of severe border controls has opened the gates to swarms of wandering refugees from other, poorer countries looking for jobs or fast deals. These new waves of migration are only one, and hardly the major cause, of what seems to be renewed ethnic conflict. Anti-Semitism and anti-Gypsy feelings have been prominent throughout most of the area, but there are also the tensions between Slovaks and Czechs, Romanians and Hungarians, and Turks and Bulgars. Of course, there is also the Yugoslav conflict which pits Slovenes, Albanians, Bosnians, Muslims, Croats, Macedonians, and Serbs against each other in violent hatred. As if that were not enough, some of the long running ethnic troubles in the Ukraine could eventually involve neighboring Romania and Poland. Finally, opening these societies to examination and the free press has revealed that infrastructures are far more dilapidated, pollution much worse, technology much more backward than anyone had realized. It is as if a scruffy old carpet had been removed, and underneath was something even worse—complete decay.

All this is very discouraging. Jan Gross, a Polish sociologist who works in the United States, put it nicely when he said that after the miracle of 1989, everyone expected there could be another and that the transition to a liberal capitalist democracy would be fast and easy. Evidently, political miracles are more easily accomplished than economic and social ones.

Now that the unrealistic euphoria of late 1989 and early 1990 has been replaced by so much gloom, it may be possible to assess the future more realistically. However, after what has happened in the last few years, it would be a very foolish specialist who would engage in precise prognosis. After all, most of us were wrong in the 1980s because we thought that communism would hold out much longer than it actually did. The overwhelming consensus in the late 1980s was that the pattern of change would be somewhat like the one that actually occurred in China: significant economic reforms leading to a gradual abandonment of socialist practice, while the entrenched communist bureaucracy continued to rule. We expected protests, but, as happened in China in June of 1989, most of us thought that the army and police would repress them if they went so far as to threaten the very existence of the regimes. Not even the most optimistic foresaw the collapse of communist power with so little bloodshed.

Humility in the face of past misjudgments is no excuse for avoiding analysis. Rather than giving precise predictions, an exercise in futility, I look at the future by comparing it to the past, and see what elements the present situation shares with old disasters in modern Central and Eastern European history, or, conversely, what signs of more optimistic outcomes may be discerned in the historical events of the twentieth century. While not wildly optimistic, I am going to claim that today's gloom is no more justified than the exaggerated euphoria of 1990.

What Happened in 1989?

However often the tale had been told by now, it is worth remembering what happened in 1989, and why. There were two long term, endogenous developments that doomed European communism, and are responsible for the weakness of communist regimes everywhere they have taken power. Then, there was a cluster of exogenous events that precipitated the revolutions. Without these external circumstances, the collapse of communism would have been more protracted, more painful, but probably just as certain.

In a recent article, Walt Rostow reminded his readers that in his classic book, *The Stages of Economic Growth*, first published in 1960, he had predicted that the Soviet model of industrialization was heading for a dead end. He had written:

The composition of Russian output must certainly change. The present higher Soviet rate of increase in GNP is the product substantially of a peculiar concentration of investment in certain sectors. If steel is not to be used for military purposes, what will it be used for? An enormous heavy industry, growing at high rates, is not a goal in itself; nor is it an intrinsic international advantage.[2]

The Stalinist model of industrialization was based on a conscious imitation of late nineteenth and early twentieth century centers of high technology: giant factories, scooping in vast numbers of workers recently migrated from the countryside, belching vast quantities of smoke, turning out prodigious amounts of steel, chemicals, electricity, and heavy machinery to make more steel, chemicals, electricity, and machinery. The Ruhr, or the American Middle West from Buffalo and Pittsburgh to Chicago, were the model. The Stakhanov movement was Taylorism run wild, an anachronism at the moment it was created. However, because this model was imposed by political means, and was entirely disconnected from the market forces that had spurred these changes in the West, once it was established it could not be adapted. The flexibility of capitalism was lacking.

Soviet-style economies never succeeded in moving into the next industrial age of automobiles and high mass consumption, and failed even more in keeping up with the next stage, the age of electronics and biotechnology. This was not produced by their inability to educate advanced scientists or capable engineers; nor was it because they were unable to see what the West, and increasingly, East Asia were doing. Although they did see, and did try to copy, Soviet engineers were almost always a little late in reproducing advanced capitalist technology, and their over-centralized, politically dominated patterns of investment and reward funneled resources to the largest, best established, laziest, and least innovative sectors. Conversely, innovation comes from flexible, small new firms, from independent thinking that defies convention, and then from the stimulus of competition that eventually forces even large firms to innovate.

It was not IBM that created the personal computer revolution, but a few eccentric young men in California and an upper-middle-class college dropout in Seattle, William Gates, and his friends. If it had been up to IBM, its near monopoly in business main-frames would never have been broken by an upstart little machine. Maverick, obsessed entrepreneurs like Soichiro Honda and William Gates, rare enough in the United States and Japan, were impossible in Soviet-style economics. Of course, there was innovation and sometimes genius in communist societies, but it was subjected to immense political and social controls, and unconventional entrepreneurial types were considered dangerous and, typically, were soon forced into more conventional behavior.

This long term problem, serious as it was, cannot explain everything. After all, European communist economies, including that of the Soviet Union, were highly successful in some ways. They did industrialize and lay the basis for highly educated, modern, urban societies. They also created the foundation for a fearsome armaments industry; the only major sector in their economies that had to match outside competition, it therefore became the most efficient of the industrial sectors.

Communism promised much more than the ability to barely keep up, or to fall behind the West slowly. It was supposed to provide a blueprint for the future, and to lead the way to a more perfect world. I am not so naive as to believe that ordinary Party members read Marx or Lenin carefully, or that they spent much time discussing the nature of alienation in capitalism and its absence under socialism. The typical Party member was far more concerned with the price of automobiles, what the waiting period was to get one, and how this compared to prices and availability of cars in West Germany and the United States. However, this does not mean that ideology was unimportant.

Initially, after the Bolshevik Revolution, there was a substantial set of enthusiasts, both among intellectuals and workers, and eventually including newly recruited, ordinary Party workers. These workers believed that somehow things were going to get much better, and that in the long run the system would bring Russia out its weak, backward condition, and make it the foremost society in the world. Later, this faith was renewed by the victory over Nazi Germany, despite all the horrors of Stalinism and the suffering of the war.

In Central and Eastern Europe, there were many who believed the same thing in the late 1940s and early 1950s. After all, even the most bitter anti-communist writers who lived through that period, such as Milan Kundera (*The Joke*), attest to this spirit of youthful enthusiasm that was successfully created by Party cadres. Though mass popular support for the communists existed only in Czechoslovakia, Yugoslavia, and probably Albania, there were true believers everywhere else, and their early successes, coming after the devastation and demoralization of World War II, gave them enough genuine legitimacy to find hundreds of thousands of loyal, dedicated supporters in each country.

It became apparent that communism was not the way of the future, that Marxist-Leninist doctrine was not a science; to the contrary, the system guaranteed only stagnation and increasing corruption, and replaced faith with cynicism. It was not Stalinism that killed European communism, or Khrushchev's "hare-brained" schemes for reinvigorating and reforming communism, but rather Brezhnevism. Ironically, Brezhnevism was exactly what the bureaucracy wanted, meaning neither Stalinist terror nor Khrushchevian instability.

What choices were there? Mao was correct to conclude in his old age that the bureaucracy blocked continued revolutionary transformation. However, the Cultural Revolution showed that revolutionary enthusiasm without bureaucracy can only produce administrative chaos and economic disintegration. There is no known way to escape from this dilemma.

As economic growth declined, as the cadres lost hope, and as legitimacy declined, all that was left was cynical self-interest among those in power. Corruption not only increased, but worse, became the only glue holding the system together. Even though a substantial minority of the population felt it had something to lose if communism were overthrown, this was not enough. If the events of 1989 prove anything, it is that once a modern, urban, well educated society deems a political system to have lost its legitimacy, sooner or later it is doomed.

This is why so few social scientists who specialize in communist systems foresaw what was about to happen. It was possible to describe in meticulous detail all of the economic problems, but these had been known for a couple of decades. Everyone knew that by 1980 there was not a single communist government capable of winning an entirely free election, but that had almost always been true. Compared to many regimes around the world, from Burma to Zaire, most European communist societies in the 1980s were economically much more successful and politically more benign. They also ruled over countries with relatively good communications, and they controlled military and police forces that were well trained, well equipped, and loyal. They were not facing active rebellions, outside threats, or catastrophic depressions. Also, from the past we knew that there were many cases in which corrupt, inept regimes had remained in power for a long time.

Today, everyone talks about the rebirth of "civil society." In Poland and Hungary, what this amounted to was the creation of alternate social institutions, outside the party-state. Intellectuals were instrumental in turning their backs on official institutions, though in Poland they were greatly helped by the existence of a strong and supportive Catholic Church. The reason this occurred was that after the crushing of the Prauge Spring in the 1968, opposition intellectuals realized that traditional forms of revolutionary activity—plots, taking to the street, planning covert military actions and assassinations— could only produce bloody repression. So, they began to turn their backs on the establishment, a trend that was greatly strengthened when the Polish military regime successfully repressed Solidarity in 1981.

There were relatively few people involved in this withdrawal into an alternate social life. Few could afford this kind of sustained withdrawal except for intellectuals, and even in Poland, where the Church provided much broader institutional protection, most people's lives were not directly affected. They went to work, stood in lines, and remained passively alienated, as before.

By beginning to turn away from the state, and refusing to take it seriously, Polish, followed by other Central European intellectuals, exposed the shallowness of communism's claims and broke what little legitimacy communist regimes still had. It is because of his early understanding of this fact, and his excellent descriptions of how this new ideology grew in Central Europe, that Timothy Garton Ash has earned his justly deserved fame.[3]

Aside from a small number of scholars who wrote primarily for specialized journals journals such as *Telos, Cross-Currents*, or similar West European journals, very few scholars paid much attention to this phenomenon, which seemed limited to the literary, journalistic, and academic fringes. Most analysts were far too hard-headed, too realistic,and too enamored of materialist social science models to take such highly intellectualized discussions seriously, especially when they did not seem to be backed by any recognizable class interest. The significance of what was going on escaped almost everyone.[4]

However small the number of intellectual protesters who were turning their backs on the establishment (they seemed particularly isolated and unimportant in Czechoslovakia), however quixotic (as in East Germany, where they concentrated on helping conscientious objectors to the draft in Europe's most militarized and disciplined society), they fatally undermined what was left of communist legitimacy. The professional, highly educated middle class, on which every modern society depends, knew about these activities, and was encouraged to turn its back, too, even if only in small ways. The intellectual opposition turned Marxism-Leninism into a bad joke, it exposed the essential lie that lay behind it all. Once it was clear the Marxism-Leninism was wrong about the future, then all of the other lies, the repression, the historical falsification, lost their magical power. It is clear that the educated Communist Party apparatus lost faith in itself, almost totally. They became ashamed and unable to act in a time of crisis. And, in 1989, a crisis occurred that required much more than alienated toleration of the system.

The two long-term endogenous developments that undermined communism were economic failure and moral collapse. However, 1989 would have passed without much incident if it had not been for the pressure of external forces.

For Central and Eastern Europe, the exogenous causes of 1989 have to do with what was going on inside the Soviet Union. After Brezhenev's long delayed death, economic and moral decay combined with the growing fear that the Soviet military was falling behind NATO's military technology produced consensus within the party that supported Andropov's attempted reform of Brezhnevism and the reintroduction of dynamism. The Chernenko anti-climax proved that Brezhnevism was too dangerous to continue because it was incapable of solving anything. So, Andropov's chosen successor, Gorbachev, was anointed.

Until 1989, all of Gorbachev's efforts were directed at reinvigorating Leninism, not at killing it. He genuinely believed that after 70 years of socialism the Soviet people, if freed of corruption and remnants of Stalinism, would enthusiastically get to work and make it work. Then, combined with a decrease in military spending and increased trade with the West, which would be achieved by negotiating an end to the Cold War, Soviet Communism could get back on the right path.

This meant, among other things, avoiding military intervention in Central and Eastern Europe. Gorbachev almost certainly wanted to preserve communist regimes in the Soviet Empire, but he urged them to follow his path of reform and relegitimization.

This proved to be impossible. How Gorbachev and his closest advisors, from the sociologist Tatiana Zasalvskaya to his friend and foreign minister Edouard Shevarnadze, could have so misread the state of public opinion and the level of disgust with Leninism, is a whole story in itself.[5]

The fact is that this group's misinterpretation was enormous, and exposed the final contradiction of Leninism. People are not willing to make revolutionary sacrifices for a future which shows no signs of ever materializing. It is possible for millions to live ordinary, miserable lives without revolting against oppression, but only if no one tries to mobilize them. In trying to mobilize the Soviets for a new effort, Gorbachev made the collapse of Leninism inevitable.

Once it became apparent, in 1989, that Gorbachev was too busy at home, and relying too much on peace with NATO, to intervene in Central and Eastern Europe, the end came quickly. It was the old Stalinists, Erich Honecker and Nicolae Ceausescu, who best understood what a false promise Gorbachev offered. Without Stalinism, Leninism could not survive, and both vociferously denied that they had anything to learn from Soviet reforms. The first was overthrown by his Politburo as he was preparing to kill thousands of demonstrators to save his regime, and the second was shot by his army after it had joined in popular demonstrations to overthrow him. The other aged Stalinist in power, Todor Zhivkov of Bulgaria, tried to humor Gorbachev and simulate reforms, but he resigned, or was pushed out the day after the fall of the Berlin Wall. If the Red Army was unwilling to defend its key strategic position in Europe, East Germany, it was not going to save an old Stalinist in a reformer's costume in Bulgaria, either.[6]

The way in which communism fell in 1989 left behind what seemed to be almost unanimous admiration for what was previously communism's main ideological enemy from 1945 to 1989: Western European and American capitalist, parliamentary democracy. Naturally, practically all of the new governments in Central and Eastern Europe, with substantial popular support, declared that this is what they wanted. No other model had ever been seriously considered by the opposition, because, when compared to "really existing socialism," Western Europe and the United States seemed to be paradise. Some of the most thoughtful and knowledgeable new politicians argued that it would be better to take the "Swedish" or Austrian" road, softening capitalism with a developed welfare state, or coming up with some sort of social compact that Western political scientists call "neo-corporatism." Others demanded harsher reliance on market mechanisms. But for a time, the scope of debate was narrowed to what were essentially all liberal solutions: moderate, democratic, and capitalist; but also, as much as possible, humane, law abiding, and peaceful.

There is a terrible historical precedent for the liberation of Eastern and Central Europe: 1918. Then, there was a liberation, too, and great admiration for Wilsonian democracy. Within a decade, however, there was only one functioning democracy in the entire area, Czechoslovakia, and then, in the 1930s, there began the nightmare of growing fascism that culminated in the atrocities of World War II. Following a short period of hope, a new set of nightmares began which was to last into the 1980s. Why should a region with such an awful historical record, with poor economic prospects, and with so little experience with democracy turn out better in this round of liberation? One way of approaching this question is to see what went wrong after 1918.

Why Did Liberalism Fail Before World War II?

The history of this region after World War II has been well researched, and there is no need to cover it in any detail.[7] But some aspects of what happened need to be reviewed in order to explain the subsequent disasters, and to highlight the difference between the two periods of "liberation," after 1918 and 1989.

There was little consensus, either among intellectuals or within the general population about what sorts of ideological models should be followed after 1918. The regimes that survived, in Romania, Bulgaria, and Serbia (which has become the strongest component of Yugoslavia), as well as in Greece, which was culturally and politically a part of Eastern Europe until it joined NATO after World War II, were all insecure monarchies. Only the king of Yugoslavia, who was a Serb, came from a native family. The others were German, and aside from being a rallying point for conservative and military elites, these monarchies, installed in the late nineteenth century, never gained deep legitimacy. Even in Yugoslavia, there lingered doubts about which of the two feuding royal families should rule, and the King of the Serbs quickly made himself unpopular among Slovenes, Croats, and Macedonian Slavs. It is doubtful that Bosnian and Albanian Muslims in the new Yugoslavia ever accepted the newly imposed Serbian hegemony with anything other than resigned passivity.[8]

To the north, in what might properly be called Central Europe (a term that has more or less come to mean those parts of Europe east of Germany and Italy that are predominantly Catholic or Protestant) all the regimes were new. Poland and Hungary began their new lives with catastrophic wars. Hungary, which lost half its territory in 1918, experienced a communist revolution that was overthrown by a Romanian military invasion. The fact that it was the Romanians who received the best of the seized Hungarian lands, Transylvania, and that Hungarians despise Romanians as corrupt and effeminate (Hungarians used to joke about the perfumed Romanian cavalry officers who rode into Budapest after this war) did not help. Poland began by claiming a far greater territory than it was to be awarded. It invaded Lithuania to take Wilno, and soon it became involved in a war with the Soviet Ukraine. The Polish army reached as far as Kiev. But Trotsky's Red Army rallied, and almost pushed the Poles back to Warsaw. It was there the Red Army was stopped, barely, by the Poles, who were receiving French aid.

Austria, which should be considered Central European as well, was stripped of its empire and left isolated, poor, and internally sharply divided between right and left.

Within Central Europe, only Czechoslovakia was entirely happy with its new borders, though these came with a very substantial German minority, a backward, somewhat hostile Slovakia, and a very backward, isolated Ruthenia populated by Ukrainians (though there are Ruthenians who claim to be a distinct ethnicity). In the Balkans, Romania and Yugoslavia had had their claims satisfied, but at the cost of their neighbors, Bulgaria, Italy (which claimed much of the Dalmatian coast that went to Yugoslavia), Russia, and Hungary. Poland's very existence, of course, was an affront to Germany and Russia.

Poland and Romania were each only about two-thirds Catholic Polish and Romanian Orthodox, with the rest of their population consisting of other linguistic and religious groups. In both countries nationalists were anti-Semitic and resentful of the disproportionate share of professional and middle class urban positions held by the Jews.

All these countries except the Czech lands of Bohemia-Moravia, and Austria had a serious "peasant" problem, that is, an overpopulated countryside where many peasants continued to cultivate with primitive tools and inadequate credit. In Hungary and Eastern Poland (where most of the peasants were Belorussians and Ukrainians rather than Poles, but where long established Polish landowners still controlled vast properties) this was made worse by the presence of huge estates that owned much of the land.[9]

The new boundaries, almost completely re-drawn in Central Europe, and substantially altered in the Balkans as well, blocked old trading patterns. Polish industry based around Warsaw lost its Russian market; Czech and Transylvanian industries lost their Habsburg outlets; Croatia and Slovenia were thrown into an economy dominated by a more backwards Serbia. The French, who became the dominant political big power in this region after 1918, lacked the economic dynamism to be a major investor, market, or source of high technology.

Considering this daunting list of problems, it is not entirely surprising that things went badly. However, contrary to what most observers of that time thought, this does not explain the disasters that occurred.

A cursory examination of the interwar economic record shows that after the political situation stabilized in the mid-1920s, all of the economies in Central and Eastern Europe experienced substantial economic progress. The Great Depression of the early 1930s hit this region hard, but by the mid-1930s, rapid growth picked up again. If the 1920s and 1930s are taken as a single historical period, all of these countries, except Austria, which did not recover from its losses until after World War II, had rates of industrial growth that were high by any historical or comparative standard. All of them increased their food production faster than population growth, and all of them experienced significant drops in infant mortality, as well as in birth rates. Even in the most backward regions, schools began to reduce illiteracy.[10]

Nevertheless, in the 1930s, in all of these countries, with the exception of Bohemia-Moravia (but including the German minority in the Czech Sudeten), the forces of the far right gained, and those of liberal democracy declined. The economic and social progress of the late 1920s and the the mid-to-late 1930s counted for little. In the Balkans there were military-royal dictatorships established to control social and ethnic protest, starting with Yugoslavia in 1929, and spreading to Bulgaria, Romania, Greece, and even Albania, where a north Albanian tribal leader, Zog, tried to establish a royal dictatorship. The conservative dictatorship, established in Hungary in 1919 to 1920, and the moderate Polish dictatorship restablished in 1926, became harsher in the 1930s. Open, virulent anti-Semitism became a major problem in Poland, Hungary, and Romania, and the latter two developed strong, violent extreme fascist movements. In Austria a kind of clerical fascism, more moderate than Nazism, but still brutally repressive, was established after a near civil war with the Left in 1934, and the Nazi Party continued to grow in popularity until Austria was absorbed into the Third Reich in 1938.

By the late 1930s, in all these countries except Czechoslovakia, but including the three Baltic Republics, governments were controlled by authoritarian, conservative regimes whose main enemies were the much more radical forces of the far right. Yet even Czechoslovakia was not really an exception, because its moderate democratic government was also threatened by rightist nationalists in Slovakia and the Sudeten Germans, who turned wholeheartedly to Nazism. Why did this happen?

The answer is not to be found exclusively within the region. There existed, throughout Europe, an intellectual and ideological atmosphere which was contemptuous of, and violently antagonistic to liberalism. There is no better way to characterize these movements, whether the Volkisch ideology that gained ground in Germany in the 1920s, and came to power in 1933, or Italian fascism, or the Action Francaise, and the many other similar movements, than as thorough rejections of the European Enlightenment. Nor was this confined to populist, frightened middle class elements, as some analysts have claimed. On the contrary, such movements had very respectable intellectual antecedents in the late nineteenth century, and these were immeasurably strengthened by the disillusionment and cynicism produced by the terrible bloodshed of the First World War and its disturbing aftermath, in which none of the old problems of modern industrial society seemed to have been solved, despite all the sacrifice.[11]

Why such a large part of the late nineteenth century intelligentsia throughout Europe, from Russia to France, turned against democracy, capitalism, and the very idea that open tolerance and a free market in goods and ideas could bring progress, is a very large question which cannot be answered in a few paragraphs. What it amounted to, however, was a philosophical rejection of modernity as too crass, too uninspiring, lacking in honor and nobility, too alienating and uprooted from tradition, and finally, too corrupt to be tolerated. Some of the same intellectual rejection of liberal bourgeois democracy, which is to be found in thinkers as divergent from each other as Durkeim and Nietzsche, eventually spread very widely, in more popularized form, to weaken the legitimacy of democratic and moderate regimes. An important part of the revival of anti-Semitism, starting in France in the last decades of the nineteenth century, was connected to this rejection of the disturbing effects of modernization. The "Jew" became the symbol of everything "alien" introduced by greedy capitalism and misplaced democratic tolerance.

The right took the rejection of the Enlightenment further, by glorifying the mythical and unique role played by the "folk." A popular and obsessive image in rightist thinking throughout Central and Eastern Europe became the glorious, sacrificial battles fought against the savage hordes from the "east."

This disgust with the fruits of capitalist democracy was not uniquely a phenomenon of the right. Though the left eventually came to reject anti-Semitism, at least formally, because it was so closely associated with the right, the rationale beneath the rejection of capitalism was quite similar at both extremes of the ideological spectrum. Bourgeois democracy was a sham because it left too much power in the hands of the rich. Capitalism was disgusting because it was based on greed and exploitation. There was no solution but the overthrow of the whole rotten structure.

The height of this mentality was reached in Germany, and captured by Oswald Spengler, who became one of the most influential writers throughout Central Europe. Peter Gay, explicating and quoting phrases from Spengler's *Preussentum und Sozialisums*, summarizes the essence of Spenglerian thought:

> Class struggle is nonsense, and the German Revolution, that product of theory, is nonsense, too. The German instinct, which, rooted in the blood, is truthful, sees things very differently: "Power belongs to the whole...the individual serves it. The whole is sovereign....Everyone is given his place. There are commands and obedience. This, since the eighteenth century, had been authoritarian—*autoritativer*— socialism, in essence illiberal and anti-democratic—that is, if we think of English liberalism and French democracy." The true German must recognize the needs of the day and, yielding to them, transform the authoritarian socialism of the eighteenth into the authoritarian socialism of the twentieth century. "Together, Prussianism and socialism stand against the England within us, against the world view which has penetrated the whole existence of of our people, paralyzed it, and robbed it of its soul."[12]

England, or sometimes, despised, distant America stood for everything that was wrong with bourgeois society. As Friedrich Nietzsche had put it earlier, in *Beyond Good and Evil*, the English were "profoundly mediocre." Their great liberal philosophers, Hume and Locke, were capable only of "mechanical stultification of the world," and their scientists capable of little more than "narrowness, aridity, and industrious carefulness." In the *Genealogy of Morals*, Nietzsche had called on Germany to unite with autocratic Russia to become masters of the world, to give up "the English principle of the people's right of representation," and above all, he added, "No American Future!"[13]

This pervasive hatred of modernity fit very well with the nationalism which prevailed throughout Central and Eastern Europe. In virtually every case, it was an angry doctrine of educated elites who felt that they had not received their just rewards, or recognition from the more powerful and jealously admired but also deeply resented great Western powers, chiefly France and England. German as well as Russian nationalism had been based on such sentiments in the nineteenth century, and this has been used to explain their aggressive romanticism, the combination of self-pity and over confidence which lay at the heart of these nations' anti-liberalism.[14] In both Germany and Russia, the bitterness among nationalists provoked by the losses of the First World War brought such sentiments to the fore. They have been used to explain the rise of Hitler, and could probably serve to explain many aspects of Stalinism, too.[15]

Whatever interpretation of Russian and German history one may accept, it is even easier to see why the notion of "resentful nationalism" describes the sentiments of much of the intelligentsia in Central and Eastern Europe, particularly in Poland and Hungary. It works almost as well for the Balkan countries, too, all of whose modern nationalisms were conceived in the nineteenth century as a retrieval of past glories. Whatever the historical mythologizing, the actual, hard circumstances were bound to produce intense frustrations, for these were all too little, poor countries, unable to offer enough positions to their growing intelligentsias, and incapable of meeting the demands of grand nationhood. This was true before 1914, but became even worse after 1918, when almost every national elite was disappointed by the outcome. Andrew Janos, in a study of Hungarian nationalism until 1945, generalized his conclusions this way:

> [I]mages and expectations are disseminated faster than the means of material improvement, creating a deep sense of relative deprivation, indeed bitter frustration...in the long run, pent-up frustrations are likely to resurface time and again, to act as the single most important destabilizing factor in peripheral societies.[16]

The inherent contradiction between reality and nationalist aspirations pushed Hungarian and other nationalism in this region (and later, throughout much of the world) inevitably toward romantic escapism.

The dominant intellectual and ideological currents in between the world wars worsened ethnic conflicts, exacerbated border disputes, and made small economic successes seem insufficient, especially if they benefited classes other than the angry intelligentsia. They weakened the image, and therefore the stabilizing influence of the two great European democracies, England and France. The internal dynamics in this region were bad enough, but their intellectuals continued to look to the great European powers for ideas and inspiration, and what they heard and read immeasurably strengthened the forces of the anti-Enlightenment right. In France these sentiments were growing, but in Germany and Italy, they were triumphant.

It would be misleading to say that the noxious influence of Germany and Italy was limited to intellectual matters. Almost from the start of his rule, Mussolini began to interfere in Balkan and Central European affairs by providing subsidies and refuge for his friends such as the Croatian Fascists. There were arms deliveries to Austria, Hungary, and Bulgaria as well.[17] After Hitler's rise to power, direct German involvement in the politics and economies of the entire region were a major part of his foreign policy.[18]

It was not until 1938 that either the Germans or the Italians were in a position to intervene directly into Central or Eastern Europe. By then, except for the Czechs, all of the countries had, of their own will, and in accordance with growing popular sentiment, moved their countries substantially to the right. The ideological groundwork had been laid long before, and by then, the forces of obscurantism and nationalist hysteria had burst the bounds of philosophical discussion. They represented the most vigorous, youthful, and promising sectors of the population, not just the frightened old elites who had been worried about socialists and the Soviet Union. The conservatives, by then, would have been happy to see the fascist movements brought under control. In fact, in both Hungary and Romania, where fascist movements were the strongest, that is exactly what their conservative governments tried to do.

The influence of the more advanced, bigger European powers was real enough, but it would have been far weaker if it had been limited to direct economic and political pressure.

When the French and British betrayed Czechoslovakia at Munich in 1938, they did something much worse than letting down a strategically important ally. They confirmed the widely held perception that bourgeois democratic idealism really was nothing but a hypocritical mask for the interests of a small minority. That explains, in large part, why Hitler was to be so surprised by British resistance to compromise from 1939 to 1941.[19]

European Cores and Peripheries

The explanation of economic backwardness that lays the blame on the exploitation of peripheries by a capitalist core has venerable theoretical antecedents. It reached a peak of popularity in the late 1970s and early 1980s because of Immanuel Wallerstein's work.[20] On the whole, long before "world system theory" became known in the United States, it was widely accepted by intellectuals in the modern world's two first full-scale peripheries, Latin America and Eastern Europe.

The best available evidence from the latest research by economic historians, however, does not confirm the central thesis of world system (or, more properly, "dependency") theory for Eastern and Central Europe. On the contrary, the more exposure there has been in this region to Western economic forces, the more economic progress there has been. This works in regional comparisons at any particular time, and in temporal comparisons within any part of the area. To be sure, the evidence is complex, and to say this is not to make any claim that contact with advanced economies offers any panacea for backwardness. Economic peripherality in the eastern parts of Europe existed throughout the Middle Ages. In fact, merely on the basis of agrarian technology, it is possible to discern a distinct western, central, and eastern European pattern, and a fourth Balkan one as early as the twelfth or thirteenth century. Once backward areas were absorbed into the capitalist Western sphere, which happened very unevenly from the fifteenth until the early twentieth century, they did, indeed, behave in a peripheral way, as the theory predicts. But they also began to modernize, so that prolonged exposure and integration with the West, where it could be maintained, gradually decreased backwardness. Furthermore, political developments within all of Central and Eastern Europe, including Prussia, the Habsburg lands, and Russia, were not shaped primarily by economic peripherality. They were, to a considerable degree, independent, which explains why political outcomes in adjoining but economically similarly positioned countries could be so different. Otherwise, the great political strength of Prussia on one side, and Russia on the other, compared to the disintegration of the Polish state in the eighteenth century, would make no sense at all.[21]

Dependency theories have tended to be resolutely materialist, and in recent decades, almost exclusively Marxist. In fact, a case could be made for a cultural world system, with a powerful core generating scientific and technological inventions, philosophical schools, social theories, and of course, ideologies. These are then adapted in various ways in different peripheries, but the influence of the central core remains important. Marxism itself is a classic example of this. Mid-nineteenth century European positivism, particularly French, also had a brilliant career in peripheries from Brazil to Japan; as did social Darwinism. After all, the book widely considered to have most influenced the intelligentsia of the Russian Revolution, Nikolai Chernyshevsky's *What Is to Be Done*, was a crude materialistic and positivistic track without any trace of Marxist influence.[22]

Western Europe was the cultural and economic "core" for most of the nineteenth century, only losing its absolute cultural dominance after 1918, and more after 1945, to the United States and the Soviet Union. Yet, even in the darkest days of the European political and economic weakness in the years following World War II, Western Europe retained considerable influence. Though Western Europe will never regain the dominance it had before 1914, it has recaptured ground. The correlation between economic and cultural power is strong, but not absolute. In fact, the Soviet Union has had more of an influence on ideology in much of the "Third World," and among many intellectuals in the "First World," than it had either direct economic or political power.

This is not to suggest that ideologies always translate well. West European political and economic liberal ideas lost their essential qualities emphasizing individual freedom and responsibility when they were transferred to most other societies. As Tibor Szamuely and others have shown, among the Russian intelligentsia, utilitarianism and Spenserian social Darwinism were taken to mean that the state should be paramount because it alone could represent the true, scientifically ascertainable interests of the population. Nor does it mean that single or simple ideological trends sweep the periphery. After all, within the European core, there were always many conflicting trends.

Nevertheless, ideas and models from the core count for a great deal. Even Lenin relied on doctrinal evidence from the West, particularly on Karl Kautsky, in his version of *What Is to Be Done*, in 1902, which transformed Marxism into a revolutionary program for action.[23] What Lenin did was to adapt Marxist concepts to the deeply elitist, collectivistic, and anti-Western attitudes of the Russian revolutionary intelligentsia, while others versions of Marxism, was well as liberalism, failed to win over a large enough proportion of that stratum.

All of this was equally true in the different regions and countries of the lands in between Russia and Germany and in the Balkans. The local intelligentsias were predisposed to being hostile to liberalism by the lack of individualistic and democratic practice in their background. Few of them were comfortable with the idea that a business middle class, which, in their countries, often meant foreigners, particularly Jews in Poland, Hungary, and Romania, should become a powerful class. All of them considered themselves a natural elite, bearers of national consciousness, and inheritors of their glorious historical aristocracies.[24]

The rise of the right in the more powerful, advanced parts of Europe after 1918, particularly in Italy, and then in Germany, but also as a strong intellectual current in France, fit with the predisposition of the Eastern and Central European intelligentsias, and was adopted as a welcome counterweight to liberalism. One might ask why these intellectuals did not lean toward Marxism. After World War II, in much of the former colonial world, that is exactly what happened, with Marxism playing a role similar to that it had played in Russian before the Revolution. The primary reason Marxism was weak in Eastern and Central Europe was that the conservative forces which came to power everywhere in the region, except Czechoslovakia, were far more fearful of communism, and of the Soviet Union, than they were of the right, or of Germany and Italy. Furthermore, in the days of the Comintern, the communists were obliged to take many anti-nationalist positions, particularly where local national-ism conflicted with Russian interests, as they did along all of the USSR's western border. Finally, in the 1930s, Stalin effectively destroyed much of the leadership of Europe's communist parties.[25] Just as the forces of the right were on the ascendant, those on the left were in decline, and the middle was vanishing.

In light of this, it is easy to understand why the situation in the 1930s went from bad to worse. It should also be clear why the situation today is so different, and why, even if Eastern Europe goes from being a Soviet dependency to becoming, once again, a periphery of Western Europe, the consequences will not be anything like what happened before World War II.

Nationalism is certainly not a spent force in any part of Europe, or elsewhere in the world. But in Western Europe, now more than ever the intellectual and ideological beacon for Eastern and Central Europe, existing nations no longer make any territorial claims on each other, and they have ceased to harbor the historical resentments so essential to the rise of the right in the early twentieth century. There are right wing movements throughout Western Europe, but their ideology revolves primarily around stopping or reversing the flow of immigrants into Europe from the poor countries of Asia and Africa. Not even in Germany, where such movements could be directed against refugees from Eastern Europe, has there been any serious claim to old territories lost in the East, much less to France. The lessons of World War II were learned much better than those of World War I, and the extreme nationalist forces that continue to exist in Eastern Europe, particularly in the Balkans, can find no comfort, direct backing, or philosophical support in Western Europe.

The decline of the right is an old story, and dates from the calamitous fall of Hitler and Mussolini, as well as the exposure of the Nazi crimes. However, the decline of the left has now become equally as great. For a long time, the seeming success of communism in the USSR and the Warsaw Pact nations contributed to the maintenance of a strong left in West European, particularly French and Italian, politics. Many European intellectuals simply refused to accept liberalism and capitalism as valid doctrines, and deprived of the right, they flocked to the left. In the end, the failures of nationalizing schemes at home, and the growing evidence about the crimes, corruption, and inefficiency of communist states to the east, eroded support for the socialist state. The abandonment of socialist ideals has been so complete that even the social democrats, who retained some vague anti-capitalist commitments until recently, have been thrown into disarray.[26]

To an extraordinary degree, Western European politics have been "Americanized," that is, turned into a competition for power between various liberal forces, ranging from moderate social democrats on the left to Thatcherite conservatives on the right.

As far as the former communist countries in Eastern and Central Europe are concerned, there is no need to discredit the left, as it will be decades before a viable left will reassert itself. The way in which communism fell, without outside intervention, but from internal failure and moral collapse, will not be forgotten any time soon. And the absence of a real left in Western Europe, or, one can safely predict, in Russia, will make it that much more difficult for the left to develop elsewhere in Europe.

Economic and social problems in the former communist countries of Europe will be as severe as they were after 1918. In some ways it will be worse, because a whole social system and a vast economic infrastructure will have to be torn down and rebuilt. The difference is that developments in Western Europe make it almost inconceivable that either the far right or far left will overcome liberal forces. On the contrary, every bit of economic, political, and ideological influence from the West will push to strengthen liberalism.

As far as economic influence is concerned, almost all of the evidence we have from economic development over the past 40 years throughout the world, and from the economic history of Eastern Europe over the previous centuries, suggests that integration into the capitalist world market is beneficial, not harmful. The specter of permanent poverty through peripheralization, appealing as it was to anti-liberal intellectuals throughout the world, is almost certainly chimerical. I understand there are many social analysts who do not accept this point of view, though by now very few of them are economists. Limiting myself to Europe, where cultural similarities between cores and peripheries are far greater than on a world-wide scale, it is clear that Ireland, Spain, Portugal, southern Italy, and Greece are all much better off than they would have been had they remained isolated. They still have many problems, but these are not as bad as they were in the past. This is why the newly liberated, former communist countries would so like to be accepted into Europe, whatever the costs involved.

Political democracy and relatively free market economies have proved to be the strongest basis for the preservation and expansion of human liberty. Whatever internal problems may exist in Eastern and Central Europe, the important external circumstances suggest that it would be premature and almost certainly wrong to be too pessimistic about the future.

The Balkan Viper Pit and Other Dangers for Liberalism

The international setting may be favorable for liberalism in Eastern and Central Europe, especially when compared to the situation after 1918, but the domestic situation is not as optimistic. This is especially so in the Balkans.

If the lands between Germany and Russia were to be divided into Orthodox Christian and Muslim regions on one side, and Protestant and Catholic ones on the other, the line dividing the two would come close to delineating the border between countries where communist politicians have retained considerable power since 1989, and those where they have virtually vanished from the scene. Serbia, Montenegro, Albania, Bulgaria, and Romania were still in communist hands for some time after 1989, and, except for Bulgaria, still are. Even in Bulgaria the communists, under a different name, remain a major political force. Names and official policies have changed, but there is no concealing the survival of the old elites in commanding positions. To some extent, this pattern holds in the USSR as well, with the Baltic countries in the forefront of liberalization and behaving more like Central Europe, except for Lithuania, and the rest of the Soviet Union resembling the Balkans. Is this, finally, a visible dividing line between "Eastern" and "Central" Europe?

This should not be interpreted as any great love of communism among the Orthodox Christian peoples, much less among Muslims in the Balkans or in the Soviet Union. In Serbia, Albanian Kosovo, Albania proper, Macedonia, Bulgaria, and Romania, as in Russia, the Caucasus, Moldavia, and both the eastern, more Orthodox, and western, more Latin rite parts of the Ukraine, there is almost as much disgust with the corruption and lies of Leninism as in Poland and Hungary. In all these places there are vigorous opposition movements that want to destroy the remnants of the old systems.

What stands out in these areas, specifically in the Balkans, is the survival of a bitter, resentful, anti-democratic, illiberal strain of nationalism. While not entirely absent in Central Europe, aside from Slovakia, it is weak.

This is not something that suddenly appeared in the Balkans in 1989. In the last decade of communism, but starting in the early 1970s in Romania, and as early as the 1950s in Albania, it was precisely these virulent strains of nationalism, taken from the prevalent ideologies of the inter-war period, that were used to sustain and legitimize Balkan communists. They worked much better than the feeble attempts by the Central European communists to revive their fortunes in the 1970s and 1980s. Nationalism deflected dissidents, made those opposed to the regimes feel that they might be endangering national sovereignty, and generally distracted opposition by providing ethnic scapegoats for all of communism's failures. There was a substantially similar policy in Brezhnev's USSR, in which classical anti-Semitism was officially sanctioned under the guise of "anti-Zionism."

In the 1970s Nicolae Ceausescu's pet intellectuals recreated a doctrine that had been popular among the pre-war fascist intelligentsia. It claimed that Romania has long been in the forefront of European culture, that it has been a bastion of high civilization endangered by less civilized Magyar, Turkic, and Slavic hordes, and that the pure Romanians had been defending their homeland since pre-Roman times, though it was admitted that the mixture of Latins and Dacians had made a positive contribution in the second and third centuries. Since December, 1989, these same intellectuals have been peddling the same filth in Romania's best selling newspaper, *Romania Mare*, except that they have added scurrilous anti-Semitism to their repertoire, and they attack their old lord and master, Ceausescu. Their writings are full of imagined plots against them by western Jews, Masons, financiers, liberals, and Americans duped by the Hungarian or Jewish lobby. They are reproducing the youthful and heartfelt views of Mircea Eliade, an Iron Guardist in the late 1930s, who ended his days as one of the most popular teachers of mystical religion to eager American undergraduates in the 1970s and 1980s.[27]

It was only slightly better in the last years of Todor Zhivkov in Bulgaria. Understanding that communism was a spent force, he began a purification campaign against the Turkish minority, which amounts to at least 10% of the population, or perhaps up to 15%, in order to "Bulgarianize" it. In the mid-1980s, hundreds were killed, and thousands imprisoned, and, toward the end, hundreds of thousands driven into exile. The excuse was that they had been forcibly Islamized five centuries earlier, so it was only right to bring them back to the proper fold, whether or not they liked it. "National homogeneity" was the official goal. The claims were justified on pseudo-historical grounds that claimed the existence of a pure Bulgarian race, an original mixture of Huns and Slavs that had remained unsullied by all the migrations through the Balkans since the eighth and ninth centuries.[28] This was somewhat reminiscent of the research branch of Himmler's SS during World War II that tried to decide who among the Slavic, or other non-German speakers in the east were really lapsed Germans in order to reconvert these populations rather than exterminating or enslaving them.

There was something quite similar in Serbia, too. It was particularly virulent among academic intellectuals, and resulted in some severe cases of academic persecution in Serbian universities, where those unwilling to toe the ultra-nationalist line were harassed and fired.[29] The policy was more than theoretical in Kosovo, which is 90% Albanian, and where the

Serbs reasserted their authority with harsh measures. (Not that the tactics of the Albanians, which had relied heavily on intimidation to force the Serbian minority out of Kosovo before the crackdown, were any more "liberal.") There were appeals to a Greater Serbia, a reborn medieval empire, with borders considerably larger than the present ones of Serbia. This remains the goal today, described as bringing Serbs living in Bosnia or Croatia back into Serbia, but retaining historic Kosovo, even if few Serbs live there. It is nationalism, not communism, that sustains Slobodan Milosvic in power. Uncompromising cultivation of Serbian chauvinism, and authoritarian, tight central control by the Serbian government and military are the essential elements of his version of socialism.

By the 1980s, Balkan communism was well on its way to becoming indistinguishable from fascism. Its interpretation of the past was based on the same kinds of historical legends, its greatest goal was ethnic purity and the recovery of past grandeur; it persecuted minorities, it was brutally authoritarian, it was hostile to democracy, and it was anti-capitalist and increasingly anti-Western. In the 1990s, the same forces are alive and well in these countries, particularly in Romania, Serbia, and poor Albania, whose re-entry into Europe has exposed Enver Hoxha's fantasies for the cruel, xenophobic sham they always were. This augurs poorly for the future of the liberalism in the Balkans, but it is certainly not the result of the events of 1989. On the contrary, it is because these are the countries in Eastern Europe that have not experienced the full revolutions that took place further north.

It is not uniformly easy to explain this. Albania was always isolated from Europe, and always the poorest part of the Continent, tribally divided, feuding, and illiterate. Its backwardness and illiberalism seem connected, and easy to explain.

Bulgaria, also relatively isolated from the West, was much less so, and much more developed than Albania. But it suffered from isolation before the late nineteenth century, and then again under communism until the 1980s. Until the 1980s, in fact, when it was passed by Romania, it seemed to be the European country most cut off from the West, except for Albania.

Romania, in its cities, particularly Bucharest, was very much a part of the Central European tradition before World War II. However, after 1940, Romania fell into a dark period, and except for a brief respite in the late 1960s and early 1970s, it was also isolated; and in the last decade of Ceausescu's rule, its intellectuals almost lost contact with the West, while Romania's economy declined. Romania became Europe's second poorest and second most isolated country.

It is plausible that having been cut off from the prevailing trends in Western Europe has resulted in the continued strength of what strikes other Europeans as archaic, primitive nationalism, and for the failure to grasp the liberalizing trend of the past forty years.

This is a poor explanation for what is going on in Yugoslavia, which was the most open communist country in the world from the 1950s until the 80s. Yugoslavia's intellectuals generated an early and promising liberal dissident movement (centered on the writings of the Praxis group). Even before that, the Yugoslav experiment with workers' management had seemed to offer a way out of Leninist-Stalinist autocratic centralism. But Yugoslavia never really worked as a country, at least not after 1929. It had the most bitter civil war in Europe from 1941–44, in which over ten percent of the population was killed, more by internal ethnic conflict than because of fighting with the Germans and Italians, who, in any case, had local allies. Added to the continuing inequality between the regions of Yugoslavia, and the ultimate failure of socialism, this legacy of conflict has obviously come to the fore, even among Serbian intellectuals, whose westernization has turned out to be weak.

In the end, the Orthodox tradition must count, too, not only for Serbia, but for Romania and Bulgaria as well. The absence of Enlightenment influences, such as those that penetrated Poland directly from France, or of an earlier Protestant Reformation, which left such a strong imprint on Bohemia-Moravia and Hungary (including Transylvania), meant that Orthodox thinkers were cut off from the individualistic and liberalizing philosophies that changed Western thought. Indeed, Orthodox thought has been marked by less flexibility, a weaker tendency toward rationalization, than either Catholicism or the Protestant sects of Central Europe.

In combination with greater isolation from the West during communist times, or, in the case of Serbia, the stress produced by the most intense, violent ethnic conflicts in Europe, the Orthodox predisposition to be less tolerant and open to liberal thinking has produced a higher degree of xenophobia and authoritarianism than in Central Europe, as well as greater distrust and resentment against outsiders.

The intolerance and extreme nationalism of the Poles and Hungarians, without mentioning the German and Austrians before World War II, might seem to put such historical reasoning in doubt; but they do not.

Most of Continental Europe drifted toward the right in those years, and Central Europe, except for the isolated island of Bohemia-Moravia (which was hardly perfect, but still stood in marked contrast to its neighbors), was part of this swing. From the late nineteenth century until the mid-twentieth, there was the most concentrated attack on the Enlightenment tradition in modern European history. It failed, and now it is different because Central Europe, still a part of Europe, has learned the terrible lessons of the twentieth century. Yet, in the Orthodox and Muslim Balkans (and, it is to be feared, perhaps in the Orthodox and Muslim parts of the USSR), this has not happened.

Although anti-Semitism remains potent and widespread in Poland, and even in Hungary, the attempts of the communists in Poland to exploit it in 1968, and as late as the early 1980s, have failed, largely because intellectuals refused to take the bait. In Hungary, the Party never tried this tactic, though in Czechoslovakia, it certainly played on the Czech-Slovak divide.

Both before and after 1989, the astonishing fact is that so few Central European intellectuals went along with ultra-nationalist positions. This was even so during the recent elections there. Despite Adam Michnik's fear and loathing of Lech Walesa, it was not Walesa but fringe forces which have now virtually vanished that tried to capture this sentiment. Even in Slovakia, which is breaking away from Czechoslovakia, there is little likelihood of violence. Thus, with rare exceptions, the anti-Semites, the hysterical nationalists, those calling for a return to pre-war racial doctrines in Central Europe have found little leadership or respectability.

Do Ideas Really Matter?

In sum, the prospects for liberalism seem reasonably good in Central Europe, in part because of the economic and political influence of Western Europe and the favorable conditions which prevail in the European Community. But of equal or grater importance, though certainly related to the enormous success experienced by Western Europe over the past four decades, is the ideological climate throughout Europe. This will even have considerable effect in the Balkans, though there, the weakness of liberal sentiment among the intellectuals, the xenophobia, and the ethnic tensions added to the ethnic tensions added to the problems of economic transition augur much more poorly.

However, in the the case of the Balkans, the fact that Europe as a whole is at peace, that there will be no support for the Balkan extremists, means that the damage can be contained. Soviet-style socialism, whatever may happen in the USSR itself, has been entirely discredited. On the other side, the extreme right, which has strength in several Balkan countries, will be isolated.

Yet such a conclusion, based on a review of intellectual currents and European ideological trends, may seem to raise more issues than it answers. What about the very real, concrete problems of economic change? There is rising unemployment. There are, in all these countries, highly self-aware working classes whose livelihood is endangered by the collapse of large state enterprises. Aid from the West will be insufficient. Profiteers and speculators, who are already thought to be having a field day, will be resented by populations unaccustomed to the ways in which markets work. The vast civil service bureaucracies will react, also, as their jobs are threatened.

The signs from Germany are not reassuring. There is the revival of a far right, as in France, largely directed against foreign immigrants. Inflation and unemployment are increasing, especially in the former German Democratic Republic. Could the conditions of the 1920s and 1930s be reproduced? Would an analysis based on the study of class interests lead to the kind of conclusion I have suggested?

Perhaps not. But the relatively optimistic future I predict, especially for Central Europe, is also a statement about social theory. Larger intellectual currents, on a world scale, and even more obviously at a continental level, are both causes of and powerful indicators of what will happen.

For much of the past half century social science theory has been overwhelmingly materialist. Cultural and ideological realities have been considered epiphenomenal, mere reflections of class and economic realities.

Without wanting to exaggerate in the other direction, I think it safe to say that the events of 1989 have larger implications than the mere failure of a particular economic system. The old European Enlightenment, written off as dead so many times by skeptical intellectuals, has survived in its most liberal and tolerant form. It is back as the world's strongest ideology, and it seems more firmly based than at any time in the twentieth century, or at least since World War I.

This does not mean that the triumph of liberalism is assured once and for all, especially in the least Europeanized and poorest regions of the world. But in Central Europe, certainly, and even in the rest of Eastern Europe, it can no longer be dismissed as the remnant of a discredited bourgeois past. On the contrary; it looks much more like the future than like the past. And this, more than anything else, greatly increases the prospects of liberal democracy in these countries.

Endnotes

1. Council for Mutual Economic Assistance—the communist trading bloc, also called COMECON.
2. Rostow, W.W., "Eastern Europe and the Soviet Union: A Technological Time Warp," Chirot, Daniel, ed., *The Crisis of Leninism and the Decline of the Left: The Revolutions of 1989,* University of Washington Press, Seattle, WA, 1991.
3. His major essays of the late 1980s have been collected in Garton Ash, Timothy, *The Uses of Adversity,* Random House, New York, NY, 1989.
4. Aside from Garton Ash, a notable exception was Tony R. Judt in a paper delivered a the Woodrow Wilson Center in Washington during the summer of 1987, and published as "The Dilemmas of Dissidence: The Politics of Opposition in East-Central Europe," *Eastern European Politics and Societies,* 2:2, 1988.
5. See Stephen Hanson's essay, "Gorbachev: The Last True Leninist Believer?" in Chirot, *The Crisis of Leninism,* pp. 33–59.
6. I offer a short analysis of what happened, though with considerably more detail than I have provided here, in "What Happened in Eastern Europe in 1989," in *Crisis of Leninism,* pp. 3–32.
7. The classic work is Rothschild, Joseph, *East Central Europe Between the Two World Wars,* University of Washington Press, Seattle, WA, 1974. Also very useful are Weber, Eugen, "Romania," Whiteside, Andrew, "Austria," and Deak, Istvan, "Hungary" in Hans Roger and Eugen Weber, *The European Right,* University of California Press, Berkeley and Los Angeles, CA, 1966. An elegant treatment of the conflicting cultural tendencies during this period is Gregor von Rezzorl's *Memoirs of an Anti-Semite,* Viking Press, New York, NY, 1981.
8. For anyone interested in the immense complexities of the Yugoslav situation, and the mistakes that were made by the Serbs almost form the beginning to compound an already tense situation, see Banac, Ivo, *The National Question in Yugoslavia: Origin, History, Politics,* Cornell University Press, Ithaca, NY, 1984.
9. Warriner, Dorreen, *Economics of Peasant Farming,* Barnes & Noble, New York, NY, 1964, reprint of 1939 edition.
10. This is based on the statistics in Mitchell, B.R., *European Historical Statistics,* Columbia University Press, New York, NY, 1978. My argument, which goes against the generally pessimistic consensus among specialists, is explained fully in "Ideology, Reality, and Competing Models of Development in Eastern Europe Between the Two World Wars," *Eastern European Politics and Societies,* 3:3, pp. 378–411, 1989.
11. This is the great merit of Nolte, Ernst, *Three Faces of Fascism,* Weidenfeld and Nicolson, London, UK, 1965. It traces the intellectual roots of these move-

ments in France, Italy, and Germany, and takes their ideologies seriously, as sets of ideas, not as superficial expressions of class-based interests.

12. Gay, Peter, *Weimar Culture: The Outsider as Insider*, Harper Torchbooks, New York, NY, pp. 86, 1970.

13. *The Philosophy of Nietzsche*, Modern Library, New York, NY, pp. 565–67, 802, 1954.

14. This is the main theme in Liah Greenfeld's massive book, *Nationalism*, Harvard University Press, Cambridge, MA, 1992. She explains Russian nationalism in "The Formation of the Russian National Identity: The Role of Status Insecurity and Resentment," *Comparative Studies in Society and History*, 32:3, pp. 549–91, 1990.

15. In particular, extreme Russian nationalism has been skillfully used in Robert C. Tucker's masterful new biography to explain many of Stalin's positions, as well as his sources of support within the Party. See *Stalin in Power: The Revolution from Above, 1928–1941*, Norton Press, New York, NY, 1990.

16. Janos, Andrew, *The Politics of Backwardness in Hungary, 1825–1945*, Princeton University Press, Princeton, NJ, p. 315, 1982.

17. Mack Smith, Dennis, *Mussolini: A Biography*, Vintage Press, New York, NY, pp. 154–56, 1983.

18. Berend, Ivan I., and Ranki, Gyorgy, *Economic Development in East Central Europe in the Nineteenth and Twentieth Centuries*, Columbia University Press, New York, NY, pp. 267–282, 1974.

19. Hitler was convinced that the British were opposed to war, and once they understood that the did not threaten their most vital interests, they would come to their senses. "I don't believe in idealism," he said in private on February 6, 1942. "I don't believe that a people is prepared to pay for ever for the stupidity of its rulers. As soon as everybody in England in convinced that the war can only be run at a loss, it's certain that there won't be anyone left there who feels inclined to carry on with it." *Hitler's Table Talk 1941–44: His Private Conversations*, Weidenfeld and Nicolson, London, UK, pp. 299–300, 1973.

20. For a fuller discussion, see Daniel Chirot and Thomas Hall, "World System Theory," *Annual Review of Sociology* No. 8, pp. 81–106, 1982. A more complete bibliography and critique of Wallerstein can be found in Charles Ragin and Daniel Chirot, "Immanuel Wallerstein's World System: Sociology and Politics as History," in Theda Skocpol, ed., *Vision and Method in Historical Sociology*, Cambridge University Press, New York, NY, pp. 276–312, 1984.

21. This is, to say the least, an academically controversial position, but it is supported in some detail by the various articles in Daniel Chirot, ed., *The Origins of Backwardness in Eastern Europe: Economics and Politics from the Middle Ages until the Twentieth Century*, University of California Press, Berkeley, CA, 1989. See in particular, the essays by Peter Gunst, Jacek Kochanowicz, and Fikret Adanir.

22. Szamuely, Tibor, *The Russian Tradition*, McGraw-Hill, New York, NY, pp. 168–72, 1973.

23. Leonard Schapiro is particularly clear about this in his article "Marxism in Russia," in his collected essays, *Russian Studies*, Viking Press, New York, NY, pp. 151–53, 1987.

24. Bauman, Zygmunt, "Intellectuals in East-Central Europe: Continuity and Change," *East European Politics and Societies*, 1:2, pp. 162–86, 1987.

25. Roy Medvedev has catalogued the destruction, particularly in the Polish Communist Party, but in the others as well, in the late 1930s. *Let History Judge: The Origins and Consequences of Stalinism,* Columbia University Press, pp. 430–36, 1989, revised edition.

26. Seymour Martin Lipset has documented the collapse of the moderate left throughout the democratic parts of the world in "No Third Way: A Comparative Perspective on the Left," in Chirot, ed., *The Crisis of Leninism.*

27. Verdery, Katherine, *National Ideology Under Socialism: Identity and Cultural Politics in Ceausescu's Romania,* University of California Press, Berkeley, CA, pp. 284–301, 1991. "Happy Guilt: Mircea Eliade, Fascism, and the Unhappy Fate of Romania," *The New Republic,*" 8/5/91, pp. 27–36.

28. See, for example, Gale Stokes, ed., *From Stalinism to Pluralism: A Documentary History of Eastern Europe Since 1945,* Oxford University Press, New York, NY, 1991. A speech by Stanko Todorov, pp. 232–34.

29. Stokes, Gale, *From Stalinism,* translated a good example of this kind of reasoning by Veljko Gubernia, a noted Belgrade lawyer, pp. 224–28.

Academe and the Soviet Myth

Robert Conquest
Hoover Institution, Stanford University

As we all know, over the past half century an influential section of Western academe became addicted, to a greater or lesser degree, to Marxism. At the same time, and mainly as part of this phenomenon, many academics became firm believers in a large array of falsehoods about the Marxist states, in particular the Soviet Union.

Not all Marxists believed the Soviet myth, though most of them did. And by no means all who misunderstood the Soviet Union were Marxists, though it is true that many of them had probably been affected to some extent by the Marxist tinge in the prevailing intellectual atmosphere.

Those who were grossly and fundamentally deceived about both the facts and the motivations of the Stalin and post-Stalin regimes in the USSR were not only academics. Journalists like Lincoln Steffens and (more cynically) Walter Duranty, and a dozen others; diplomats and politicians like Joseph Davies and Harry Hopkins: a whole spectrum of those responsible for purveying the facts and playing a role as formers of governmental and public opinion here, played a major role.

However, the academics may in the long run have been the most influential in peddling falsehood, if only from their particular claim to special knowledge and to the disinterested pursuit of truth, and also from the fact that politicians, media and public took this seriously, and each ill-formed politico and editor maintained a supposed expert to support his own preconceived opinions.

It was in the 1930s, just when the Soviet system was in its very worst phase, that major validation of the enormous set of falsifications with which this was concealed came for the first time from Western academics of the highest standing.

The stars were Sydney and Beatrice Webb, the deans of Western social science. The motivations of the Webbs are clear enough, and may be divided into two main attitudes, which we find in different forms throughout Western pseudological writing on the Soviets. First of all, for them "Socialism" was the society of the future, in which government representing the people would provide a planned economy, with beneficial results. They thought they saw socialism in the USSR, as indeed they did. This led, as is normal in academic self-deception, to their excusing some of the undemocratic reality and denying the rest. Subsequently, their work was of a genre common in literature, but hitherto never applied to a real country: Utopian fantasy.

The Webbs' second contribution to our field was also to persist until quite recently in some academic circles: They accepted as true the facts, figures, and so forth published by the Communists. They thought that the electoral system, the trade unions, and the cooperatives existed in reality in the forms which in fact existed on paper only.

The Webbs' book, seen as the last word in serious Western scholarship, ran to over 1200 pages, representing a vast amount of toil and research, all totally wasted. It was originally entitled, *Soviet Communism: A New Civilization?*; but the question mark was triumphantly removed in the second edition which appeared in 1937, at precisely the time the regime was in its worst phase of gloomy, all-embracing terror.

Their view of what they reckoned as the exile of a million odd families of 'kulaks' was that "the Soviet government could hardly have acted otherwise," and indeed that "strong must have been the faith and resolute the will of the men who, in the interest of what seemed to them the public good, could take such a decision." When it comes to the artificial famine of 1933 in the USSR, whose mere existence was then denied by the regime, but is now officially reckoned as taking six or seven million lives, they say there was merely some local food shortage due, anyhow, to "sabotage" by the peasant population. On the faked Moscow Trials, they take the view that the confessions of the accused were due to their "behaving naturally and sensibly, as Englishmen would were they not virtually compelled by their highly artificial legal system to go through a routine which is useful to the accused only when there is some doubt as to the facts." Another leading British academic, the highly influential Professor Harold Laski, took a similar view, with particular praise for Stalin's villainous prosecutor Andrei Vyshinsky, who was "doing what an ideal Minister of Justice would do if we had such a person in Great Britain."

It is significant that the Webbs (Laski too) had little knowledge of history and approached the evidence from the point of view of analytical social and political science. We shall come across later examples of this often long and laborious, but essentially worthless, type of approach.

Another leading British academic of the period did not even have their excuse of arrogant ignorance. Sir Bernard Pares, Britain's leading Russianist, had opposed the Soviets, but changed his mind on arriving in Moscow late in 1935, and instantly feeling that the Bolsheviks "were Russia." He went on to believe the Soviet version of the trials, adding his own fatuous contribution that "the bulky verbatim reports were in any case impressive." Once again this inability to imagine that official documents could be a pack of lies; and we shall find this to be true even in the 1990s!

Throughout the 1940s and 1950s, much truth about the USSR became available in the West, and there were a number of academics who were, in one way or another, directly and personally involved in the real politics of the war and post-war period. The fantasy, to emerge again in the next academic generation, was much less in evidence.

One of those writing was Merle Fainsod who, in 1953, produced his excellent study *How Russia is Ruled*, and revised it well in 1963. Here, alas, we are led into the modern period. After Fainsod's death, the task of producing a new edition fell to a young scholar, Jerry Hough.

An academic scandal well known in the Sovietological field ensued. Hough changed the title to the more polite *How the Soviet Union is Governed*, and used the prestige of the original, adding; "By Jerry F. Hough and Merle Fainsod. Revised and enlarged by Jerry F. Hough." The "revising" consisted of reversing and distorting the whole work. To take a particularly revealing example: Fainsod's index gives over 60 references to Forced Labour Camps; Hough's revision gives none. Again while Fainsod spoke of millions of victims of Stalinism, Hough gave a totally contrary view. I remember at Columbia more than twenty years ago, Stephen Cohen saying to me; "There's someone here who thinks Stalin only killed ten thousand people." "No, there isn't," I said, confidently. Steve led me over to where Hough stood and asked; "Jerry, how many people did Stalin kill?" "Ten thousand, or so," he replied. In his pseudo-Fainsod he takes the same view, though there and later admitting a possibility of "a figure in the low hundreds of thousands." Of course, even then the question was how many millions, or tens of millions, as is now fully confirmed in Russia. A single one of the mass graves lately dug up there holds more than Hough's whole estimate.

It should be noted that, parasitical on the success of Fainsod's original, Hough's version was and still is a textbook for many students.

Hough also described Brezhnev's Soviet Union in strange terms: "The Soviet system [is] a very participatory one;...the regime has become more tolerant of individual iconoclasm, including political dissent, than it was...in the Khrushchev era;...Brezhnev came to power promising normalcy, and it was a pledge that he kept"; the Soviet Union is "a parliamentary system of a special type." "Pluralist" was a phrase also much used, not only by Hough. Hough is to be taken into account, if only because he still figures, or did so until recently, as a guru on television and in the other media.

Hough is to some extent a freak, even among oddball Sovietologists. But he was an influential precursor of the "revisionist" Sovietology which became vociferous in the mid-1980s. These persons formed a group which claimed to present a truer picture of the Stalin period than that prevailing among what they call "Cold War" Sovietologists. Their general thesis was that the terror had been fairly minor: their chief American proponent, J. Arch Getty, wrote of "thousands" executed and "tens of thousands" imprisoned. Playing down the extent of the terror was not the only point; they also held that terror was not in any case of major importance, since institutional and social changes were the true essence of the period, though terror affecting millions directly and the whole population indirectly might also be thought of as a social phenomenon. They were also interested in the rise of new cadres, but not in the criteria for their selection—servility, brutality and coarseness of mind, constituting what is now called in Russia a "negative selection" of the new ruling class. Nor were the revisionists interested in the methods of personnel change – the denunciation and execution of their predecessors. Others of this school wrote of the collectivization in a similar vein, as a social change, and they praised the party emissaries from the cities who effected it – i.e., bullied the peasants into submission.

Part of the trouble was that revisionists such as Getty were, like Hough, sociologists by training, rather than historians, and sought (in rather the same context as that which produced Marxism) the structural rather than the essential, the form rather than the content. This also led them, like the Webbs before them, into accepting official documents as better evidence than what they referred to as "anecdotal" accounts – that is, the first hand testimony of actual witnesses which contradicted the official picture. As we now know, this unofficial evidence was vastly superior to the official, and even when not conclusive was not simply one vast fake like the Communist product.

Then, a plaint common to all these people is that some of us allegedly used the "totalitarian model" in describing the Soviet Union. This merely shows the limited nature of their conceptions. They assume that everyone has "models." In reality we used the *word* "totalitarian" as generally descriptive of Stalinist society. Leszek Kolakowski and Giovanni Sartori have argued at length that the word is indeed a useful one, and Gorbachev and Yeltsin have both employed it to describe the old Soviet system.

Myopic obsession with official data often goes hand in hand with an openly expressed desire to avoid the "judgmental." This has led, and not only in revisionist circles, to a mediocrity in the teaching of Soviet studies. One result is that students have been actively discouraged from the more profound areas in which serious moral or political judgments are unavoidable, and play safe with "objective" themes like cotton prices in Uzbekistan.

The idea is that opinions, even strong ones, are incompatible with the most conscientious treatment of the facts. Historians of any sense have long known that this is an absurd error. Gibbon wrote of the fanatical Jensenist Tillemont that he was nevertheless completely "scrupulous" about evidence. Trevelyan saw that not "dispassionateness" but "good faith" was the real crux. The supposed neutrality of an academic is very often, in fact, no more than the acceptance of the effects of unadmitted prejudices of his time or his circle.

One book put the view that "the building of real conceptual bridges between comparative politics and Soviet studies...would have demonstrated more forcefully than any argument that the Soviet Union was not an outsider in the family of nations, or pariah. In destigmatizing the Soviet system, it would have moved specialists on Soviet subjects more squarely into the midstream of the discipline of political science."

A prominent British professor similarly complained that a judgmental approach to Soviet history was "more reminiscent of propaganda than of social science," and added that; "Economists have learned more about resource allocation from a single issue of the official statistical handbook than from all the writings of Solzhenitsyn, Zinoviev, et. al." This was written in 1987, just before the official figures were publicly exposed as fakes in Moscow.

In fact the whole question of Soviet economic strength had long been obfuscated in Western study. Alain Besançon pointed out in 1980:

> The Soviet economy is the subject of a considerable volume of scholarly work, which occupies numerous study centres in Europe and the United States and which provides material for a vast literature and various academic journals. But those born in the Soviet Union, or those who approach Soviet society through history, literature, travel or through listening to what the emigres have to say, find that they cannot recognize what the economists describe. There seems to be an unbridgeable gap between this system, conceived through measurement and figures, and the other system, without measurement and figures, which they have come to know through intuition and their own actual experience. It is an astonishing feature of the world of Soviet affairs that a certain kind of economic approach to Soviet reality, no mater how well-informed, honest and sophisticated, is met with such absolute skepticism and total disbelief by those who have a different approach that they do not even want to offer any criticism, it being impossible to know where to begin.

The fullest study, sponsored by the CIA, was totally misleading, as the Moscow analyses released a couple of years ago made absolutely clear. The CIA's experts did not actually accept official Soviet figures. However, they accepted them as the basis of analysis because they were the only figures available, with the assumption that they were distorted or exaggerated in certain aspects, but still useful. In fact, they were not distorted, they were *invented*. Once again, there was a defect in the imagination of the Western researchers.

In the novel *1984*, Orwell has Winston Smith reading in the official newspaper of a minister announcing to triumphal trumpets that 50 million pairs of boots had been produced last year. Winston Smith, quite apathetically and with no special political attitude, says to himself that for all he know no boots at all were produced. Orwell understood Soviet statistics; academic economists did not. I have more than once been asked in Russia how it was that a writer like Orwell grasped the essentials of the Soviet regime and so many supposedly trained Western Sovietologists did not. The answer seems to be that he had the necessary imagination. They could not believe that statistics could be totally falsified nor that millions of citizens could be killed and tortured, since such things were outside their own narrow range of experience.

Of course, when you get to the real kooks, there is stuff even odder than the CIA's, as with John Kenneth Galbraith, in the true Webb tradition, telling us in 1984 that the "Soviet system has made great economic progress in recent years....One can see it in the appearance of solid well-being of the people in the streets," adding that, in particular, unlike Western economies, the Soviet Union, "makes full use of its man-power." A staggering misstatement.

The extent to which this fetishism of official documents and attitudes prevailed may be seen even in the supposedly rigorously numerical field of demography. Two demographers, with little knowledge of Soviet matters, published in the mid-1980s analyses of the Soviet human losses in the 1930s. They began with assumptions about quite different populations, and applying these to the USSR found that high death rates were implausible. A pointless exercise.

In a controversy with them, I referred to the 1939 Soviet census as a "fake." They replied that no censuses were perfect, and that I was not thereby entitled to pick and choose which census I accepted. My objections to the 1939 census were: that a census taken in 1937 had been suppressed and the Census Board shot for "diminishing the population of the Soviet Union," so that the new Census Board had some incentive to exaggerate the numbers; that these new figures were announced in 1939 before the new Census board had delivered its figures; and so on.

All obvious enough, and Soviet publications have since confirmed the obvious: that the millions reported in the 1939 document "existed only on paper." Yes, official "documentary" evidence was totally worthless and a tiny modicum of common sense should have made this plain even to an academic.

Of course, Soviet material published in the late 1980s and early 1990s have destroyed these and similar delusions. Or so one might think; but this would be underestimating the skill of the academic mind in devising evasive stratagems. Even in the true sciences, deep intellectual investment in what turns out to be fallacy is not easily given up.

Without frankly repudiating their errors, survivors of the revisionist writers now tend to concentrate on the period's detailed documentation at the lower level now becoming available in the USSR, though they take the view that statements made by activists and others in the localities represent evidence of "grass roots" feelings rather than being at least somewhat constrained by the Stalinist ambience. This work on such details is not without its uses. Above all else, it signals that the researcher is working away, being scholarly.

Meanwhile, a last ditch defense by the misinterpretators of the USSR is that while those who took a soft view of the regime were mistaken, those who took a hard view believed that the regime could not be changed. This is untrue. I, and as far as I know all those who took the hard view, have continually expressed agreement with Orwell's remark that it would "either democratize or perish."

'Houghites', and so forth, now claim that they predicted the liberalization of the USSR. No; they said it was liberal already, and becoming more liberal. This they attributed to the political good will of the rising generation of rulers. No, the end of the old regime was due to its complete inherent rotteness and non-viability, and when the facts left no alternative its new rulers tried by new policies to save rather than to abandon the system.

What were the plausible motivations for this whole intellectual disaster? First, as we have earlier said, fetishism of the word socialism. Along with that, hostility to the West and to the United States in particular, manifested in praise of its opponents. Then, in the case of the younger lot, a desire to be original, to avoid endorsing established views. The revisionist attitude was, indeed, not original in the sense that it echoed the Webbs and other earlier dupes. But it was, in the 1980s, "challenging" and appealing to editors who wanted "provocative" pieces; and, in the long run, helpful in careers. Nor should we neglect mere vanity; the feeling that it would have been impossible for *them* to be deceived.

As to Marxism proper this has exerted a wholly destructive influence on serious study of the USSR or of any other polity, including our own. It its pure form, it will soon so doubt only be found, like the spotted owl, in a few sanctuaries on the Pacific Coast. However, its remnants still distort the study not only the USSR, but of practically all the humanities.

One remarkable phenomenon is that as the influence of Marxism started to collapse, it left an influential detritus, especially in the English departments, at a lower intellectual level still. Marx and Trotsky, Gramsci and Lukacz may be been fanatics and pseudoscientists, but at least they believed that rational discourse was possible, and held that some literature transcended class attitudes. Now we have the quasi-Marxism of the deconstructionism in academe. I have suggested elsewhere that Lenin's phrase "Left-wing Communism and Infantile Disorder" might apply, except that in the present late period of the ideology it should be described as "A Senile Disorder."

I have concentrated on the theme of academic unwillingness to face reality in the case of the Soviet Union. Academe still suffers from the effects of this, but also of the more general Marxist and quasi-Marxist simplicities. Perhaps this is because the academic mind prefers the comforts of unifying formulae to the discomforts of reality and of serious thought. Among lesser beings there is word for this: stupidity. It is, and has been, a dangerous stupidity. Insofar as it had an effect on public policy, it was thoroughly negative. Insofar as it penetrated education, it was anti-educative.

Why Didn't We Anticipate the Failure of Communism?

Seymour Martin Lipset
George Mason University

The basic question which social scientists have to deal with in reacting to the collapse of Communism in the Soviet Union is why they, and, it must be admitted, other non-academic experts, such as the intelligence agencies of the great Western powers, did not anticipate that this would happen, or even that it could occur. The evidence is fairly clear that the world was taken by surprise by the transformations which emerged under Gorbachev and even more by the outlawing of the Communist Party after the coup against him. There was, of course, a failure to anticipate that the Eastern European Communist regimes would give up power.

These events, both in the Russian empire and in the Soviet Union itself, seemingly challenged a fundamental assumption of Marxism as well as various generalizations made by non-Marxists. The Marxist one is that no ruling class gives up power without being forced out, most typically by a revolution. The non-Marxist assumption was that the unique all-controlling, all-encompassing totalitarian systems in the Communist world were basically stable, that they could not be overthrown, that they would not give up as right-wing authoritarian systems did in Spain, Greece, Portugal, Argentina, Brazil, Chile, etc. Jeane Kirkpatrick's differentiation between non-Communist dictatorship, which were inherently unstable and could be overthrown, and Communist totalitarianism, which held absolute power and would never yield, seemed valid. The fact is, as we now well know, that the analysis was wrong. Communism could and did collapse, much more quickly and totally than anyone thought possible.

The basic problem with the analyses of the Soviet Union, both academic and non-academic, is that they were fraught with ideology and politics. Both the Left and the Right made judgments about the Soviet system which derived from their political beliefs. The Right believed that the Soviet Union was an "evil empire," that it was an oppressive totalitarian regime ready to use all resources under its control to retain and even to extend its power. Given its strength, including complete domination of means of communication, of propaganda, and education, and the willingness to spend considerable funds on repressive institutions, the military and the secret police in particular, plus the apparatus and ideological commitment of the Communist Party, there seemed no way the system could be overthrown from within. The Right was certain that the system was exploitive, that it violated the logic of economics and of human nature, that there was considerable opposition to the regime, but few thought this might produce a breakdown. The Right also believed that the system was militarily efficient, that morale in the armed services was reasonably high since they were treated well, and that therefore the Soviets were a serious threat.

The Left differed in its assumptions or beliefs about the nature of Soviet society. At one extreme, the various wings of the Communist movement agreed that the system was a good one, a progressive one that was leading to improvements in productivity and the standard of living of the population and that the people supported Communism. The non-Communist Left varied considerably in its judgments, from assessments which were close to those of the Communists to much more critical ones, and in some cases evaluations which were not far from those of the Right. Basically the various parts of the Left saw the Communist world as on their side, as representing some form of socialism, as efforts to create a more egalitarian and ultimately freer social system. Many felt that this effort was distorted, was corrupted, but the Soviet system was regarded essentially as part of their world, as on the Left. In interpreting the reasons for the Cold War, the Left put much more of the responsibility on the West. They did not believe that there was a Soviet military threat. But again regardless of feelings about the nature of the system, the Left agreed with the Right that the Soviet regime would not be overthrown and that any consideration of its breaking down from within was a near impossibility.

The research literature reflected different political viewpoints. The Sovietologists, academic experts on the Soviet Union, like most American social scientists, have been overwhelmingly liberal and left. Their pre-Gorbachev writings tended to be "soft" with respect to the nature of the Soviet Union, to see it as progressing, even though many did report various black spots. But these tended to be blamed on Russian history, on economic and cultural backwardness, and/or on Stalin. The Sovietologists, on the whole, underestimated the significance of the terror, of the purges, of the role of the secret police. They regarded the repressive apparatus as less important in preserving stability than the system's supposed ability to produce a steadily improving economic, cultural and educational way of life. They were, of course, for the most part aware of the considerable inequality in standards of living which existed within the Communist world, but saw this as a consequence of the lower productivity of these societies, as compared to the highly industrialized nations.

These experts were highly critical of the underlying assumptions of the Cold War, of the reliance on nuclear armament, of the effort to create the technology associated with S.D.I., Star Wars. My judgments about their opinions, of course, refer only to modal patterns of behavior. There were a number of prominent, usually policy-oriented, Sovietologists associated with negative evaluations of Soviet society. These included historians like Martin Malia and Richard Pipes, political scientists like Zbigniew Brzezinski and Samuel Huntington, sociologists like Mark Field and Paul Hollander, and demographers like Murray Feshbach and Nicholas Eberstadt. Basically, however, academic judgments concerning the Soviet Union tended to view it in a much more favorable light than the more policy-oriented experts did.

Any effort to evaluate the theoretical implications of the Soviet collapse should examine the assumptions of people who anticipated its failure in the long run, if not by an implosion. Much of the grand theory predicted Communism would produce a reactionary and oppressive society, and concluded that the system would fail. Here I am thinking of the writings of classical sociologists such as Max Weber, Robert Michels, the Italian elite theorists such as Vilfredo Pareto, and, in more recent times, Raymond Aron. Classical liberal economics, of course, also produced major theoretical works attesting to the inherent failure of socialism. Ludwig von Mises, Friedrich Hayek, and Joseph Schumpeter all concluded that a socialist planning system and government ownership of industry were necessarily inefficient. They argued that a capitalist market system was inherently much more productive than its rival.

These views, it should be noted and acknowledged, coincided to a considerable extent with those of the fountainhead of socialist theory and of Communist ideology, Karl Marx. Marxism is a materialist theory of society and history. The nature of society, the structural possibilities, are determined by the level of technology. Social structures, class relations, power systems, ideologies, are derivative from, are closely tied to, the productive apparatus. Marx, therefore, rejected as utopian proposals to build communism prior to the emergence of highly industrialized countries. Marx and Engels distinguished between utopian and scientific socialism in *The Communist Manifesto* and in Engles' work, *Socialism: Utopian and Scientific*. The concept of utopian socialism referred to efforts in the Middle Ages to create egalitarian communes and to the writings of men like Fourier and Owen, who favored creating cooperative communities in the 19th century. And following from Marx's assumption, the major Marxist theorists did not believe that socialism could be built in a non-industrialized country like the Czarist empire. These included, prior to the Revolution, Russians like Lenin, Trotsky, Plekhanov, and Martov, the last two the theoreticians of the Mensheviks, and, outside Russia, major figures like Karl Kautsky and Rosa Luxemburg.

Underdeveloped, primarily agrarian, countries did not meet Marx's materialistic requirement for socialism. He consistently emphasized that socialism could only come to power and take shape in a society which produces economic abundance, that is, has the appropriate material substructure. Marx was convinced that an exploitive class society is the inevitable consequence of scarcity. In societies in which the equitable distribution of resources means the equitable distribution of poverty, inequality is inevitable. Those in directing positions have to be over-rewarded in order to motivate them to organize the society. Surplus value has to be extracted from the lower classes in order to produce economic growth and to support the institutions of the ruling class, of government, of political organization, of defense against natural and human enemies. To repeat, socialism can only emerge in a society in which technology is so advanced, so productive, that the goal of equality is a realistic one. As Marx implied in *The German Ideology*, socialism would be a system in which machines did the work, so that people could hunt, fish, and enjoy the fruits of creative culture. Utopian, unrealistic efforts to create socialism, to form an egalitarian society prior to abundance, must fail.

In *Das Kapital*, Marx noted that "the most advanced society would show to the less developed the image of their future." Ironically, this meant that the first socialist country would be the United States since it was the most developed country from the late 19th century on. And many Marxists, ranging from Friedrich Engels to Daniel DeLeon in the U.S., Paul Lafargue, Marx's son-in-law, in France, August Bebel in Germany, and Maxim Gorky in Russia, concluded that America had to be the fist socialist country. They continued to believe this up to World War I, even when they saw large socialist movements developing in Europe, but not in the United States.[12] Lenin, however, was able to switch the party's orientation. He argued that Russia was the weakest link in the chain of capitalist nations as a result of the military defeats it had suffered in the war. He felt and hoped that a Russian revolution would provide the spark for the revolution in the industrialized West, particularly in Germany, but elsewhere as well. And it was his belief that if the working class, if the socialist movement, came to power in the more developed countries of Western Europe that Russia could be helped along by them. No one, certainly not he nor any of the other Marxists, thought that socialist institutions could be erected in the backward material conditions of the Czarist Empire. He did not really believe that the Bolsheviks would hold power unless the West joined in. There are reports that on the seventy-first day after the seizure of power, Lenin danced in the snow because they had outlived the Paris Commune of 1870, which had lasted only seventy days.

We do not know what went through Lenin's mind as it became clear that the revolution would not succeed in the West, that the Bolsheviks were isolated in what had become the Soviet Union. For the first few years, he and the other Bolsheviks kept looking for the revolution to emerge in the industrialized West, in harmony with Marx's anticipations. But as it became clear that this was not happening, that they were isolated in their economically backward realm, one which showed little evidence of response to the equalitarian norms introduced under Communism, Lenin became increasingly pessimistic. And he put the blame for domestic shortcomings not only on war conditions and underdevelopment, but also on the low cultural level of the Russian people, on Asian traditions which made for passivity.

Lenin did not live long enough to react to the long-term isolation of the Revolution. But Karl Wittfogel, who had been an important Marxist historical analyst and member of the German Communist Party, was to present a dramatic view of Lenin's private outlook supposedly derivative from an aspect of Marx's work. Wittfogel was interested in Marx's writings on "oriental despotism." This concept applied to certain countries, such as ancient Egypt and China, where the state rather than property was the principal source of power and class. In these societies, according to Marx, the need to control large-scale water resources—the Nile Delta, the Yangtze—led to centralized state domination over the economy. The peasantry were the largest class, but they lived in "self-sufficient, dispersed and isolated rural communities," which formed the base of oriental despotism. The dominant strata maintained their position by virtue of their relationship to the all-powerful state. Wittfogel, after he broke with the Communists in the early forties, described Communist societies as modern versions of oriental despotism. In the last chapter of his book, *Oriental Despotism* (1957), he notes that Lenin, in a number of writings in 1922–23, shortly before his death, portrayed the Soviet Union in words which were almost identical to those used by Marx to describe the social structure and economic systems of oriental despotic societies. Lenin never used the term in analyzing the Soviet system, nor did he ever overtly imply that this was what was happening. But Wittfogel argues that the use by Lenin, who certainly knew his Marx, of such language could not have been accidental. He suggests that Lenin was trying to convey an Aesopian message that the Soviet Union was becoming an oriental despotism, not a socialist society.

We will never know whether in fact Lenin had such ideas in mind, or whether his use of this language was some sort of ironic coincidence. But in any case Soviet developments may be linked to Marx's analysis of utopian socialism. Marx's theory implied the effort to build socialism in a less developed society would result in a sociological abortion. And if those words do not describe what happened in the Soviet Union, nothing does. Karl Marx anticipated that the premature creation of a socialist state would be a fetter on the means of production, not a goal, would be repressive and reactionary. But Marx would not have believed that the ruling class of the sociological abortion would give up as benignly as it has.

Some orthodox Marxists, focusing on organizational variables, came up with equally pessimistic predictions about the future of an effort led by an elite party, the Bolsheviks, to build socialism in Russia. Leon Trotsky, in the period after the Revolution of 1905, rejected the Mensheviks as too moderate, but regarded the Bolsheviks as too authoritarian. Analyzing the internal structure of their organization and Lenin's power within it, he predicted that a Bolshevik seizure of power would inevitably lead to an authoritarian regime, in which one party controlled everything, with a dictator who dominated the party. He of course gave up this analysis when he joined the Bolsheviks in 1917.

The Polish-German Marxist Rosa Luxemburg also debated with Lenin in the early years of the twentieth century. She rejected his idea that a small revolutionary elite party would lead the working class into socialism. In two articles published under the title "Leninism or Marxism?" in 1904, she argued against Lenin's organizational views. She attacked Lenin's emphasis on a centralized elite party, one which she thought implied contempt for the working class, suggesting they could not come to revolutionary consciousness on their own. Like Trotsky, she anticipated a future in which the Party would dictate to the masses, the Central Committee would dictate to the Party, and a leader would ultimately dictate to the Committee. After the Bolsheviks had come to power and established a dictatorship, she again polemicized against Lenin's views in a pamphlet on *The Russian Revolution*. She wrote, among other things: "Freedom only for the supporters of the government, only for the members of one party—however numerous they may be—is no freedom for all. Freedom is always and exclusively for the one who thinks differently." And she predicted that "without general elections, without unrestricted freedom of press and assembly, without a free struggle of opinions, life dies out of every public institution, becomes a mere semblance of life in which the bureaucracy remains the only active element.... [The system becomes] a clique affair, a dictatorship to be sure, not, however, the proletariat, but only a handful of politicians.... Such conditions must inevitably cause a brutalization of public life: attempted assassinations, shooting of hostages, et cetera."

The idea that socialism could only emerge in an advanced industrial society, which was a fixed dogma of Marxism prior to 1917, almost disappeared afterwards, given the existence of the Soviet Union. It should be noted, however, that the justly esteemed Italian theoretician, Antonio Gramsci, wrote from prison in the middle twenties in line with that traditional Marxist gospel, that his country, Italy, must "Americanize" in order to become socialist. That is, Gramsci argued Italy must first become an advanced bourgeois industrial country like the United States before it could move on to make a socialist revolution. Gramsci did not refer critically to the situation in the Soviet Union—as a Communist he could not—but he may very well have had it in mind, since it was even more backward than Italy.

While a member of the German Social Democratic Party, Robert Michels put forth a major critique of socialism that was to become extremely influential. His book *Political Parties*, which first appeared in 1911, emphasized inherent oligarchic tendencies within political parties, especially within the socialist parties and most notably within the most important one of them at the time, his own German party. Michels noted that the socialists claimed to be the greatest advocates of democracy in the polity and the economy. Their coming to power would supposedly lead both to greater democracy and classlessness. Michels, however, documented in abundant detail that the internal structure of the socialist parties was not democratic, that the parties were controlled by an elite which was able, through its control of the organization and political resources, to dominate the membership. He also emphasized that the party bureaucrats were not workers, even if some of them had been such before they became party employees and leaders. Hence he argued, as did Rosa Luxemburg from a different perspective, that the program of the party reflected not the social situation of the working class but the position and interests of the socially privileged party elites. The basic theory of organization which Michels developed stressed that all organizations are dominated by their elites, not by their members, even if they have nominally democratic structures. Since this was particularly true of the socialist parties, Michels concluded that socialist parties might triumph, come to office, but that socialism as an egalitarian system never could occur, that there would always be a dictatorship, control by the party bureaucracy, who would be the ruling class in a socialist society.

While Michel's classic work was written years before the Russian Revolution, it was seriously discussed in what for a time was the major theoretical tome of the Russian and international Communist movements, *Historical Materialism*, written by Nikolai Bukharin in 1924. Bukharin, well versed in sociological theory, knowledgeably evaluated the writings of Durkheim, Weber, and Michels. He dealt with the criticisms of Marxism by various bourgeois political scientists. In his book, he summarized Michels' argument, but then surprisingly did not reject it. Rather he acknowledged that the beginnings of a new ruling class or stratum could be seen in the Soviet Union. He stated, however, that it would not lead to the failure of socialism or to the growth of a new dominant class because one of the major variables that Michels stressed as making for elite dominance did not exist in the Soviet Union, namely, the lack of political competence and education of the working class. Bukharin argued that the working class was being raised by a socialist society to a higher level of knowledge, of sophistication, and consequently also of political participation than had ever occurred before. These skills would enable the workers to resist what he accepted as inevitable, the tendency of the dominant strata of a socialist society to try to become a new ruling class. Bukharin believed that a sophisticated proletariat would prevent this from occurring. It is obvious, however, that Bukharin was concerned that socialism might fail, that it might produce a new exploitive class.

Historical Materialism, which was used as required teaching material in the Communist movement for a few years, was to disappear completely, and Bukharin himself, like almost all the Revolutionary fathers, was to be executed by Stalin as a traitor in the Second Moscow Trial in 1938.

Michels' *Political Parties* was to have a considerable effect on young American radicals in the 1930s and early forties, including two who were to become sociologists, Philip Selznick and myself. We had been Trotskyists, which meant that we were critically aware of the exploitive authoritarian character of the Soviet Union, but as we observed autocratic tendencies in the Trotskyite movement itself, we came to accept Michels' analysis that oligarchy and dictatorship seemed to be inherent in the organizational structure of revolutionary movements, a belief which was to lead us out of the movement and to be severely critical of the Soviet Union.

Max Weber, the great sociological critic of Marx, in his writings about socialism and capitalism, also contributed important insights for understanding the nature of and subsequent failure of the Soviet Union. He was, in fact, the mentor of the young Michels and inspired his study of political parties. Weber emphasized bureaucracy as the characteristic mode of large-scale social organizations in modern society, including both government and industry. Weber, however, generalized beyond politics to argue that whether the means of production were privately owned as in capitalism or publicly or socially owned as under socialism would make little difference for the position of the lower strata. The socialist revolution would, in fact, intensify the bureaucratic character of modern industrial society, resulting in the increased oppression of the working class and other repressed strata. Weber formulated a theory of alienation under bureaucratic conditions, which differed from Marx and was subsequently explicated in the writings of scholars like Erich Fromm, C. Wright Mills, and David Riesman. Weber emphasized that in a bureaucratic system the people lower in the hierarchy have to "sell" their personalities to impress their superiors. Bureaucracy produces what was later to be called organization men or marketeer or other-directed personalities. People in bureaucracies market their personalities rather than their manufacturing skills. The theory implies that they are even more alienated from their true selves than is suggested by the Marxist analysis of alienation resulting from economic powerlessness. Weber, who lived to see the beginnings of the Soviet rule, argued with students in Germany about the future of socialism, predicting that it would not produce a decent or egalitarian system, but rather one more oppressive than capitalism because it would be more bureaucratic. He concluded one of his lectures by saying "Let us meet again in ten years to see who is right." Unfortunately, he only had a short time to live.

The writings of Weber and Michels were to have an influence on analyses of the Soviet system during and after World War II. James Burnham, who had been a leading American Trotskyite, wrote two books, *The Managerial Revolution* and *The Machiavellians*, which advanced the idea that the managerial bureaucracy was not only becoming the new ruling class of the Soviet system, but was also taking over throughout Western industrial society, which he thought would become statist and managerial. Burnham argued that power lay in the hands of the managers of industry who would be the new ruling class of a post-capitalist society. These ideas had appeared earlier in the writings of another former Trotskyite, Bruno Rienzi, and subsequently in the works of Max Schachtman, who also had been a Trotskyist leader. Burnham was to give up his belief in the dominance of the managerially controlled state and become an advocate of pure market economics.

The free market critique of socialism and even more strongly of the Communist system presented by economists like von Mises, Hayek, Schumpeter, and Friedman essentially emphasizes that a socialist state planning system cannot work and that inequality of reward is inherent and necessary. Basically, as is well known, they have argued that a free economy, the product of hundreds of thousands of individual decisions by different entrepreneurs seeking to maximize profit, is much more likely to produce innovations, organizations that are economically productive, than a system characterized by a central planning agency, a Gosplan, or government monopolies in each industry. The basic logic is fairly simple: namely, that any one bureaucracy or planning agency can at best only be right part of the time, that it is less likely to innovate, to support new ideas, new plans, than a competitive market system in which different players seek to win out over each other. If ten people try to build an automobile or whatever, it only takes one of them to come with an innovative successful approach, the others may go bankrupt. From this perspective, the more controlled, the more authoritarian a system, the less choice that consumers and producers have, the less likely a system is to grow, to develop. Economists also argue that a system with differentiated economic reward, unequal reward, is necessary to secure high productivity. They believe, as did Marx, that inequality is inherent in scarce economic resources. This logic also underlies the explanations of inequality to be found in sociology, in the writings of Weber, as well as the functionalist theorists from Durkheim through Kingsley Davis and Talcott Parsons. Unless one can reach abundance, a meaningless concept to non-Marxists, it follows from all of these approaches that inequality and social classes are inevitable and necessary. In the sociologists' analyses, status, prestige, will always be a scarce resource, since the competition for status is a zero-sum game. The market economists, in any case, predicted that a system like the Soviet one would not work, that its economy would slow down or decline, that it would stagnate.

To move from different theoretical approaches for the failure of socialism generally or of the Soviet Union in particular to empirical analyses, I have already mentioned that Sovietology in general has not been very useful in anticipating recent developments. As I noted earlier, the tendency of academic social scientists, particularly the more research-oriented among them, to be on the left has greatly affected the quality of scholarly analysis of the Soviet Union and, one might add, of China as well. There are, however, some works to which these criticisms do not apply. One of the most significant such analyses in my judgment is by Murray Feshbach, a demographer who has been interested in health statistics. Feshbach, in a number of noteworthy papers written in the seventies and eighties, brought together a variety of data demonstrating how miserable Soviet living conditions were. Particularly noteworthy was his stress on the fact that infant mortality had been going up in the Soviet Union while longevity declined. Such tendencies could not be found in any other country. While there are many countries which are low on both, the direction in industrialized countries has always been upward, except under Communism. Feshbach also noted, documented, the tremendous extent of alcoholism in the Soviet Union. Another demographer, Nicholas Eberstadt, drawing in part on Feshbach's work but also on his own, noted evidence of considerable alienation, particularly work alienation, within Soviet institutions. Some time after I first became aware of these efforts, I read an article by a Soviet emigre describing conditions in the Soviet Union more or less in line with these writings, but to which he added the contention that the lack of morale, alcoholic addiction, low work capability, not only affected the civilian economy but also penetrated the military and police. He claimed that the KGB was essentially a very inefficient force, that Soviet dissidents found no difficulty in dodging them whenever they wanted to have a meeting of their own. He reported considerable alcoholism and lack of interest in work among the guardians of the system.

A devastating critique of the Soviet system was presented by a Soviet emigre, Andrew Amalrik, in his essay *Will the Soviet Union Survive Until 1984?* (1969). Amalrik wrote during an earlier period of liberalization, that of Khrushchev. He suggested that the "liberalization" was a function of "the growing decrepitude of the regime, rather than its regeneration," that "the logical result will be its death, followed by anarchy." Many of his criticisms surprisingly read like those made of Gorbachev, that economic reform from the top was a "half-measure," which was being "sabotaged by the party machine," for its own success would mean the end of the machine. Basically he argued that the strata who most benefitted from the system, largely the educated professionals, want democratic reforms, greater freedom, and the rule of law. The masses, the workers without rights, the collective farmers, all exhibit "pervasive discontent" with their lot. Though the 1960s showed a slow growth in the standard of living, Amalrik predicted that "a halt or even a reversal in the improvement of the standard of living [such as in fact occurred from the seventies on] would arouse such explosions of anger, mixed with violence, as were never before thought possible." Such developments would occur because of the "ossification" of the system, and would affect industrial output. He saw the regime becoming "progressively weaker and more self-destructive."

Beyond changes in class relations, Amalrik noted that the Stalinist expansion into Eastern Europe and its "fostering of international tension" created a danger for the regime. The USSR would not be able to hold down the forces of nationalism. Any event which undermined domestic stability "will be enough to topple the regime. It will open the door to the various nationalities who will demand and secure independence." He anticipated a breakdown in the 1980s.

Awareness that the nationality question, ethnic tension, would undermine the system, is at the heart of the analysis by one of us, Randall Collins. In a paper he wrote in 1980, but had difficulty in publishing in academic journals until it appeared in his own book of essays in 1986, Collins wrote that the Soviet Union "had already reached its limit...and was entering a period of...decline...with the likelihood of extensive decline becoming very high before the 21st century." He concluded that the country was overextended economically, militarily, and politically, that it would not be able to control "the Baltic, the Ukraine, the Caucasus and the Central Asian Moslem territories." These would follow on the "breakdown of the central power of the Russian state." As a Weberian, he emphasized legitimacy, and suggested that the Soviet Union had major legitimacy problems, since the failures of the system had produced a loss of faith in Marxism, in Communist ideology. The privileged no longer had faith.

Most Sovietologists did not agree with these judgments. They believed that the system was improving, that after Stalin's death it had become less repressive, that conditions of life were better for the masses. Relying to some extent on Soviet data, they concluded that the Soviet economy was doing well to the point where, as Martin Malia notes, "by the 1970s, the conventional wisdom came to be that the Soviet GNP was some 60 percent of the American."

Russian emigre economists were disturbed by the overestimation of their economy. One, Igor Birman, argued that "American academia and the CIA fail to take into account not only the unreliability of Soviet statistics, but, even more important, the low quality of the whole Soviet national product." He concluded that the Soviet consumption level was a quarter to a fifth of the U.S. level. As Henry Rowen and Charles Wolf report, a Soviet economist, Alexander Zaichenko, indicated that "given the volume of goods and services consumed per capita, the Soviet Union ranks between fiftieth and sixtieth in the world." Even these estimates may be too high, since, as Alex Inkeles notes, they are based on averages which "may disguise major inequities in distribution" and quality. In the last few years, ex-Soviet economists have emphasized the exaggerated character of Soviet statistics, that these were "non-statistics" designed to conceal the fact that "socialism was one of the greatest economic disasters of the 20th century." As Yuri Maltsev, former senior researcher at the Institute of Economics of the USSR Academy of Sciences, noted: "By the mid-1980s, the deterioration of the Soviet system reached a critical point. More than 50 percent of state business enterprises were permanently unprofitable, but survived due to the provision of huge subsidies...." (109).

Gorbachev did not create the crisis; his policies were reactions to it. He was placed in office with the Politburo's knowledge that he would attempt drastic reforms to deal with the declining economy. As Henry Rowen and Charles Wolfe noted:

We should...ask why the Soviet leadership has been behaving recently in ways that may reduce its military power, weaken its influence in

Eastern Europe, stimulate latent desires for independence in many of its republics, cause its citizens to question the legitimacy of the system, and put its future in question. The answer, evidently, is that *not* to embark on such a risky path is considered even more dangerous. To be sure, one should not attribute all of the motivation for change to poor economic performance. The Afghan war, environmental degradation, rigidification of the social structure, and the awful dreariness of life in the Soviet Union doubtless all contributed. But these conditions would have been much less pressing had the economic welfare of the population been improving. The picture that emerges on the state of the economy is bleak.

Gorbachev, and his mentor Andropov before him, hoped to reform Communism, to get people to work harder by granting them more freedom, by appealing to their faith, by exposing the corruption in the party and state bureaucracy generally. But though he and his advisors knew that private market incentives were necessary, they could not bring themselves to take on the party, to open up the society to the explosion which would inevitably follow moving to a free enterprise system, closing down inefficient plants, creating large-scale unemployment and inflation. And *glasnost*, as Amalrik, Collins, and others anticipated, opened the door to ethnic and national aspirations which could not be repressed.

Finally, in all honesty I must note that some American politicians on both the Right and the Left seem to have known what was happening in the Soviet Union and based their policies on this knowledge. In four major speeches delivered in 1982, 1983, 1987 and 1988, Ronald Reagan said the system was going down. At Westminster in 1982, he noted as simple fact that "of all the millions of refugees we've seen in the modern world, their flight is always away from, not toward, the Communist world," and he consigned Marxism-Leninism to the "trash heap of history." In 1983, he said Communism is a "sad, bizarre chapter in history, whose last pages even now are being written." In 1987, at the Brandenburg Gate, he stressed: "In the Communist world we see failure, technological backwardness, declining standards of health, even want of the most basic kind—too little food." And he proclaimed that his cold war policies were based on the assumption that the Soviet Union was a "basket case." Economics, Reagan believed, was the Soviet Union's primary failing. As a good pupil of the market economists, he explained that weakness as derivative from the fact that "it's hard for government planners, no matter how sophisticated, to ever substitute" for the judgment of "millions of individuals," for the "incentives inherent in the capitalist system."

From the Left, Daniel Patrick Moynihan, in a series of prescient statements made from the late seventies on, gave even more emphasis to the terrible weakness of the Soviet Union. Asked to predict what would happen in the 1980s, he stated in 1979 that the Soviet system "could blow up." He pointed to the economic downturn, the *"rise* in mortality rates, the nationality strains." In a speech in the Senate in January 1980, Moynihan noted: "The indices of economic stagnation and even decline are extraordinary. The indices of social of social disorder—social pathology is not too strong a term—are even more so.

The defining event of the decade might well be the breakup of the Soviet Empire." In 1984, he pointed to the absence of legitimacy, "that the Soviet idea is spent...it summons no loyalty." Again in that year, he commented, "the Soviet Union is weak and getting weaker," and in October 1984, before Gorbachev took office, Moynihan proclaimed: "The Cold War is over, the West won....The Soviet Union...has collapsed. As a society it just doesn't work. Nobody believes in it anymore." Moynihan differed from Reagan in drawing policy implications. His strategy "for dealing with the Soviets is to wait them out." They will collapse.

Given these judgments of the Soviet future made by political leaders privy to intelligence information, the question is, why were they right and so many of our Sovietological colleagues wrong? My answer again must be ideological. Reagan came of a rightist background, and Moynihan, much like the leaders of the AFL-CIO, from a left anti-Stalinist social democratic milieu, both of which were disposed to believe the worst; most of the Sovietologists were left-liberal in their politics, an orientation which undermined their capacity to accept the view that economic statism, planning, socialist incentives, would not work. They were also for the most part ignorant of, or ignored, the basic Marxist formulation that there is no way to build socialism in impoverished societies.

One may ask, what about Asian Communism? Why is it surviving? I obviously do not have to deal with this issue, but I would note that China and Vietnam are following the strategy advanced by Trotsky before World War I for revolutions in underdeveloped societies, to preside over market-driven economies. Most of the Chinese economy is now private and is becoming even more so. Its most successful regions are the most privatized. Vietnam is predominantly a capitalist economy. And as, or more, important is the fact that it is 43 years since the Chinese party came to power and only 17 years for Vietnam, as compared to the 74 years that the Communist regime lasted in the Soviet Union. The men who made the Asian revolutions are alive and at the summits of their power structures. Communism still has its revolutionary legitimacy for them, one that decrepitude and biology had reduced, if not eliminated, in the USSR.

Finally, I would note that though Marx was right about the failure of efforts to create socialism in pre-industrial societies, he was wrong in anticipating the socialist revolution in advanced industrial ones. The United States apart, they all have significant socialist or social democratic parties, but without exception all of these have now given up socialist objectives; they all endorse the market economy as the best means to produce increased productivity and a higher living standard for the underprivileged. Socialism and Marxism may be considered failures not because of developments in the formerly Communist world, but because of their inability to point the way for the advanced countries. "The most developed nation shows the way to the less developed." That nation for the past century has been the United States.

Does modern sociology have anything to contribute to the analysis of developments in the former Communist world? I hope I have shown that it does. But if you doubt it, may I note that while the party still held power, at a three-day conference on "the party and *perestroika*" at the Higher Party School in Moscow in 1989, attended by Communist scholars and intellectuals from all over the Soviet Union, a review of the stenographic record by S. Frederick Starr reports few references to Marx and Lenin, while statements by Max Weber and Talcott Parsons were invoked more frequently to justify various proposals for reforms.

Endnotes

*This is a preliminary version of a longer work, "Anticipations of the Failure of Communism" by Gyorgy Bence and Seymour Martin Lipset, which will appear in the journal *Politics and Society*. I am grateful to the John C. Olin Foundation for a grant which helped to facilitate the research and I appreciate the assistance of Jeffrey Hayes.

1. They looked to America as the country that would show others the way to socialism, in spite of the glaring weakness of socialist parties in the United States. As Howard Quint points out, they "found the United States, of all the countries in the world, most ripe for socialism, not only in the light of Marxian law of economic development, but also by the express opinion of Friedrich Engels." Karl Kautsky, considered the leading Marxism theoretician in the Germany Social Democratic Labor Party, announced in 1902 that "America shows us our future, insofar as one country can reveal it at all to another." He

elaborated this view in 1910, anticipating "the sharpening of class conflict more strongly" in the U.S. than anywhere else. The British Marxist H.M. Hyndman noted in 1904 that "just as North America is today the most advanced country, economically and socially, so it will be the first in which Socialism will find open and legal expression." Werner Sombart emphasized this point in his classic book, *Why Is There No Socialism in the United States?* (1906): "If...modern socialism follows as a necessary reaction to capitalism, the country with the most advanced capitalist development, namely the United States, would at the same time be the one providing the classic case of Socialism, and its working class would be supporters of the most radical of Socialist movements." Maxim Gorky, who supported the Russian Bolsheviks from 1903 on, wrote in 1906 of his conviction that "socialism would be realized in the United States before any other country in the world." August Bebel, the leader of the German Social Democrats, stated in an interview in 1907 in the American socialist paper *Appeal to Reason* that: "You Americans will be the first to usher in a Socialist Republic." His belief—at a time when his party was already a mass movement with many elected members of the *Reichstag*, but the American Socialist Party secured less than 2 percent of the vote—was based on the fact that the United States was "far ahead of Germany in industrial development." He reiterated his opinion in 1912, when the discrepancy between the strength of the two movements was even greater, saying that America would be "the first nation to declare a Cooperative Commonwealth." Paul Lafargue paraphrased Marx on the flyleaf of his book on America by asserting that "the most industrially advanced country shows to those who follow it on the industrial ladder the image of their own future."